REGION, NATION AND HOMELAND

The ISEAS – Yusof Ishak Institute (formerly Institute of Southeast Asian Studies) is an autonomous organization established in 1968. It is a regional centre dedicated to the study of socio-political, security, and economic trends and developments in Southeast Asia and its wider geostrategic and economic environment. The Institute's research programmes are grouped under Regional Economic Studies (RES), Regional Strategic and Political Studies (RSPS), and Regional Social and Cultural Studies (RSCS). The Institute is also home to the ASEAN Studies Centre (ASC), the Singapore APEC Study Centre, and the Temasek History Research Centre (THRC).

ISEAS Publishing, an established academic press, has issued more than 2,000 books and journals. It is the largest scholarly publisher of research about Southeast Asia from within the region. ISEAS Publishing works with many other academic and trade publishers and distributors to disseminate important research and analyses from and about Southeast Asia to the rest of the world.

REGION, NATION AND HOMELAND

Valorization and Adaptation in the Moro
and Cordillera Resistance Discourses

MIRIAM CORONEL FERRER

ISEAS YUSOF ISHAK
INSTITUTE

First published in Singapore in 2020 by
ISEAS Publishing
30 Heng Mui Keng Terrace
Singapore 119614

Email: publish@iseas.edu.sg
Website: bookshop.iseas.edu.sg

The responsibility for facts and opinions in this publication rests exclusively with the author and her interpretations do not necessarily reflect the views or the policy of the publisher or its supporters.

ISEAS Library Cataloguing-in-Publication Data

Names: Coronel Ferrer, Miriam.
Title: Region, nation and homeland : valorization and adaptation in the Moro and Cordillera resistance discourses / by Miriam Coronel Ferrer.
Description: Singapore : ISEAS – Yusof Ishak Institute, 2020. | Includes bibliographical references and index.
Identifiers: ISBN 9789814843713 (paperback) | ISBN 9789814843720 (PDF) | ISBN 9789814881036 (epub)
Subjects: LCSH: Mindanao Island (Philippines)—History—Autonomy and independence movements—Study and teaching. | Cordillera Administrative Region (Philippines)—History—Autonomy and indigenous peoples' movements—Study and teaching. | Discourse analysis, Narrative—Philippines—Mindanao Island. | Discourse analysis, Narrative—Philippines—Cordillera Administrative Region. | Ethnicity—Political aspects—Philippines.
Classification: LCC DS686.5 F38

Typeset by Stallion Press (S) Pte Ltd

Contents

Preface

The chapters in this book came from my long engagement with the Cordillera and Moro movements. I recall vividly the articles that we, as editors of the *Philippine Collegian*, the student paper of the University of the Philippines, bravely published on the developments in the Cordillera and Mindanao at the height of martial rule in the late 1970s. One month after graduation, I joined an international delegation that travelled to the hometown of Macli-ing Dulag, the revered chieftain of the Butbut tribe in Kalinga and the face and voice of the opposition to the Chico River Dam. In April 1980, soldiers assassinated Dulag, and our group travelled to Kalinga to show solidarity with the local people's struggle against the dam. Writing for the *Diliman Review* in the late 1980s, I had the opportunity to interview, among others, Conrado Balweg of the Cordillera People's Liberation Army and famed American historian and long-time Mountain Province resident William Henry Scott. During this tumultuous period, I had met and had discussions with many cadres from the Communist Party of the Philippines; I have had an inside track.

My direct involvement with the Moro movement came later, as part of my peace advocacy and new academic interest in conflict resolution and peace studies after the fall of the Marcos dictatorship. In the early 2000s I met Moro Islamic Liberation Front leaders Ebrahim Murad, the late Ali Lanang, and Mohager Iqbal as part of my advocacy work on the international campaign to ban landmines. In the Philippine Campaign to Ban Landmines, we urged different armed groups like the MILF to commit to a landmine ban. Little did I know that I would be thrust into a major role involving the MILF. In July 2010 I was appointed first as a member of President Benigno Simeon Aquino III's negotiating panel in talks with the MILF. From November 2012 to June 2016 I was the chair of the government panel that signed the Comprehensive Agreement on the Bangsamoro in March 2014.

This appointment took place after I had completed most of the research and had written the chapters that make up the bulk of this book. I have updated the 2010 drafts to take account of recent developments and other materials that have followed over the last few years. My visits to the Cordillera region in 2019 for another project allowed me to revalidate my analysis.

I had conducted field research and written and published several book and journal articles on the Cordillera and Moro movements before, but none of my past work involved the application of critical discourse analysis. In applying it here I have veered away from the positivism that marked my earlier work.

I am grateful to the University of the Philippines Diliman for providing me a home for the last three decades. This book was made possible through the various research loads and extension service credits, study leaves, research grants and secondment that the university granted me during my tenure as faculty member at the Department of Political Science.

For the publication of this book, my special thanks go to the ISEAS — Yusof Ishak Institute, especially to Ng Kok Kiong and Stephen Logan who oversaw the editorial aspects of the publication process.

And on a personal note, my thanks again to Anthony, who always let me be.

Metro Manila
July 2019

Abbreviations

ADDA	Anti-Dam Democratic Alliance
AFP	Armed Forces of the Philippines
AHJAG	Ad-Hoc Joint Action Group
AMANPHIL	Asian Muslim Action Network in the Philippines
AOPG	All-out Peace Groups
ARMM	Autonomous Region in Muslim Mindanao
ASG	Abu Sayyaf Group
BARMM	Bangsamoro Autonomous Region in Muslim Mindanao
BDA	Bangsamoro Development Agency
BIAF	Bansamoro Islamic Armed Forces
BIBAK	Benguet, Ifugao, Bontoc, Apayao, Kalinga
BIBAKA	Benguet, Ifugao, Bontoc, Apayao, Kalinga, Abra
BJE	Bangsamoro Juridical Entity
BMILO	Bangsa Muslimin Islamic Liberation Organization
BMLO	Bangsa Moro Liberation Organization
CAB	Comprehensive Agreement on the Bangsamoro
CAR	Cordillera Administrative Region

CBA/CBAd	Cordillera Bodong Administration
CEB	Cordillera Executive Board
ConCom	Constitutional Commission
CPA	Cordillera People's Alliance
CPDF	Cordillera People's Democratic Front
CPGF	Cordillera People's Guerilla Forces
CPLA	Cordillera People's Liberation Army
CPP	Communist Party of the Philippines
CRC	Cellophil Resources Corporation
CRCC	Cordillera Regional Consultative Commission
DATAKO	Demokratiko a Timpuyong Dagiti Agtutubo ti Kordilyera, or Democratic Movement of the Cordillera Youth
ECOSOC	United Nations Economic and Social Commission
FAB	Framework Agreement on the Bangsamoro
FPA	Final Peace Agreement
GRP	Government of the Republic of the Philippines
HiAct	Highlander Activists
ICAR	Interim Cordillera Autonomous Region
ICCPR	International Covenant on Civil and Political Rights
ICESCR	International Covenant on Economic, Social and Cultural Rights
IGO	Igorot Global Organization
IHL	international humanitarian law
ILF	Igorot Liberation Front
ILO	International Labour Organisation
IP	indigenous peoples
JI	Jemaah Islamiyah
KBPPHA	Kalinga-Bontok Peace Pact Holders Association
KKK	Kilusang Kabataan ng Kabundukan, or Highlander Youth Movement; also Kilusang Kabataan ng Kordilyera, or Mountain Youth Movement

KM	Kabataang Makabayan or Nationalist Youth
MILF	Moro Islamic Liberation Front
MIM	Muslim Independence Movement; also Mindanao Independence Movement
MINSUPALA	Mindanao, Sulu and Palawan
MNLF	Moro National Liberation Front
MNLF-RG	MNLF Reformist Group
MNS	Montañosa National Solidarity
MOA-AD	Memorandum of Agreement on Ancestral Domain
MORO	Moro Revolutionary Organisation
MWL	Muslim World League
NAPOCOR	National Power Corporation
NDF	National Democratic Front
NP	Nacionalista Party
NPA	New People's Army
OIC	Organisation of the Islamic Conference/(since 2011) Organisation of Islamic Cooperation
OPAPP	Office of the Presidential Adviser on the Peace Process
PANAMIN	Presidential Assistant on National Minorities
PCBL	Philippine Campaign to Ban Landmines
PD	Presidential Decree
PIGSA	Progressive Igorot Students Association
PK	Partido Kordilyera
UP	University of the Philippines
WGIP	UN Working Group on Indigenous Populations/ (since 1988) Peoples

Maps

Autonomous Region in Muslim Mindanao (August 2001–February 2019)

CORDILLERA ADMINISTRATIVE REGION

1

Introduction: Text and Resistance

"(D)iscourse as a political practice is not only a site of power struggle,
but also a stake in power struggle..."

— Norman Fairclough, *Discourse and Social Change*
(Cambridge: Polity Press, 1992), p. 67.

Resistance discourses construct an alternative analysis of society,
critique the power relations that govern that society, and condemn the
resulting oppression of the population that the resistance promises to
liberate. They propose the ways and means social change can be done,
and elaborate the shape of a new polity. While the dominant societal
discourse reflects dominant power relations and helps reproduce the
status quo, anti-state resistance movements and their discourses are
counter hegemonic. They aim to realign state power and institutions
by mobilizing people around their critique of the status quo and in
support of their alternative vision.

In this book, I examine the resistance discourses within the Moro
and Cordillera armed movements. 'Discourses of resistance' have been
described as those that highlight difference and affirm 'resistant space'
in opposition to the institutionalized frame.[1] Critical discourse analysis is
particularly relevant as a framework and method of analysis, given its
concern with "the radical changes that are taking place in contemporary
social life: with how discourse figures within processes of change, and

with shifts in the relationship between discourse ... and other social elements within networks of practices".[2] The narratives of the Moro and Cordillera armed resistance are basically narratives of difference from the Filipino majority population. Both the Moro and Cordillera identity entrepreneurs waged what we can call ethnopolitical mobilizations that were directed against the Philippine state.

Ethnopolitical mobilizations are movements whose discourses claim or reclaim ethnicity-based identities in order to advance a political project that will recognize and institutionalize their identity claims. In the Philippines, and probably in most other contexts, ethnopolitical mobilizations are distinct from, although related to, class-based and other ideological struggles. They are distinct because of the pre-eminence that the asserted 'ethnic identity' plays in their claims. Their construction of their ethnic identities and corresponding claims are embodied in their discourses, and their discourses in turn also set the direction of their struggle to constitute and create new socio-political relations. Thus, an analysis of the narratives and/or discourses[3] of such movements is crucial to understanding the nature and trajectory of these movements.

The Cordillera and Moro ethnopolitical mobilizations in the Philippines stand out for their nature as armed resistance. The more prominent of the two is the Moro liberation movement in the southernmost part of the country, in the major island grouping of Mindanao and the adjacent Sulu archipelago where the majority of the estimated 10–15 million Philippine Muslims from some thirteen ethnolinguistic groups live. Its origin as a resistance goes back to the colonial period. The Moro population fought against incorporation under the Spanish and American regimes and asked not to be included in the independent Philippine Republic. In the late 1960s a new wave of ethnonationalism emerged leading to the founding of a series of Moro organizations demanding independence from the republic. At the height of the resistance in the early 1970s, an estimated fifty thousand people were killed in the conflict.

Meanwhile, the ethnic mobilization in the Cordillera in the Northern Philippines emerged in the late 1970s. In contrast to the Moro autonomy struggle in the Southern Philippines, the armed conflict in the Cordillera is tightly linked to the communist insurgency. The revitalized Communist Party of the Philippines (CPP) and its new military arm, the New People's Army (NPA), were constituted in the late 1960s.

The CPP-NPA have since been waging a people's war against what they describe as the "semi-feudal, semi-colonial" Philippine state and society. The CPP's ideological moorings lie in Marxist-Leninist-Maoist thought with a strong anti-US imperialism content. It has a command structure founded on Leninist principles: the party as vanguard of the revolution; democratic centralism as its decision-making principle; and the committee system as the organizational framework. Its analysis of Philippine society is an application of Marxist political economy with strong Maoist overtones. Its guerrilla strategy is largely taken from Mao's injunction to "encircle the cities from the countryside". Its narrative is not at all rooted in ethnic complexities.

In the Cordillera, however, the ethnicity/identity factor provided a variant context for the struggle between the communist insurgents and the Philippine government. Religion was not one of the identity markers, since Christianity had already spread to the region beginning with the American period. Rather, threats to the survival of the indigenous population in the Cordilleras provided the pool for generating a CPP-led anti-government regional resistance. Because of its geographically defined scope, it has similarities with the Moro liberation movement. However, unlike the Moro movement, the Cordillera resistance was never secessionist in nature. Moreover, 'Cordillera' identity-making has been less salient in the last two decades compared to the older 'Moro' or 'Bangsamoro' (as it is now more often referred to) project. Still, 'Cordillera' has been established interchangeably as an administrative, geographic, cultural and ethnopolitical marker.

Discourse analysis is consistent with the view that it is principally the subjective experience of conflict that drives reactions and behaviour, especially during times of acute tension.[4] Thus, in understanding the phenomenon of armed ethnic mobilizations, we need to look into the "social and psychological processes by which subjective differences between cultures produce clashing frameworks for action that are at the core of the current conflict".[5] In discourse analysis, such subjectivities are understood by examining the linguistic resources behind the processes. Or, as has been said elsewhere, discourse analysis "offers a social account of subjectivity by attending to the linguistic resources by which the sociopolitical realm is produced and reproduced".[6] The importance given to discourse analysis is congruent with the new social constructionist model of ethnic identity formation and mobilization. The latter theoretical approach stresses the fluid, volitional and situational nature of ethnicity. It emphasizes the contemporary bases (demographic, social, political, economic processes) of the phenomenon that give rise to perceptions of oppression and resentment.[7]

The Written Texts

Utilizing mainly the written texts of the Cordillera and Moro armed groups, I have examined in this volume their respective claim-making on the aspects of nationhood (one people) and territory (homeland/region). My choice of written texts as the material for discourse analysis is based on the assumption that written texts — especially manifestos and books authored by movement intellectuals — fulfil a social function in specific ways. They consciously distil and put together movement demands in order to provide the 'master frame' of the resistance and become, in the process, the main source of 'repertoires', their 'valorized' view of the world, and the guidelines for action of their ardent supporters. I am very much aware that members, supporters and communities sympathetic to the cause do not necessarily share the totalizing perspectives provided by these movement texts and their leaders. However, these texts' valorized, even 'official', standing in the ranks vest the texts with authoritative stature. The written materials provide cohesion to otherwise differentiated beliefs, understandings and knowledge among the movement membership or the communities under their respective influence. As such, they serve as the foundation of other articulations and discursive practices. The salience of written movement texts can be gleaned from the way, for instance, the Communist Manifesto and the collected works of Mao Tse Tung influenced not only the socialist revolutions in their long march but also the socialist states and societies that were born from these revolutions. We also see the continuing salience, after several centuries, of the Qur'an and the Holy Bible in serving as the foundational source of their adherents' world views and guides to action.

Since I wanted to examine transformations in discursive practices within and across the selected movements and across time, the texts as the source material provided a reliable and practical unit of analysis in plotting valorization and 're-framings' in the movements' discourses.

This examination across time in turn provided the window to illuminate the dynamic interplay between and across discourses and actors, evidencing in the process a main thesis in critical discourse analysis that discourse is both constituted and constitutive; that is, discourses are determined socially but they also have social effects.[8]

The specific texts I have analysed in examining the Moro/Bangsamoro movement's discursive practice are the May 1968 Manifesto and June 1968 Draft Constitution and By-laws of the Muslim/Mindanao Independence Movement,[9] and the April 1974 Manifesto of the Moro National Liberation Front (MNLF).[10] Two articles written by Nur Misuari in the mid-1970s were also used. These articles were collected in the publication, *The Bangsa Moro People's Struggle for Self-Determination (Towards an Understanding of the Roots of the Moro People's struggle).*[11]

Apparently, the Moro Islamic Liberation Front (MILF) does not have a founding document that articulates its position. Key books on the Moro struggle do not refer to any such founding document, nor do informed sources. At best there is the letter from Salamat Hashim dated 24 December 1974 addressed to the OIC (Organisation of the Islamic Conference, since renamed Organisation of Islamic Cooperation) on why the group was breaking away from Nur Misuari. In 1985, Bangsamoro Publications released the document entitled *The Bangsamoro Mujahid: His Objectives and Responsibilities* written by Salamat Hashim. Hashim's speeches and interviews have been collected in three volumes by the MILF. The first volume, entitled *The Bangsamoro People's Struggle against Oppression and Colonialism*, was published in October 2001. The second collection, *Referendum: Peaceful, Civilized, Diplomatic and Democratic Means of Solving the Mindanao Conflict*, was published in April 2002. I do not have a copy of the first volume. The third volume entitled *We Must Win the Struggle!* was published posthumously in 2005. The second volume includes messages and interviews from 1986 to 1999; and the third volume compiled MILF Central Committee/Hashim's resolutions and messages from 2002 to 2003. Extensive notations in the third volume were provided by Nu'ain Bin Abdulhaqq, head of the MILF Agency for Youth Affairs.

Interestingly, the earliest, most developed MILF text systematically expounding their analysis is the "Position Papers of the [MILF] Technical Working Groups on the Six Clustered Agenda" written around 2000/2001 in view of the peace negotiations with the government.[12] That this text was written for purposes of negotiations should be kept in mind. While not an organizational text, the books, *Bangsamoro, A Nation under Endless Tyranny* (1999, 3rd ed.) and *The Long Road to Peace* (2007), both written by Salah Jubair, pseudonym of MILF Central Committee member Mohager Iqbal, will also be correlated, especially in sourcing MILF discourse on the accommodation of political negotiation and expanded autonomy in the 1990s.

Jubair/Mohagher Iqbal[13] wrote the first edition of *Bangsamoro, A Nation under Endless Tyranny* in Pakistan, on a mission in 1982 for the MILF chair Hashim to precisely write a pamphlet that could help explain the Bangsamoro struggle to the world. He claimed he had very limited references available to him during this assignment, and as such he largely based the book on his thesis submitted to Manuel Quezon University for his master's degree in political science.[14] For this job well done he earned the praise of Hashim Salamat, who wrote about him in *The Bangsamoro Mujahid*, albeit without identifying him: "Being in the battlefront should not deter us from learning. In fact, dedicated service to the Front can make experts out of MILF members. A case in point is an information officer who has been doing his assignment with zeal for the past ten years or so."[15]

Jubair/Iqbal chose to use a pseudonym, Salah Jubair, because according to him if a member of the MILF claimed authorship people would consider it biased. *Salah*, from the Arabic word *salih*, means purity. There was no specific reason for the choice of the pen name except for the fact that it was not any of his underground names. A thousand copies of the first edition in English were printed in Pakistan in March 1984, and the book has supposedly been reprinted once or twice. A Turkish translation was also circulated in Turkey. A thousand copies of a second expanded edition came out in October 1997, published by the Islamic Research Academy in Lahore, Pakistan, with the word *Bangsamoro* dropped from the title "for brevity and more importantly to do away with the technical confusion.... Bangsamoro is literally translated into 'Moro Nation' and therefore to retain it [would be] redundant."[16] The third and significantly expanded edition published in 1999 in Kuala Lumpur reinstated *Bangsamoro* in the book's title, "in answer to several suggestions, both solicited and unsolicited, from readers and friends who wish[ed] this work to state in categorical terms which nation is referred to and, more importantly, to do a fine job of imparting some of the hard facts of the seemingly endless bloody human drama in Mindanao".[17]

The Position Paper written by the MILF Technical Working Group, Hashim's *The Bangsamoro Mujahid* and collected messages and interviews, and Jubair's books were my main sources in elucidating how the MILF articulated its struggle.

Two papers will serve as the main source documents for analysing the divergence in the resistance discourses of the Cordillera People's Democratic Front (CPDF) and the Cordillera Peoples' Liberation Army's (CPLA). These are the 1986 General Program of the CPDF, and the 1986 CPLA position paper that was co-authored by the Cordillera Bodong Administration (henceforth, CBA[18]) and the Montañosa National Solidarity (MNS).

The December 1986 CPDF draft was a product of several years of revision. The first draft was produced in 1981, and several revised versions came out in 1983 and 1985. The 1986 draft can thus be considered as reflective of the outcome of years of debate within the CPP on the 'correct line' and forms of organization to address the national minority question in the Cordillera. The draft was presented at the January 1987 'First Political Congress' of the CPDF held in Sagada, Mountain Province. The congress was held at a highly emotional time when the Northern Luzon revolutionary forces were already suffering from the schism and the overall marginalization of the national democratic left due to its boycott of the 1986 'snap election' called by Ferdinand Marcos.[19] The CPDF Program was again revised in March 1989 during the 'First Organizational Congress' of the CPDF. A constitution was also passed.

The CPLA-CBA-MNS paper "Towards the Solution of the Cordillera Problem: Statement of Position" was presented to President Aquino during the talks held on 13 September 1986 at the Mt. Data Lodge in Bauko, a municipality in Mountain Province.[20]

Organization of the Book

How did these texts define the resistance? Though both the Moro and Cordillera armed movements were framed in the discourse of autonomy and the right to self-determination, the articulations diverged. What patterns in and across statements were there? What was passed off as common knowledge or truths? What argumentation strategies were used? How did the breakaway groups build on the mother organization's discourse and yet draw resources from it? These are the questions I will answer over the course of the book.

Before plunging into the discourse analysis proper, chapter 2 provides an overview of the beginnings of the Moro liberation movement and chapter 3 does the same for the Cordillera autonomy movement. Unlike most expositions of the movements or the movement organizations concerned, these overviews focus on the ideological and organizational cleavages that emerged, as articulated by the groups themselves or as explained by external observers/scholars. These chapters provide the necessary background for the analyses that follow in chapters 4 and 5, which examine the two sets of organizational discourses using different foci.

Chapter 4 examines the intertextuality in the Bangsamoro resistance discourse. It traces and analyses the weaving of texts upon texts in the articulation of the programmes of the two Moro liberation fronts. Simply put, the mother organization, the MNLF, drew on the 1960s anti-colonial, 'Third World' discourse founded on the right to self-determination. The breakaway faction, the MILF, superimposed on this framing the newer evolved rights of indigenous peoples, bolstering their claims on the basis of both homeland and ancestral domain rights. Influenced in their ideological quest by a religious scholar, the MILF also deepened the Islamic content of their programme and organization and aligned themselves to the global Islamic revivalism of the 1990s. In contrast, the MNLF leadership was more secular. However, as the analysis will show, both organizations remained basically ethnonationalists.

Chapter 5, on the Cordillera resistance discourse, traces the privileging of the identity marker *Cordillera* over earlier markers like *Igorot*. Through an analysis of their respective written programmes and other articulations, it surfaces the ideological differences between the CPP-affiliated CPDF and the breakaway, ethnonationalist founders of the CPLA, as manifested in how they mapped the territory and populations of what comprise the contested/claimed Cordillera region and the shape of the autonomous region they demanded be put in place. Both organizations, nonetheless, drew their inspiration from and capitalized on the rise of 'Cordillera' as the spatial site of resistance and recovery against the Marcos dictatorship in the 1970s to mid-1980s.

In all, the chapters trace the evolution of the movement organizations and how they built on their respective resistance discourses over three to four decades. We will find that the MILF manifested the richest intertextuality. Although the basic foundation of the MILF discourse is similar to that of the MNLF, they borrowed heavily from different discourses over the decades. The CPLA broke away from the CPP's class-based national democratic ideology and put more emphasis on its ethnopolitical critique of the majority-minority relations. At the same time, the CPDF successfully wove the more contemporary 1980s discourse on indigenous peoples and ancestral domain into their repertoire of claims, even as they remained within the ambit of the CPP's national democratic discourse. I illustrate the evolution and adaptation of the organizations' discourses over time in Figure 1.1.

Dispute or conflict narratives, it has been pointed out, "effect and transform social realities" in several ways.[21] They constitute knowledge, create the narrated event and reconstruct reality in order to present a more coherent and compelling account. They transform entitlements and shift authorship. They catalyse personal experience. Narratives are not only mirrors of action going on elsewhere, they themselves also constitute "important opportunities for and means of carrying

FIGURE 1.1
Evolution and Adaptation in the Resistance Discourses of the Movement Organizations

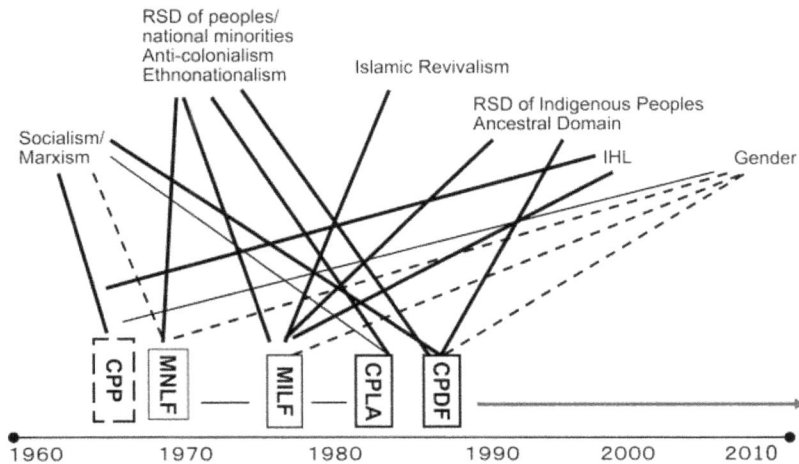

Notes: RSD: Right to Self-Determination; IHL: International Humanitarian Law.

out such action".[22] The essence and fate of any movement, and their transformation throughout time, as these essays manifest, depend significantly on their narratives and the discursive practices that have defined and propelled their aspirations.

Notes

1. Amanda Kottler and Carol Long, "Shifting Sands and Shifting Selves: Affirmations and Betrayals in the Process of Institutional Transformation", in *Culture, Power and Difference: Discourse Analysis in South Africa*, edited by Ann Levett, Amanda Kottler, Erica Burman and Ian Parker (London and Cape Town: Zed Books and University of Cape Town Press, 1997), p. 56.
2. Norman Fairclough, *Analysing Discourse: Textual Analysis for Social Research* (London: Routledge, 2003), p. 205–6.
3. A narrative has been described as "a discourse, or an example of it, designed to represent a connected succession of happenings" (Webster's Dictionary [1966], cited in Amai Lieblich, Rivka Tuval-Masciach and Tamar Zilber, *Narrative Research: Reading, Analysis and Interpretation* [Thousand Oaks, CA: Sage, 1991], p. 2). This definition appears to make narrative a form of discourse. On the other hand, a narrative can also employ different discourses, a feature highlighted in the definition of narratives as "informational schemata in that they contain complex, interrelated subject matter" (Gulich Gulich and Uta M. Quasthoff, "Narrative Analysis", in *Handbook of Discourse Analysis*, vol. 2, *Dimensions of Discourse*, edited by Teun A. Van Dijk [London: Academic Press, 1985], p. 175). Philip MacNaghten ("Discourses of Nature: Argumentation and Power", in *Discourse Analytic Research*, edited by Erica Burman and Ian Parker [London: Routledge, 1993], p. 53) provides an equally broad definition of discourse that may very well refer to narratives: "the means through which human meanings and experiences are manufactured." More simply, Dorothea Hilhorst (*The Real World of NGOs, Discourses, Diversity and Development* [Quezon City: Ateneo de Manila University Press, 2003], pp. 8, 32) defined discourse as the "more or less coherent set of references that frame the way we understand and act upon the world". Given the overlaps, we will interchange the use of the two words and draw theoretical and methodological inspiration from writings on both, even as we privilege the word *discourse*.
4. Peter T. Coleman, "Characteristics of Protracted Intractable Conflict: Toward the Development of a Metaframework — I", *Peace and Conflict: Journal of Peace Psychology* 9, no. 1 (2003): 6.
5. Marc Howard Ross, "The Political Psychology of Competing Narratives: September and Beyond", in *Understanding September 11*, edited by Craig

Calhoun, Paul Price and Ashley Trimmer (New York: The New York Press, 2002), p. 423.
6. Burman and Parker, *Discourse Analytic Research*, p. 3.
7. Joane Nagel, "Constructing Ethnicity: Creating and Recreating Ethnic Identity and Culture", *Social Problems* 41, no. 1 (1994): 150.
8. See Norman Fairclough, *Language and Power* (London: Longman, 1989), p. 163; also, Norman Fairclough, *Discourse and Social Change* (Cambridge: Polity Press, 1992), pp. 56, 72–96.
9. The MIM Manifesto is appended in W.K. Che Man, *Muslim Separatism: The Moros of Southern Philippines and the Malays of Southern Thailand* (Quezon City: Ateneo de Manila University Press, 1990), pp. 187–88; and in Salah Jubair, *A Nation under Endless Tyranny*, 2nd ed. (Lahore: Islamic Research Academy, 1997), pp. 306–7. Che Man titles the document, "The Manifesto of the Muslim Independence Movement", while Jubair preferred to use the later name of the organization, the Mindanao Independence Movement. The MIM Draft Constitution and By-laws are appended in Jubair, *A Nation under Endless Tyranny*, pp. 309–13.
10. The copy amended in Che Man was used (*Muslim Separatism*, pp. 189–90).
11. The articles were published as one volume of the *Philippine Development Forum* (vol. 6, no. 2, 1992). The PDF copy of the volume that I accessed was produced by the College of Arts and Sciences, University of the Philippines–Manila. The main articles cited were the lead (and longest) article of the same title (pp. 1–41) and "Appeal to Islamic World for Support of the Moro People in Southern Philippines" (pp. 61–94).
12. As reprinted in *Kasarinlan: A Philippine Quarterly of Third World Studies* 15, no. 2 (2000): 245–70.
13. Jubair is his pen name and Mohager Iqbal is his nom de guerre. His birth name is Datucan Abas.
14. Interview with Mohager Iqbal, 7 November 2008, MILF Compound, Crossing Simuay, Sultan Kudarat, Maguindanao.
15. Hashim Salamat, *The Bangsamoro Mujahid: His Objectives and Responsibilities* (Mindanao: Bangsamoro Publications, 1985), p. 45. This portion was humbly pointed out to me by Iqbal during my interview with him.
16. Jubair, "Preface", in *A Nation under Endless Tyranny*, p. ix. I am grateful to Soliman Santos, Jr for lending me a copy of this edition.
17. Ibid., p. vi. In the same preface, he acknowledged Soliman Santos, Jr "for suggesting to the author to reinstate the original title of the book".
18. This was the acronym used by the organization itself. We will adopt it for this section onwards, instead of the previous CBAd. The Cordillera Bodong Association (also CBA), made up of those groups and individuals who sided with the CPP-NPA, eventually disbanded.

19. The cheating in the elections led to "People Power", the overthrow of Marcos and the installation of the Aquino government in February 1986. Because it boycotted the electoral exercise, the CPP-NDF was marginalized in the upheaval that followed.

20. "Towards the Solution of the Cordillera Problem: Statement of Position", presented to Her Excellency Corazon C. Aquino, President of the Republic of the Philippines, during the Cordillera Peace Talk held on 13 September 1986 at Mt. Data Lodge, Bauko, Mountain Province, by the Cordillera Bodong Administration, Cordillera People's Liberation Army, and Montanosa National Solidarity. The paper can be found in Ed Garcia and Carol Hernandez, eds., *Waging Peace in the Philippines* (Quezon City: Ateneo Center for Social Policy, UP Center for Integrative and Development Studies, International Alert and Coalition for Peace, 1989), pp. 207–13.

21. Donald Brenneis, "Telling Troubles: Narrative, Conflict, and Experience", in *Disorderly Discourse: Narrative, Conflict and Inequality*, edited by Charles L. Briggs (New York: Oxford University Press, 1996), pp. 46–49.

22. Ibid.

2

The Moro Liberation Movement: From Secession to Autonomy

"Whereas, the MNLF, led by Professor Nur Misuari, inspired by the quest for peace and prosperity, had in the past asserted the right of the Moro people to freely determine their political status and pursue their religious, social, economic and cultural development..."

— The Final Agreement on the Implementation
of the 1976 Tripoli Agreement between
the Government of the Republic of the Philippines
and the Moro National Liberation Front (para. 2),
2 September 1996

"Underlying the CAB is the recognition of the justness and legitimacy of the cause of the Bangsamoro people and their aspiration to chart their political future through a democratic process that will secure their identity and posterity and allow for meaningful governance."

— The Comprehensive Agreement
on the Bangsamoro (para. 3),
signed by the Government of the Philippines
and the Moro Islamic Liberation Front, 27 March 2014

The events and circumstances that gave rise to the armed conflict in Mindanao are multiple and complex. Some scholars, the popular media and protagonists alike have described the conflict as a "religious war".

This perception may have been fed by the way the Spaniards framed and justified their colonization campaign in the past that resulted in deeply ingrained prejudices held between the Christianized natives and the indigenous followers of Islam. The perception was bolstered with the rise of communal conflicts in parts of Mindanao in the early 1970s involving vigilante groups among the settler and indigenous communities, often arising from land-related disputes or contestation over political and/or territorial control.[1]

Seeds of Discontent

The hostility draws on historical antecedents that saw the Islamic population in the south marginalized from the centre of politics and society located in the northern capital on Luzon island. Moreover, policies undertaken by the American colonial regime and the Philippine Republic significantly changed the demographic composition and social structure of Mindanao. Notably, the series of resettlement programmes of populations from Luzon and the Visayas to Mindanao initiated by the American colonial regime transformed many segments of the indigenous population into minorities. The succeeding Philippine government pursued the same policies. Mindanao thus developed into a settler colony from the early to the mid-1900s. Homestead arrangements for migrants and the infusion of American capital for the plantation economy in the region hastened the loss of control over land and tribute collection in the hands of the original inhabitants. Moro National Liberation Front (MNLF) founding chair Nur Misuari thus described the resettlement programme of the government as the "Filipino Trojan Horse".[2]

Spontaneous and organized migrations to Mindanao were encouraged as part of state policy to increase food production, develop uncultivated areas, balance population distribution, and diffuse land tensions in other parts of the country. From 1913 to 1919, seven agricultural colonies were established in Cotabato Valley and Lanao. Basilan was opened up for agricultural expansion by virtue of acts passed by the American colonial government. The Philippine Commonwealth set up the National Land Settlement Administration to administer the same thrust. After World War II, the Philippine Republic continued with the resettlement programmes through agencies like the Economic Development Corporation, the Land Settlement and Development

Corporation — which handled the resettlement of Huk guerrillas (for Hukbong Mapagpalaya ng Sambayanan) from Luzon — and the National Resettlement and Rehabilitation Administration in 1954. Migration to Mindanao peaked from the 1930s to the 1950s.

State laws overwrote customary laws and upset existing property ownership and relations. Under the Philippine Bill of 1902 (also known as the Cooper Act), Spanish cadastral laws were upheld. Individual ownership of land was limited to 16 hectares, while corporations were permitted up to 1,024 hectares. A 1903 law on the homestead system legalized the sale or lease of lands to Filipinos, Americans and other foreign interests. In 1905, the Public Land Act declared all unregistered lands effectively public land. Thus, prior occupancy no longer provided sufficient basis to claim ownership. Homesteaders were allowed private titling of up to 24 hectares of land, whereas titling of non-Christian lands was limited to up to only 10 hectares by the Public Land Act of 1919. In 1931 the maximum hectarage was reduced to 15 hectares for homesteaders and a mere 4 hectares for the original inhabitants.

Although some *datus* were able to title lands under their names, many indigenous Muslims who traditionally enjoyed usufruct rights failed to acquire land titles due to disagreement with or lack of appreciation for and understanding of the new laws. Others did not have the resources to finance cadastral surveys, which, under the Cadastral Act of 1910, became mandatory before the granting of titles. In succeeding decades, migrants and foreign corporations acquired land through the discriminatory legal processes, if not through outright land-grabbing.[3] A 1988 study reported that plantations, logging and mining concessions, and industrial tree plantations occupied 51.47 per cent of the total area of Mindanao. Of these lands, 30.26 per cent were in the hands of 145 big corporations, including 54 that were foreign or foreign-affiliated.[4]

As a frontier area far from the national centre, a state of relative deprivation vis-à-vis other regions prevailed. Typically, the region was left out of or deprioritized in national development programmes and budgetary allocations. These feelings of relative deprivation became potent generators of resentment against the central state. In their 1935 petition to the US Congress, Moro leaders complained that "Christian Filipinos have taken control of our insular funds in which by right we have equal share", and that most funds had been appropriated for Luzon and the Visayas, resulting in Mindanao being left behind. They saw the 1935 Constitution as bereft of provisions responding to their particular welfare and they expressed the fear of losing more lands. "Where shall we obtain the support for our family if our lands are taken from us?", the petition asked.[5]

By the time of the 1948 census, 80 per cent of Muslim Filipinos were found to have no definite source of income and no property.[6] Human development in the region also lagged. In the early confrontational years of the 1970s, the infant mortality rates in Central and Western Mindanao regions were 152.1 and 133.2 per 1,000 live births, respectively, whereas the national average was 90.2. Only 12 per cent of the Muslim population enjoyed electricity in their homes, and only 20 per cent had piped water.[7]

The inequities persisted throughout the century. Collectively, the median income in the five provinces of the Autonomous Region in Muslim Mindanao remained way below the median of the National Capital Region, as well as those of other regions in Mindanao. Only 6 out of 10 residents aged 10–64 years in the four provinces of the first Autonomous Region in Muslim Mindanao (ARMM) enjoyed functional literacy, compared to 9 out of 10 in the National Capital Region.[8] All other development indicators put the ARMM provinces at the bottom of human development among the country's seventy-seven provinces. They were among, if not the highest, in income poverty. At the same time, they were the lowest in life expectancy, percentage of high school graduates, primary and high school enrolment rates, functional literacy, and population using improved water sources.

As the demographic shift took place irreversibly in the twentieth century, the settlers overwhelmingly captured the colonial bureaucracy and local elective government posts. From governing indirectly through friendly *datus*, the United States tightened its control by creating the Moro Province, which it put under American military governorships from 1903 to 1913.[9] In 1914, a civilian government was inaugurated. The Moro Province was renamed Department of Mindanao and Sulu.[10] The 'Filipinization' of administrative posts began, with Christian-Filipinos appointed governors in four of seven provinces.[11] By 1920, Christian-Filipinos occupied all governorships. Some Moros were appointed to government posts, but only up to the provincial board level. Non-Moros also occupied the posts of secretary-treasurers and constabulary commanders. In 1920, a Christian Filipino was appointed director when the department gave way to the Bureau of Non-Christian Tribes under the Department of Interior, and later, in 1936, to the office called the Commission on Mindanao and Sulu. All government units became increasingly centralized under the national political centre. Some of these officials were abusive and not entirely competent.[12] By 1971, all elected officials in the South and North Cotabato provinces were Christian migrants.[13]

In all, very few Mindanaoans, and even fewer Muslims, have made it to the nationally elected Senate or have been appointed to the cabinet or the Supreme Court. No Muslim has become president of the country. The indigenous population has thus felt discriminated against and abused at the hands of the 'outsiders'. Moreover, military campaigns, often led by non-Moro officers, have been waged against those who resisted further state incursion. It has only been in recent decades that Muslims have been appointed to bodies like the Commission on Elections and the Commission on Human Rights, and to posts such as secretary of the Department of Agriculture and the Department of Public Works. Muslims have felt discriminated against in almost all areas, such as in employment in the predominantly settler provinces of Mindanao and elsewhere;[14] with regard to credit facilities;[15] the mass media; and history books.[16]

Eruption of Violence

Scholars on and activists of the Muslim resistance typically point to the series of violent events from the late 1960s to the early 1970s as the catalysts for the formation of a more organized Moro liberation movement. The immediate significant events include the so-called Jabidah Massacre that took place on Corregidor Island;[17] violence staged by vigilante groups, including the 1971 'Manili Massacre' where sixty-five civilians were murdered in a mosque in Manili, North Cotabato by a vigilante group of Visayan settlers; and the declaration of martial law in September 1972.[18] Che Man described the 1960s mobilization as "[l]ike other Moro wars in the past centuries,... [it] was motivated by an endeavor to defend Islam, bangsa (nation) and homeland."[19]

Canoy wrote: "Throughout the country, Jabidah became a cause celebre. Muslim students took to the streets to voice their indignation, while the intellectuals and political leaders published inflammatory manifestos in the newspapers."[20] MNLF founder Nur Misuari reportedly reminisced in 1975 that his radical political awakening took place during demonstrations in front of Malacanang Palace with fellow Muslims condemning the massacre of the Tausug military trainees on Corregidor.[21] In his own writing, Misuari described this "colossal crime of Marcos in 1968" as "(t)he most decisive immediate factor which has heightened the present revolutionary upsurge."[22]

The eruptions of communal violence that followed in the early 1970s saw more than a hundred thousand refugees forced out of their villages, hundreds of homes burned, and hundreds of Muslims and Christians killed, especially in Cotabato and Lanao, the most affected provinces. The Philippine Constabulary and local warlords fighting over prime land or electoral posts were largely responsible for these communal killings. Consequently, the violence garnered international attention and sympathy. The Organization of the Islamic Conference (OIC) and several of its member states, such as Libya, provided military training and logistical support to Moro rebels. Reflecting on the significance of these events in generating the contemporary resistance among the Islamic indigenous population, Jubair wrote: "The Manila government was to them still a 'government of outsiders' and was not only indifferent but, even more so, appeared to be the main force behind a move to 'liquidate them'...".[23]

In September 1972, Marcos declared martial law using the threat of communism and the secession posed by Moro rebels among his justifications. Fighting was most intense in the early years of the regime — that is, from 1972 to 1976. During these years approximately 75 per cent of the Philippine army, which had grown four-fold to become 250,000 strong, was deployed in Mindanao.

From Traditional Moro Elites to Revolutionary Counter-elites

The other track of the twin policy that accompanied the Philippine colonial and postcolonial state's use of repression is integration of the Filipino Muslims in the state and society. The presumed benevolent aspects of these integrationist approaches consisted of recognizing and respecting religious difference, providing special educational assistance that aimed to enable Muslim citizens to 'catch up' with their Christianized counterparts and effectively become Filipinos themselves, and providing representation in the national legislature. This type of integrationist approach that began during the second half of the American colonial regime produced a new crop of secularly educated Muslim elites, most of whom initially came from the traditional aristocracy.

As the integration process gained momentum, Moro traditional leaders made last ditch efforts to be incorporated in just terms into the independent Philippine republic. In 1934, prior to the drafting of the 1935 Philippine Commonwealth Constitution, more than two hundred leaders from Lanao, led by Hadji Abdul Kamid Bogabong, appealed in a letter to the US governor-general to guarantee, among other things, the free exercise of their faith and laws, the turning over to them of all unoccupied lands in the province, a twenty-year grace period to apply for the titling of these lands, and the appointment of "Mohammedan Filipino" in all appointive positions in the province. Should these demands not be addressed in the constitution, they preferred Mindanao and Sulu to remain under American rule "until we become educated".[24] When none of these demands were taken into account, in 1935 they sent the petition to the US Congress to exclude Mindanao and Sulu from the granting of Philippine independence that was to take place ten years after the promulgation of the Commonwealth government. This appeal was likewise rejected.

Consequently, the fathers and scions of the traditional aristocracy learned to manoeuvre in the new political environment. They succeeded in securing the narrow spaces opened up for Muslims in the legislature and the few remaining local governments where they remained the dominant populations. However, the rise of new non-Moro local elites in the settler areas and the political dynamics among the national powerbrokers further encroached on their already reduced bailiwicks.[25] Social and political tensions in these localities gave way to short-lived rebellions.[26] The old leaders failed the next generation who were in search of their identities and had been awakened by the resurgence of state violence against their kind. Jubair offers an explanation for the failure of the traditional Moro elite to rise up to the challenges. According to him, the traditional, aristocratic elites only offered lip service to what was a serious and real problem that required immediate and concrete action. As politicians or high government officials, they had become too preoccupied with the present. They made too many compromises. In addition, the "lure of the world and the inability of the aristocratic leaders — most of them belonged to the so-called royal class — to shed off their traditional privileges, must have contributed to this unfortunate frame of mind".[27]

Catalysed by the 'trigger events' discussed earlier, the Moro leaders advocating independence organized more political mobilizations. Aristocratic Muslim elites who were unhappy with their subordinated relationship with the national state moved out of their pragmatic and shifting alliances with the competing national elite factions. In varying circumstances, they supported, led and abetted anti-state activities. These young educated Muslims from aristocratic and non-aristocratic families forged alliances and formed the basis of the 1960s generation of Moro resistance leaders.

A brief description of the origin and status of the key resistance organizations from the 1960s follows.

The Muslim/Mindanao Independence Movement

The formation of the Muslim Independence Movement (MIM) was announced on 2 May 1968 by Datu Utdog Matalam, who served five terms as governor of the then undivided Cotabato territory. It became the first post-1946 Moro organization to advocate armed struggle, secession and the formation of an Islamic state. Later, the organization was renamed the Mindanao Independence Movement. The name change was reportedly aimed at accommodating the non-Muslim inhabitants of the claimed territory.[28]

A traditional Moro aristocrat, Matalam was angered by the Jabidah controversy. More personal sources of Matalam's disenchantment with the Philippine political system, however, preceded the landmark controversy. These were the killing of his son in August 1967 by an agent of the National Bureau of Investigation, interference of then president Ferdinand Marcos in Cotabato politics, and his feeling of betrayal by fellow-Muslim politicians. Marcos was running for re-election in 1969 under the Nacionalista Party (NP) and he wanted to break the clout of the Liberal Party's Matalam and Pendatun clans in the province. He did this by supporting Datu Abdullah Sangki, a relative of the Ampatuan royal clan, as the NP's standard-bearer for governor. To beat the Sangki challenge, Matalam's brother-in-law, Representative Salipada Pendatun, ran for governor, with Simeon Datumanong as vice-gubernatorial candidate. The two won, but Pendatun chose to return to his post in Congress and turned over the governorship to Datumanong (who was an Ampatuan relative). Datumanong subsequently transferred the provincial capital from Pagalungan, Matalam's traditional stronghold, to Cotabato City. The Matalam patriarch's loss of the post hurt the 'Grand Old Man' who "had agreed to step aside only because with his brother-in-law at the helm, the provincial government would still be in the hands of the family".[29]

Matalam's other sons, exposed to student activism in Manila and Muslim nationalism in the Middle East and Africa, were said to have influenced their father that the Muslims in the Philippines could only find justice in a Muslim state, and not through the student demonstrations they were waging in Manila. Deferring to his sons and cognizant of his political stature, Matalam thus reportedly issued the May 1968 MIM Manifesto.[30]

There is doubt, however, as to whether it was Matalam who wrote the manifesto. Recollections among scholars and writers shared in the e-group Kusogmindanaw in late June/early July 2008 point to "a UP [University of the Philippines] group" of young Moros — notably, Jalaludin 'Joel' de los Santos, a protégé of the late Muslim historian Cesar Majul, along with other young Moro university students like the Abbas brothers and Abul Khayr Alonto — as the drafters.[31] However, according to Mindanao-based writer Patricio P. Diaz and Cotabato Muslim scholar Abhoud Syed Lingga, the manifesto was written by two protégés of Matalam; namely, the young lawyers Musib Buat and Hussin Pangato.[32]

The MIM was a loose, nominal organization that harnessed the anger and captured the imagination of the upcoming generation of the many educated Moro elites, but it did not provide real leadership. Rather than a real anti-government group, Macapado Muslims described the MIM as a paper organization, and the so-called MIM Blackshirts that launched attacks on settler communities and army units were suspected of being government agents tasked to heighten the violence and justify state militarization.[33] The MIM, too, did not seem to be an influence on or the force behind the pocket uprisings that took place when martial law was declared, such as in October 1972 when Maranao youths with support from their elders attacked the headquarters of the Philippine Constabulary in Marawi and succeeded in laying siege to the Mindanao State University campus for a day. Matalam's name is not among the founders of groups such as the Islamic Directorate of the Philippines that raised funds for the defence of the Moros.[34] The Directorate helped forge collaboration among established and rising Moro leaders. In their declaration of unity, they "declared the readiness of the Muslims to defend Islam, the Homeland, and their people against all forms of aggressions against the Ummah".[35] There is thus some doubt as to whether Matalam and the organization he founded really intended to pursue secession. Muslim contends that up to about mid-1972 there was no talk of secession in Muslim areas, although military training was taking place.[36]

Looking back in 1986, Salamat Hashim said that "The demand for secession [of the MIM] was made only to attract the attention of the government ...[and] the leaders ... did not continue the struggle against the Philippine government."[37] Misuari, more kindly, said: "Initially, the MIM could have developed into an umbrella organization which could take under its share other aggrupations, especially the younger elements, voicing similar objectives."[38]

Jubair also offered a more sympathetic view of the intentions of the 'Old Man' Matalam:

> The desire for power was quite remote. He was already the governor of the biggest province in the entire country. Neither could his action be attributed to the desire for more wealth, for revolution does not pay off. Whether or not he was serious is not within our competence to judge. But one thing is certain. The MIM did not gain much momentum and few outside his home province of Cotabato listened to him seriously enough. But the reaction of the government was a different story. From all indications, it did not take the MIM challenge lightly. Subsequently, one of his advisers, Atty. Hussain Pangato, was killed sometime in 1970 by PC troopers at Tinidtiban, Pikit, Cotabato.[39]

Jubair also credited the MIM for the revival of "the spirit of independence: among the Moros, especially the students and professionals".[40] Similarly, for Canoy, Matalam "had set powerful forces in motion".

Che Man, for his part, assessed the MIM thus: "The MIM aimed at bringing together the Moro provinces as an independent Muslim state. It had the effect of raising the Moro struggle to a more advanced level. But its strength was limited because the organization revolved around only a few aristocratic political leaders."[41]

In any case, the MIM became insignificant when Matalam and Marcos reconciled. As Jubair recounted: "But after much rumblings, the MIM itself may have succumbed to the threats and enticements of the government. In December 1971, Pres. Ferdinand Marcos and Datu Udtog Matalam met in Manila, after which only the name was left of this organization."[42] Canoy traces the reconciliation to much earlier, to the 1969 presidential elections, when Marcos reportedly presented Matalam with a gold watch, a gift accepted by the patriarch. In their exchange, the *datu* reportedly said that what he really wanted was not independence but self-governance under a federal system. "With this admission", Canoy wrote, "Matalam wrote *finis* to the Mindanao Independence Movement."[43]

Matalam and most other aristocratic leaders of his generation who were more inclined to collaboration and were not ready to fight the martial law regime effectively surrendered the leadership of the resistance to the upcoming generation of educated Muslim youth. Whether from an aristocratic background like Macapanton Abbas and Abul Khayr Alonto, or of non-elite origins like Nur Misuari, or religious-trained like Salamat Hashim, these emerging Moro leaders all headed major student organizations that in the 1960s were increasingly radicalized. Misuari, Abbas and Hashim were, respectively, officers of the Maoist-leaning Kabataan Makabayan, the National Union of Students of the Philippines, and the Philippine Students' Union in Cairo in 1962. Jubair aptly used the subtitle "Rise of Moro Students' Power" in his book to describe the new resistance leadership that emerged during this time.[44]

While initially addressing national political and economic issues alongside the rest of the student activists in the 1960s, Jubair recounted that the Moro activists increasingly realized, "albeit quite late, that although there were common serious national issues confronting the Moros and the Christians that they could both cry about, the fact was that the Moros themselves had a particular tune to sing". Thus began the Moro-focused articulation of the restless youth.

The Bangsa Moro Liberation Organization

Then house representative Haroun Al-Rashid Lucman of Lanao
organized the Bangsa Moro Liberation Organization (BMLO) in 1969
"as an umbrella organization of all the liberation forces".[45] So named,
the BMLO thus preceded the MNLF in adopting 'Moro' as an identity
label and in advancing the notion of a Moro nation.

The BMLO interestingly straddled two generations and Moro
social strata (politician-aristocrats and commoners). Lucman headed
the Supreme Executive Council, Macapanton Abbas was its secretary,
Utdog Matalam Jr. was head of the Military Committee for Kutawato
(Cotabato), while Abul Khayr Alonto and Nur Misuari headed the
military committees for Ranao and Sulu, respectively. Except for the
older Lucman and Abbas, the rest belonged to "a dynamic group of
young Moro intellectuals who were then deeply involved in student
activism in Manila" and who provided the ideological underpinnings
to the BMLO.[46]

Lucman reportedly got the support of the sympathetic governor
from Sabah Tun Mustapha and the Malaysian government headed by
Tunku Abdul Rahman to provide military training to young Moros in
Malaysia.[47] Mostly recruited from among Moro youth organizations,
the first 'Top 90' batch left in 1969.[48] The group of 90 was made up
of 67 Maranaos, 8 Maguindanaos and 15 Suluanos.[49]

Through the Islamic Directorate, Lucman and other Moro politicians
like Senator Domocao Alonto and Senator Salipada Pendatun brought
the case of the Moros to the OIC and sympathetic governments like
Libya, which promised to provide monetary support.

Soon after the declaration of martial law in 1972, the politicians
in the BMLO chose to cooperate with the Marcos government, with
the avowed purpose of "inject[ing] the rationale of the Moro struggle
into government policies in order to lay the basis of the legitimacy
of the Moro struggle".[50] In 1973, Abbas joined the Presidential Task
Force for the Reconstruction and Development of Mindanao. In 1974,
Marcos acknowledged Lucman as the "paramount Sultan of Mindanao
and Sulu".[51] However, the next year the two politicians broke ties with
Marcos and tried, unsuccessfully, to reunite with the MNLF. Around
1977, the BMLO leaders tried to broker unification of the different Moro
factions, but the more radical groups rejected the overtures.[52] In 1984,

the BMLO changed its name to Bangsa Muslimin Islamic Liberation Organization (BMILO) and rejected the term Moro, supposedly because of its colonial origins.[53]

The Moro National Liberation Front (MNLF)

The secret founding of the MNLF and its military arm the Bangsa Moro Army in 1969 is generally attributed to the young Tausug Nur Misuari and other BMLO recruits who were on military training on an island of Perak state. These founders included Abul Khayr Alonto, Salamat Hashim, Muslimin Sema,[54] Al-Jabbar Narra, Dambong Sali, Abdurahman Jamasali, Alaverez Isnaji,[55] Hussein Mohammad, Al Caluang and Al Haj Murad Ebrahim.[56] Alonto became vice-chair to Nur of the Provisional Central Committee, and Salamat Hashim was chosen to head the Cotabato provincial committee. Other major portfolios were held by Otto Salahuddin of Basilan, Ali Alibon of Davao, Lumet Hassan of Cotabato and Sali Wali of Zamboanga.[57] In the second half of 1972, a meeting was held in Sabah to install a permanent chair of the Central Committee and, according to Jubair's account, Hashim gave in to Misuari.[58]

The grouping now came from the same generation but from across the different social strata of Muslim society in Mindanao. Canoy described the coming together of Misuari, Alonto and Salamat as an "odd triumvirate".[59] Misuari came from humble beginnings; his parents were Tausug/Tau Sug and Sama fisherfolk from Tapul Island. Abul Alonto, who was said to have willingly played second fiddle to Misuari, was the son of the former Lanao governor and Philippine ambassador to Libya Madki Alonto, and nephew of Princess Tarhata Lucman (wife of BMLO founder Raschid Lucman) and of former senator Domocao Alonto. The Islamic scholar Salamat was related to powerful Cotabato clans surnamed Matalam and Pendatun. How Misuari earned the leadership has been attributed to his being "a master of words" and his charisma that "shone in his eyes as he spoke".[60]

Despite their mixed class composition, the younger grouping also had more radical ideas about democratizing the Moro's stratified society. The young Moro intellectuals were by then exposed to Marxism and national democratic ideas carried by student activists at that time.

They were also in 'united front' talks with the national democratic communist left. However, these engagements never got far enough to lead to a convergence, and their respective movements grew independently.

As to how they adopted the name MNLF, there are several accounts as to who should have the main credit. According to Canoy, the adoption of 'Moro' took place during the training of the Top 90 batch in West Malaysia: "The Tau Sug, Maranao and Maguindanao plotters wanted to preserve their respective tribal identities. Abul Khayr Alonto broke the deadlock by proposing they use the term 'Moro'. For lack of anything to call themselves, it was adopted. The MNLF thus turned a colonial insult into a rallying cry."[61] But, as the chronology shows, the BMLO had appropriated the term first, and given the overlap in people in the two organizations, the term was already there for pragmatic adoption among the different groupings of revolutionaries.

When the 'Top 90' trainees returned to Mindanao,[62] most of them went on with their work in their legal organizations that aimed to bring together Moro youth. Alonto and Salamat recruited more members in Lanao and Cotabato. Misuari organized students from various schools in Jolo into a group called "Paambuuk", which means united in Tausug. Many of these students came from prominent Sulu families. They included the sisters Desdemona and Eleonora Rohaida Tan, daughters of the Abubakar political clan,[63] and Dr Farouk Hussein, then Jolo's municipal health officer.[64] Misuari ran and lost in the 1970 elections for members of the Constitutional Convention, with an agenda for the creation of a federal state. The succeeding takeover of the constitutional drafting process and the shutting down of Congress when martial law was declared left armed struggle as the only viable arena remaining for them to pursue their goals.

Misuari established good ties with Sabah's chief minister Tun Mustapha, a native of Sulu who migrated to Sabah after World War II. Tun Mustapha allegedly nurtured a dream to create an independent Muslim state made up of Sabah, Sulu, Taw-tawi and Palawan. With his help, Misuari established a training camp in Jamperas and two other smaller camps in Sempurna and Kota Kinabalu, all in Sabah.[65]

Lucman's influence in Lanao reportedly made the MNLF relatively weak in that province.[66] In 1972, Lucman claimed that he and the BMLO had been betrayed by Misuari and Hashim by their arranging to meet with the Libyans themselves in Sabah for the handing over of financial support, allegedly to the amount of US\$3.5 million.[67] The opportunity allowed the young revolutionaries to introduce the MNLF to the Libyan leadership. Che Man posited two reasons why Muammar Al-Qaddafi chose to support the emerging as opposed to the traditional Moro leadership: that as a revolutionary government, he pinned more hopes on the younger generation to lead the Moro revolution; and that he did not want funds to be ineffectively used by politicians.[68]

With martial law in place, Moro resistance was pushed to a higher stage as arrests of opposition leaders combined with various other grievances and conflicts assumed a violent face. Moreover, the attempts by Marcos to confiscate loose firearms threatened the Moro populace.[69] In 1973 the MNLF began constituting the Bangsa Moro Army, and the existence of the MNLF became public.[70] The first major fighting erupted in Cotabato in February. In the same year, Misuari established his headquarters in Sabah. Several months later, Hashim left for Libya and became the head of the MNLF's Foreign Affairs committee. Libya generously provided logistical support to procure armaments.

The MNLF's 28 April 1974 manifesto — ratified at the First MNLF Congress, held in Zamboanga — envisioned a Bangsa Moro Homeland covering Mindanao, Sulu and Palawan (MINSUPALA). It castigated the "oppression and tyranny of Filipino colonialism" and accused the state of "criminally usurping our land ... threatening Islam through wholesale destruction and desecration of its places of worship and its Holy Book, and murdering our innocent brothers, sisters and folks in a genocidal campaign of terrifying magnitude". It promised to institute a democratic system of government. The MNLF fought Marcos's army and claimed that the war had reached a stalemate in late 1975, which supposedly prompted Marcos to pursue negotiations.[71]

Peace Negotiations for Autonomy

The MNLF earned formal recognition as the representative of the Moro people in the OIC in July 1975. The OIC urged the Marcos government to negotiate with the MNLF. In talks brokered by OIC countries, notably Libya, the MNLF agreed to scale down its demand for separation to arrangements for autonomy in thirteen Mindanao provinces.[72] This was stipulated in the December 1976 Tripoli Agreement signed by the MNLF and the Philippine government, with the OIC as witness.

Why did the MNLF agree to scale down its demands to autonomy covering only a portion of Mindanao? Among the reasons given by analysts were the pressure from the OIC to accede to the compromise; the hesitation of Middle Eastern countries to pump in more money for war efforts; and the MNLF's dependence on and its subservience to their foreign patrons. The Tripoli Agreement was thus hailed as a diplomatic victory for the Philippine government.[73]

In January 1977 the two parties signed a ceasefire agreement. Shortly thereafter, Marcos held a rigged referendum, created two autonomous regional bodies (Regions 9 and 12) instead of one, and put these regional administrations under the control and supervision of the national government. In effect, no real autonomy was granted. Moreover, the Armed Forces of the Philippines (AFP) waged military operations to destroy MNLF bases.[74] The ceasefire broke down and the MNLF reverted to its call for a free and independent state. Fighting resumed, although it never reached the same intensity as in the early 1970s. In 1986, when Marcos had been ousted and Corazon Aquino had taken over the presidency, the MNLF resumed negotiations for regional autonomy.

Factionalization in the MNLF

Since this time, the MNLF has witnessed several splits and fallouts with the government. Many MNLF fighters laid down their arms and availed of the martial law government's amnesty programme. In March 1978, then MNLF vice-chair Abul Khayr Alonto and his followers returned to the country, paving the way for Hashim to become vice-chair. However, it seems that as early as August 1977 Hashim had already formed the 'New Leadership', with fifty-seven other men, "to pursue a state based on Islamic principles".[75] In 1984 they formally established the Moro Islamic Liberation Front (MILF). Why they split from the MNLF will be examined further in the next section.

One organizational loss was followed by another. In June 1982, Misuari's then vice-chair, Dimasangkay Pundato, declared the formation of the MNLF-Reformist Group. Pundato and forty-two others signed a petition asking for organizational reforms, including the functioning of a real and representative Central Committee and Executive Committee, unity with the other organizations such as the BMLO and the Hashim Salamat faction, and the localization of the leaders and commands of the provinces.[76] Misuari rejected the petition outright. The MILF and the MNLF-RG had a brief period of unity in early 1981, but this became moot when most members of the Reformist Group, including Pundato, joined the government.[77] Pundato based himself in Kuala Lumpur and courted Malaysia's support against Misuari.[78]

Canoy attributed the defection of top field commanders to the wholesale bribery offered by the government in the form of amnesty with cash rewards and government posts; their political, cultural and ideological differences with Misuari, whom they accused of having communist leanings; and alleged kickbacks in the purchase of arms that went to Misuari, a charge that the government allegedly perpetuated through disinformation campaigns.[79] Other than leaders, the Marcos government also harvested 'rebel returnees' from the rank-and-file. Jubair gave several reasons for the falling out of fighters from Misuari's MNLF. For one, the fighters' thirst for revenge for the crimes of the Constabulary-Ilaga against them in the 1960s and 1970s had been quenched by the numerous victorious attacks against government troops, and the wounds from these depredations had healed. Also, those who joined for adventure or the glory of banditry had been satisfied, and many had already had the opportunity to fight with their brothers and sisters against a common enemy. At the same time, Jubair offered another explanation from a military point of view. He claimed that the positional warfare that demanded much strength and resources was hard to sustain at a "clearly guerrilla state of the struggle" in 1972–75. This contributed greatly to the "early exit of the vacillators and pseudo-revolutionaries".[80]

On the whole, the series of splits that weakened the MNLF after it successfully negotiated the 1976 Tripoli Agreement (and then again, after the signing of the 1996 Comprehensive Peace Agreement with the Ramos administration) reflects the internal weaknesses in the MNLF. It failed to meet what Che Man considered criteria of a strong revolutionary organization — mainly, established mechanisms and structures. According to Che Man, the MNLF created a region-wide network of groups fighting the Marcos regime but failed to institutionalize a chain of command. Its Central Committee was based in a foreign country and was run by a few strong leaders who concentrated their efforts on generating funds and international support. Loyalties of members were largely built under the three provincial revolutionary commands in Sulu, Cotabato and Lanao (which coincided with the three major ethnic groups, Tausug, Maguindanao and Maranao, respectively). These were in turn led by their respective elites. Citing other sources, Che Man also noted the gap between the field commanders and the Central Committee and the latter's failure to control the behaviour of the many groups under it. Moreover, aristocratic elites allegedly felt threatened by the commoner Misuari's predisposition for a radical change of Moro feudal society. Nonetheless, the MNLF enjoyed mass support, which made the recruitment of trainees easy.[81]

Based on the issues raised by the Hashim faction and Pundato's MNLF-Reformist Group, Misuari's poor and personalistic style of leadership and Tausug bias alienated his comrades. The issue of poor and personalistic leadership would again manifest in the aftermath of the 1996 Peace Agreement signed between the MNLF and the Ramos administration, which saw Misuari sitting as an incompetent and corrupt governor of the revitalized ARMM[82] from 1997 to 2001.

The Rise of the MILF

Salamat Hashim is the acknowledged founder of the MILF. A Maguindanaon born in 1943 in Pagalungan, Maguindanao province, he was educated in Philippine public schools and village madrasahs. In 1959 he left for Egypt to study theology at Al-Azhar University. Coming from an aristocratic and religious family, he was described as one who belonged to the traditional and religious elite, unlike Misuari who was classified as a member of the secular elite.[83] During his student days in Cairo, Hashim was involved in student activism and was exposed to Islamic and revolutionary trends. He served as president of the Philippine Muslim Student Association and secretary-general of the Organization of Asian Students in Cairo.[84]

Jubair, in his retracing of the MILF, claimed that as early as 1962, Moro students in Cairo led by Hashim had already formed a nucleus aimed at freeing the Moro homeland, implying they must have been the first to conceive of the idea of establishing a liberation organization.

However, "they may not have called it MNLF, more so considering their religious background; but certainly they would have put up an organization along Islamic perspectives".[85] In a 1986 interview, Hashim also retraced the roots of the MILF to Cairo — prior to the formation of the MNLF. Although the MILF was declared only in 1984, "(t)he organization was founded in 1962, when we were students in Cairo. At that time it was just called Moro Liberation Front." When these Cairo students returned to the Philippines, they joined forces with Misuari's MNLF.[86]

Hashim supposedly was responsible for covertly arranging the military training of the Top 90 recruits that eventually formed the core group of the MNLF.[87] In 1970 he returned to Mindanao to help organize the second batch of trainees known as Batch 300. He then became the first chairman of the Kutawato Revolutionary Committee, whose jurisdiction covered Maguindanao, Cotabato, South Cotabato, Sultan Kudarat and four municipalities of Lanao del Sur.[88] The declaration of martial law in September 1972 forced him to go underground. In 1974 he became a member of the MNLF's Central Committee and was posted to Libya, where he chaired the Committee for Foreign Affairs. It appeared that he was being excluded from Central Committee meetings and he found himself disagreeing with Misuari on almost all policy issues. In September 1977, shortly after the MNLF's talks with the Marcos regime broke down, the Kutawato Revolutionary Committee petitioned the OIC and the Muslim World League calling for the ouster of Misuari as MNLF chair and the recognition of Hashim.[89] Hashim's supporters then tried to wrest the leadership from Nur Misuari at a meeting in Mecca in December 1977. In response to the "popular clamor of the leaders in the field", Hashim allegedly executed an 'Instrument of Takeover', which Misuari of course rejected.[90]

The OIC and the Muslim World League separately attempted to mediate a reunification in succeeding years, but they failed. Both Egypt and Libya provided support to the MILF, even though Libya was openly supporting the MNLF.[91]

Reasons for the Split

In the petition, the breakaway group stated that they had been alienated by the "arrogant, secretive leadership" of Misuari. They said he had arrogated to himself the "policies, plans, and decisions and dispositions — political, financial and/or strategic" of the organization.[92] Other than the organizational differences, Hashim had also disagreed with the MNLF's veering towards "Marxist-Maoist orientations" and away from Islamic goals.[93] Moreover, according to Canoy, Hashim came under tremendous pressure from the *ulama* to break away from Misuari, whose supposed communist-leanings they did not like.[94]

Lingga similarly highlights the MILF's ideological justification for leaving the MNLF. He wrote that "the split was basically caused by the different ideological outlook between the two leaders. Salamat categorically defined the ideological line he follows as LA ILAHA ILLA ALLAH MUHAMMAD AL-RASUL ALLAH, meaning that God alone must be worshipped and the worship must be carried out according to the teachings and examples set by Prophet Muhammad, peace be upon him. He is committed to the application of this ideology in all aspects of the life of the Bangsamoro people which can only be possible through the establishment of an Islamic government." Salamat's goal "is not just the liberation of the Bangsamoro homeland from what the Bangsamoro fronts perceived as Philippine colonial rule but the application of the Islamic ideology similar to the goal of Islamic movements in different parts of the world".[95]

In forming the MILF officially in March 1984 with Islam as its official ideology, Lingga wrote, "The word 'national' was permanently dropped in favor of 'Islamic' to emphasize the Islamic ideological line which Salamat originally and invariably espoused during the founding years of the revolution."[96]

Salamat's and Misuari's ideological differences and their divergent backgrounds were reportedly also reflected in how they conducted their international work. "A political scientist, Misuari chose to touch base with the foreign ministers and heads of state through the OIC. Salamat, the theologian, preferred to link up with the world confederation of Islamic religious leaders, the Rabita", wrote Canoy.[97] Hashim moved around Egypt and Pakistan to generate support for the MILF for much of the 1980s.

Writer Soliman Santos, Jr consequently distinguished the MNLF as the "secularist-nationalist-modernist stream" from the MILF, which he described as the "radical Islamic revivalist stream".[98] The MILF established Islamic-modelled organs like the Supreme Islamic Revolutionary Tribunal and the Majiles Shura.[99] The *ulama* played a major role in mobilizations and in articulating Islamic unity and laws "as an anti-thesis to familiar politics and social inequities".[100] Allied Muslim professions have formed organizations working for "Islamic unity and revival".[101] The community-based camps they had established in Central Mindanao were said to serve both as a symbol of the resistance and as models of the envisioned Islamic community.[102] Among the tasks of the village committees and the Internal Security Force in the village was to ensure that the teachings of the Qur'an and the Sunnah were observed.[103]

Weight is also given to the fact that while Misuari is a Tausug, Hashim belonged to the Maguindanao ethnolinguistic group. The Sulu archipelago, where the Tausug are the largest ethnic group, has remained the stronghold of Misuari's MNLF. The MILF developed a larger base straddling Maguindanao and North and South Cotabato.

Writing in 2002, Lingga provided another angle for the split: "The Bangsamoro people at one time were united under the leadership of the MNLF but after it abandoned the goal of regaining independence and accepted autonomy within the framework of Philippine sovereignty and integrity, Salamat and other field commanders bolted out and formed a faction it initially called the New MNLF Leadership and then renamed it MILF to continue the struggle for independence."[104] This seems to me a popular but mistaken assumption for one of the fundamental reasons the Hashim faction broke away; namely, the ideological difference with and disdain for Misuari's undemocratic and personalistic leadership style. It should be noted that Hashim and his allies were part of the negotiations that led to the 1976 Tripoli Agreement. They were just as bitter that Marcos reneged on the implementation.[105] Indeed, Jubair's more or less official MILF account made no mention of Hashim disagreeing with the negotiations for autonomy.

Hashim's willingness to negotiate in lieu of the independence track was again made evident when the opportunity arose with the downfall of the Marcos regime. The MILF was expecting that a conjoined MNLF-MILF panel would negotiate with the newly installed President Corazon Aquino in 1987.[106] But Aquino chose to meet with Misuari only, in Sulu on 5 September 1986, and her representatives signed the Jeddah Accord with the MNLF to formally resume talks in January 1987. Both instances took place without the MILF. In retaliation, the MILF staged tactical offensives in Central Mindanao provinces for five days in January 1987 "to convey the message that it was not a pushover organization".[107]

It is true that the MILF continued to campaign for independence as a strategic goal, but it more decidedly pursued a 'genuine autonomy' track when it engaged the government in formal negotiations beginning in 1997. This track achieved its peak when the Comprehensive Agreement on the Bangsamoro that provided for an autonomous Bangsamoro region was signed in March 2014, with this author as co-signatory on behalf of the Philippine government then headed by President Simeon Benigno Aquino III.

Under Hashim Salamat's Leadership

As a counterpoint to Misuari's leadership style, the MILF under Hashim's leadership instilled the practice of consultation and collective decision-making. Hashim wrote in 1985: "One of the hallmarks of the MILF is its policy of CONSULTATIVE and COLLECTIVE LEADERSHIP. Essentially, this policy means that no major decisions could be formulated and implemented without resorting to Shurah (consultations) in general meetings attended by Central Committee members in the homeland and representatives from different regions."[108] This dictum is fairly consistent with his criticism of Misuari's leadership as personalistic and undemocratic. Admittedly though, this process also leads to delay in some action or policy responses.[109]

The ideological difference was further fortified in a ten-year programme launched in 1980, and extended to 2000. The programme identified four priority fields of concern: Islamization, organizational build-up, military build-up, and self-reliance.[110] By the 1980s the MILF and its armed wing, the Bangsamoro Islamic Armed Forces (BIAF), had become a much stronger force, not only in terms of the number of Moro fighters but also as a revolutionary organization with a network of supporters and organizations lodged in different sectors of society: the *ulama*, the youth, and professionals. Lingga credited the MILF's growth to Hashim's leadership: "Under his leadership, the MILF embarked to strengthen its political organizations, reorganized and trained its military forces that gained reputation as disciplined revolutionary forces, undertook economic and logistical self-reliance, and vigorously promoted Islamic values and education which made it grow and become the biggest liberation organization in Southeast

Asia and one of the biggest in the world with functional political and military organs."[111] Lingga also praised Ustadz Hashim as the "ideologue of the Bangsamoro liberation movement" whose guidance on military, political, social and spiritual matters are sought by the mujahideen all over Mindanao, earning for him the title of Amirul Mujahideen.

Hashim's 1985 monograph, *The Bangsamoro Mujahid: His Objectives and Responsibilities*, codified the organizational guidelines for MILF fighters that he had issued in various lectures. The teachings sought to strengthen the MILF as a revolutionary force primarily by strengthening an awareness, commitment and unity based on Islamic ideals. "The crowning objective of every Muslim true to his faith is to go to Paradise ... a blessing not only to the Muslim Ummah but to the whole of mankind."[112] The force of such religious underpinnings in waging the war cannot be underestimated. Hashim extolled all mujahid Bangsamoro to live the life of faith in Islam based on knowledge of the teachings of Islam and the history of the Bangsamoro people, and with the conviction to live "a life of obedience and submission to the Will of God".[113] He argued that joining an Islamic organization like the MILF is obligatory for all believers because "the situation is such that the government in our homeland is itself the enemy, the oppressor".[114] Devotion to Islam is a major criterion in bestowing honour and in promotion through the ranks of the MILF, along with loyal service, exemplary performance of duties, intellectual contributions and uprightness of character.[115] Categorically, he wrote, "The core of our political and social program is the ISLAMIZATION of the Bangsamoro people."[116] Since the Moros are already Muslims, he most likely meant their deeper conviction to live the faith and wage jihad.

Hashim ruled by example. He practised Islam faithfully, both in his personal devotion and as his guiding leadership of the practical affairs of the movement. Mohager Iqbal described Hashim as very organized and disciplined.[117] He must have followed the regimen he preached to the mujahid.[118] This spiritual discipline is complemented by his organizational acumen.[119] He was said to have motivated people effectively. According to Abhoud Syed Lingga, who conducted extensive interviews with Hashim in the 1990s for his master's thesis on "The Thoughts of Salamat Hashim", the MILF chair never pressured people to join the MILF; he would only say to them, do something good for the Bangsamoro.[120] Hashim permanently returned to Mindanao from exile in 1987.

In 1994 the AFP estimated MILF strength at 5,420 fighters. In December 1999, AFP chief of staff Angelo Reyes claimed the MILF was 15,690 strong, or almost 300 per cent of the size of their 1984 estimate. The MILF had at least one camp each in Basilan, Bukidnon, Davao del Sur and Tawi-tawi; two major camps in Lanao del Norte and Lanao del Sur (Camp Busrah Somiorang and Camp Bilal), and in South Cotabato and Sarangani provinces; three major camps (Camps Rajah Muda, Madirago and Usman) and several sub-camps in North Cotabato; and five major camps and ten sub-camps in Maguindanao, including Camps Badre and Omar Ibn Al Khatab, its general headquarters at that time, Camp Abubakre, and its current headquarters in Camp Darapanan.[121]

In June/July 2000, the AFP under President Joseph Estrada launched Oplan Mindanao II/Black Rain. As a result, Hashim was said to have been forced "to implement a Qur'anic injunction to reposition the MILF forces as a 'strategem of war' from the urbanized communities of Camp Abubakre as-Siddique to its heavily forested military fortifications."[122] Nearly 10,000 residents of the camp moved to town centres of Maguindanao province and Cotabato city. The MILF lost several camps in the war that followed, including its headquarters, Camp Abubakre. Since then, the AFP has come up with conflicting estimates of MILF strength ranging from 5,000 to 15,200 — the latter based on the claim that they suffered casualties of 500 men in the 2000 military offensives, although other accounts indicate much higher casualties for both the MILF and the government.

On 13 July 2003, Hashim died of a heart attack at Camp Busrah Somiorang. The series of government bombings of the Islamic Center at Buliok in Camp Rajah Muda that began on 11 February (referred to among MILF members as 2/11) had forced Hashim to leave the camp, where major meetings of the Central Committee were held.[123] In his journey back to Camp Abubakre as-Siddique, he stopped by Camp Busrah. On 29 May the AFP struck at Camp Busrah for several hours but missed the leader, who, reportedly, subsequently issued a recorded audio message saying that "he was not afraid to die any time because he was certain to have planted the seeds of Jihad in the hearts and minds of the Moro people and you who will continue the glorious struggle for their freedom and independence".[124]

Ameerul Mujahideen Ash-Shayk Ash-Shaheed Salamat Hashim is revered by the MILF, not only with this title but enthusiastically, with platitudes such as "the illustrious Imam of the oppressed Bangsamoro people". Located in the context of the Islamic world he was "one of the greatest freedom fighters ever produced by the Muslim Ummah in modern times".[125] His followers take pride in his scholarship, as witnessed by the many writings and *khutab* (sermons; which were audio-taped) in English, Arabic and the Maguindanaw languages. In his effusive tribute, successor Ebrahim Murad called him the "Grand Old Man of the Bangsamoro", a "Great Reformer", "Scholar", "Visionary", "Thinker", "Great Leader", "Elder Brother and the Mother-and-Father combined of the Bangsamoro People and Struggle".[126] MILF Youth Agency chair Nu'ain Bin Abdulhaqq said that given Hashim's formidable leadership and the power of his pen, he could be considered "the Ibn Khaldun or Shaykhul Islam Ibn Taymiyya of this Moro generation" and the "modern day Sultan Kudarat of his generation".[127]

Using the metaphor of China's Long March as an analogy, MILF Youth Agency chair Abdulhaqq marked Hashim's death as the end of the sixth and last leg of the shaheed's lifetime struggle.[128] The first leg in this rendering of Hashim's thirty-year struggle began in 1958 when the young Moro left his hometown of Cotabato City to study in Egypt, where he organized the League of Cotabato Students in Cairo and then in 1962 the Philippine Students Association in Cairo and the Solidarity Council of the Southeast Asian Students Association in Cairo. The second leg of Hashim's Long March was spent in various European countries where "the young man educationally developed and politically advanced at par with his contemporary Thinkers, Scholars and Revolutionaries in the Middle East, Asia, Latin America and Europe".

The third leg in this legend-like recounting was the return to the homeland during the Marcos regime and back again to several countries in the Middle East to establish the MNLF's foreign offices in Islamabad, Cairo and Jeddah. According to the tract, Hashim had already finished writing his dissertation on "The Rise of Islam in Southeast Asia" but could not ship it to Egypt because his house in Mindanao had been burned by government forces. Among the successes credited to him was the shipment of European-made arms of World War II vintage that armed the MILF's Top 90 and Batch 300 trainees. This third leg stretched up to the parting of ways with Misuari, which the account dated as taking place in December 1977, followed by the setting up of the new MNLF leadership the next year. It also covered the formation of the MILF in March 1984, and in 1985 the issuance of "Hashim's masterpiece on the Moro struggle — *The Bangsamoro Mujahid: His Objectives and Responsibilities*, which became the Islamic Front's written guidelines in pursuing the struggle for self-determination".

Hashim's permanent return to Mindanao in 1987 "on a still classified route and circumstances" constituted the fourth leg. He stayed in Camp Abubakre as-Siddique and pursued the four-point programme mentioned earlier, which the author credited for the building of thousands of mosques where Hashim delivered his Friday *khutab*, hundreds of Islamic schools, the establishment of at least forty-six military camps-cum-Islamic communities and of the MILF's legislative and judicial systems, the training of thousands of *da'wah* workers, and the cultivation of agricultural land which supposedly made the MILF self-reliant. Thousands of firearms were reportedly acquired, and the Abdhulrahman Bedis Memorial Military Academy in Camp Busrah was established to train the MILF's freedom fighters. All these allowed the MILF to operate "a shadow Islamic state and government complete with police and military forces [who were] respected and obeyed by its citizens and feared by her enemies". This leg lasted up to early July 2000, shortly after the launching of Oplan Mindanao II/Black Rain by the AFP under President Joseph Estrada.

The fifth leg began on 12 July 2000 when Hashim declared 'all-out jihad' against Estrada's 'all-out war'.[129] The author claimed that in so doing Hashim became only the second Moro leader to do so, next to the seventeenth century Sultan Kudarat who issued a general call to arms and jihad. The MILF shifted from positional to guerrilla warfare. Hashim built several satellite camps. He exercised command from Camp Rajah Muda in Buliok, his birthplace, and he was here on '2/11' in 2003 when Macapagal-Arroyo renewed offensives. During these offensives, "Chairman Salamat roamed freely the Ligwasan Marsh. His mastery of the marsh allowed him to establish several command centers.... Various sultans and datus of Magindanaw had similarly used the marsh as wide open fortifications against the Spaniards, the Americans and the Japanese. In fact, Chairman Salamat used to meet the MILF Central Committee in his submersible mobile command centers in the marsh." Major meetings with the Central Committee were held at Camp Rajah

Muda, while the 16th and 17th general assemblies held in September 2001 and November 2002, respectively, were reportedly held in the forests of Camp Abubakre.

The sixth leg began with his departure from the marshland of Camp Rajah Muda to find safety in Camp Abubakre. Stopping over at Camp Busrah, "Allah Subhanahu wa Tqa'ala took his soul".

A few hours before he died, Hashim was said to have told his attending physicians: "My heart could have been bypassed easily had it not been due to the oppression inflicted against us by the Philippine colonial government." Shortly after listening to a brief update from his secretary, Muhammad Ameen, he relaxed his back, uttered a few words of prayers, put his right hand over the left, closed his eyes, and took a deep breathe "that suddenly broke the deafening silence of the legendary Makaturing and Pangulintangan sierra madre".[130]

Commiserating on his death, MNLF's Nur Misuari proclaimed him as a "Great Bangsamoro National Hero".[131]

Murad: Successor to Hashim Salamat

The MILF announced Salamat's death only on 5 August, by which time they had held their 18th General Assembly at Camp Madinah, allegedly a satellite camp of Camp Abubakre, on 27–29 July 2003. Murad Ebrahim's audio message, broadcast over Suara Mindanaw, a radio programme of the Institute of Bangsamoro Studies in Cotabato City, also revealed that he had succeeded Hashim as MILF chair.[132] Murad was the chair of the Kutawato (Cotabato) Revolutionary Command of the MNLF when he left it to join Hashim. Murad led the MILF panel in talks with the government until Hashim's death, after which he was replaced by fellow Central Committee member and head of the information/propaganda office Mohager Iqbal. Murad's father is a religious leader, but, unlike Hashim, he was secularly educated, with a degree in civil engineering from a local university.

Murad, then the vice-chair for military affairs, contended for the top post with Alim Abdulazziz Mimbantas, then the deputy chair for internal affairs, founding member and former chief negotiator of the MILF from 1997 to 2000;[133] and Ghazali Jaafar, deputy chair for political affairs. When Murad became the MILF chair, Mimbantas assumed the post of vice-chair for military affairs while initially holding on to his post as head of internal affairs in a concurrent capacity. According to Jubair, Hasim did not nominate his successor. The MILF's rules reportedly state that in case of permanent vacancy of the post the Supreme Shariah Court, acting as caretaker for thirty days, shall call for a meeting of the Central Committee to deliberate and nominate the replacement from among the three deputies. The Central Committee shall then hold a general meeting to confirm the nomination. The most senior member other than the chairman-elect, in this instance Ghazali Jaafar, would issue the official announcement.[134]

According to Jubair, the three gentlemen deferred to each until the intramural "stopped when Abdulazis, in a show of splendid selflessness and statesmanship, approached and practically begged Murad to accept the chairmanship of the MILF. 'You deserve to be the next chairman,' he told Murad in terse voice and in near tears."[135] The humility and hesitancy to assume the responsibility seemed consistent with Hashim's words in 1985 that "We must be wary of members who, by overt or covert acts, aspire for any position in the Front."[136] It can also be recalled that Hashim was said to have deferred to Misuari for the chairmanship in the 1970s. To Jubair, such humility and test of character is "a tradition bequeathed by Islam that no one shall actively seek a position for himself".[137]

In effect the MILF procedure was largely followed except that the Supreme Shariah Court did not act as caretaker for thirty days (if it did at all), since the Central Committee meeting and general assembly took place consecutively from 26 to 31 July 2003 in Lanao del Sur and Murad effectively took over the helm before the thirty-days anniversary of Hashim's death. Whilst they were taking place, the proceedings were kept confidential from the media and the government and they resulted in a smooth transition.

Another more dramatic account of how Murad became the new chair was given by Abdulhaqq in the posthumous collection of Hashim's writings compiled by the MILF's Agency for Youth Affairs in 2005. Vice-chair Alim Abdoulaziz Mimbantas, who was at Hashim's deathbed, reportedly called up his co-chair, Al Haj Murad, and immediately informed him of Hashim's death. In the same phone conversation, Mimbantas allegedly pronounced the traditional pledge of allegiance (bay-ah) to Murad as Hashim's successor. "And then, both cried, firstly, for the demise of the Chairman, and secondly, for the great responsibility bequeathed and entrusted to them...".[138] The Central Committee meeting eventually chose Murad "by unanimous decision".[139]

The first policy declaration of the new leadership was issued on 7 August 2003, which basically said that the reorganized Central Committee would respect and pursue the programmes and policies of the late chairman in order "to provide and maintain continuity in the exercise of all authority and in the performance of all functions for the attainment of the objectives of the Bangsamoro people".[140] Indeed, the MILF continued to practise consultative and collective leadership, the practice ingrained by the late chair.[141]

Despite the current more secular leadership, religious leaders, notably the *ulama* based in communities, remain influential inside the MILF. The Supreme Islamic Tribunal has jurisdiction to pass judgment on an erring MILF member, although the Central Committee also possesses the power to suspend members guilty of negligence, insubordination or indulgence in immoral practices.[142]

Under Murad and the more than seventy other members of its Central Committee, the MILF continued to be the biggest and most organized non-state armed group in the country despite the serious losses suffered during the war under the Estrada administration and the offensive launched in 2001 by President Gloria Macapagal Arroyo's then defence chief Angelo Reyes. It had regular provincial, municipal and village committees that operated side-by-side with the armed commands (see Table 2.1 indicating the armed structure of the MILF in 2004).

In 2008, when the Supreme Court nullified an initialled but unsigned major agreement called the Memorandum of Understanding on Ancestral Domain, the ceasefire broke down. Several commanders attacked villages in Maguindanao and Lanao in protest over the decision. Eventually, one of these commanders, Ustadz Umbra Kato, would break away and form the Bangsamoro Islamic Freedom Fighters, taking with him a chunk of the 105th Base Command.

The MILF leadership under Murad doggedly continued on-off negotiations with the Philippine government. After seventeen years of negotiations that began in 1997 and spanned the administrations of four presidents, it succeeded in forging a Comprehensive Agreement on the Bangsamoro with the government during the term of Simeon Benigno Aquino III. Under the March 2014 agreement, the MILF agreed to the

TABLE 2.1
MILF Camps as of October 2004

Before	Now	Commander	Area
1st Field Division	105th Base Command	Jack Abdullah	Liguasan Marsh, Maguindanao
2nd Field Division	104th Base Command	Tops Jalhamie	South Cotobato (including Lumad tribal highlands and Christian population centres; stretches of coastline of Sultan Kudarat and Sarangani provinces where Khadafi Janjalani was believed to be hiding)
HQ Division	101st Base Command	Gordon Saifullah (allegedly with ties to Jemaah Islamiyah)	Camp Abubakre (inc. Maguindao Lanao borderlands)
1 Battalion of National Guard Division	Part of 106th Base Command	Samir Hashim	North Cotobato
206th Brigade	109th Base Command	Amelil Umbra	Camp Omar, Maguindanao
101st Brigade (1st Division)	107th Base Command	Cosain 'Sonny' Soso	Davao Region
4th Field Division	108th Base Command	Aloy Al-ashrie	Zamboanga Region (mixed population — Maguindanao, Tausug, Sama, Iranon, Kalibo, majority Christian)
3rd Field Division (under Alim Solaiman Pangalian)	In 102/103 Base Command	Rajahmuda Balindong (Commander Bravo)	Lanao
ISF elements (under Abdulaziz Mimbatas)	In 102/103 Base Command	Tayah Luksadatu (also deputy chief of staff to Gambar)	Lanao

Source: Data from International Crisis Group, *Southern Philippines Backgrounder: Terrorism and the Peace Process*, ICG Asia Report No. 80, 13 July 2004.

legislation of a new autonomy law that replaces the ARMM with a new autonomous government with greater political and fiscal autonomy and a parliamentary form of government. Once the Bangsamoro government is fully established, the MILF would have decommissioned all its forces and weapons and converted military camps into civilian communities. In August 2018, the Bangsamoro Organic Law was passed by Congress creating the Bangsamoro Autonomous Region in Muslim Mindanao and providing for a Bangsamoro Transition Authority led by the MILF until 2022. Thus, the MILF closed one chapter of their jihad to move on to another form of struggle, no longer as a non-state armed group but as a state actor at the helm of a transition government, and as a political party gearing up for elections in 2022.

Notes

1. Among these vigilante groups was the Ilaga, made up initially of Tiruray (a non-Islamicized tribe in Cotabato who resented taxation exacted by Muslim *datus*) and later of Ilonggos, settlers from an ethnolinguistic group from the Visayas group of islands. The Ilaga was led by an Ilonggo settler called Commander Toothpick. The Blackshirts and Barracudas were Muslim armed bands whose services were used by powerful Muslims and Christians. The Blackshirts have been linked to Datu Utlog Matalam's MIM, although this is disputed, while the Barracudas are identified with House Rep. Ali Dimaporo of Lanao del Norte. For an MILF account of the Ilagas, including a "list of Massacres committed by the ILAGAS in Mindanao", see Salah Jubair, *Bangsamoro, A Nation under Endless Tyranny* (Kuala Lumpur: IQ Marin, 1999), pp. 135–37, 141. Jubair said most of his sources were "from MILF files".
2. Nur Misuari, "The Bangsa Moro People's Struggle for Self-Determination (Towards an Understanding of the Roots of the Moro People's Struggle)", *Philippine Development Forum* 6, no. 2 (1992): 30.
3. Political scientist Macapado Muslim claims that the turmoil and criminal activities in the 1960s were due "mainly to naked landgrabbing, not the much written about 'conflict between the traditional Muslim system of land ownership and the secular Philippine land laws' explanation that follows the 'encounter of cultures' model". According to a 1963 Senate Committee Report on National Minority, which he cited, the land-grabbers included rich and well-connected Christian Filipino capitalists and government officials. See Macapado Abaton Muslim, *The Moro Armed Struggle in the*

Philippines: The Non-Violent Autonomy Alternative (Marawi City: Mindanao State University, 1994), pp. 89–91.

4. *Bantaaw: Economic and Social Indicators of Mindanao* 3, no. 8 (1988), a publication of the Alternative Resource Center cited in Muslim, *The Moro Armed Struggle*, pp. 28–29.

5. Cited in Muslim, *The Moro Armed Struggle*, pp. 85–86.

6. Cited in Ibid., p. 89.

7. Various studies cited in Muslim, *The Moro Armed Struggle*, 89–91.

8. Data taken from the 2000 Census. The first ARMM established in 1990 was made up of Maguindanao, Lanao del Sur, Sulu and Tawi-tawi by virtue of Republic Act 6793 passed in 1989. When the Organic Act was amended in 2001 by Republic Act 9054, another referendum resulted in the inclusion of Basilan province and Marawi City in addition to the original four provinces.

9. The Moro province was made up of 5 districts: Davao (with 5 organized municipalities — Davao, Mati, Cateel Baganga, Caraga; and 6 tribal wards); Cotabato (with 2 organized municipalities — Cotabato and Makar; and 18 tribal wards); Lanao (with 2 organized municipalities — Malabang and Iligan; and 13 tribal wards); Sulu (with 3 organized municipalities — Jolo, Siasi, Cagayan de Sulu; and 9 tribal wards); and Zamboanga (with 2 organized municipalities — Zamboanga and Dapitan; and 5 tribal wards and 56 sub-districts).

10. Agusan and Bukidnon were also placed under the jurisdiction of the new department.

11. Muslim called the process "Indioization" (*The Moro Armed Struggle*, pp. 73–74). The Spanish regime called natives "indios", but the distinction between Christianized natives and the Moros is emphasized in the choice of the root word. The same applies to "Filipinization", the word more commonly used to refer to the taking over by Filipinos (Christianized natives) of the administrative, political and legislative arms of the Philippine state that was undergoing the transition from colonialism to independence.

12. In a 1927 address, Senator Juan Sumulong from Luzon castigated indiscretions committed by government officials and employees who were sent to Mindanao, which he claimed had become the dumping ground of undesirables in government. He counselled the appointment of more Moros to government positions. Cited in Muslim, *The Moro Armed Struggle*, pp. 77–78.

13. Muslim, *The Moro Armed Struggle*, p. 124.

14. See the July 1972 University of the Philippines-Mindanao State University Report cited in Muslim, *The Moro Armed Struggle*, p. 120.

15. See the 1979 Eugenio Demegillo study cited in Muslim, *The Moro Armed Struggle*, p. 119.

16. Muslim intellectual Ibrahim Jubaira wrote: "Against overwhelming odds you stuck to your life, to your religion.... It is a sad fact, however, that in so doing, even at the cost of your lives, you have been marked Moro pirates, juramentados, while your Christian brothers have been acclaimed heroes. By whom? By what? By Christian history." *Philippines Free Press* article of 1955 cited by Muslim, *The Moro Armed Struggle*, p. 127.

17. The 1968 'Jabidah Massacre' revolved around the extrajudicial executions that allegedly took place on 17 March 1968 of Tausug trainees recruited by the army for secret training on Corregidor Island. The secret operation, called Jabidah Project or Merdeka, was believed to have been part of a plan by former president Ferdinand Marcos to invade Sabah using a force of secretly trained Muslim recruits. The trainees reportedly complained about delays in payment of their salaries and of the harsh training conditions on Corregidor Island. Also, it is claimed, they wanted to back out when they learned their mission was to attack Sabah, the people of which they considered fellow Muslims and fellow ethnic Tausugs. Misuari, notably, highlighted the religious reason. In his recounting of the events, Misuari wrote: "After the initial phase of the training in Simunul island was over in December 1967, the trainees were transported to Corregidor island on Manila Day, allegedly for further specialization. But there the real purpose for recruiting them was revealed, just when they were about to be dispatched to invade the State of Sabah. The Muslim trainees protested. They refused to be used as pawns in a clandestine operation of Marcos against their Muslim brothers" (Misuari, "The Bangsa Moro People's Struggle", p. 16). He did not mention the issue of non-payment of salaries. In any case, although the recruits were reportedly told they could resign, several of them were instead taken and killed in groups. Estimates of how many of the 180 recruits were killed range from 14 to 68. The Senate's investigations were never concluded and the accused were exonerated. Until now, the nature of the operation and the circumstances of the killings remain only partially known. For the different estimates and accounts, see William Larousse, *Walking Together Seeking Peace: The Local Church of Mindanao-Sulu Journeying in Dialogue with the Muslim Community, 1965–2000* (Quezon City: Claretian, 2001), pp. 102–3; Salah Jubair, *Bangsamoro, A Nation under Endless Tyranny*, 3rd ed. (Kuala Lumpur: IQ Marin, 1999), pp. 131–33; and Marites Vitug and Glenda Gloria, *Under the Crescent Moon* (Metro Manila: Anvil, 2000). In March 2008 a group of civil society organizations commemorated the twentieth anniversary of the

massacre with a visit to Corregidor Island accompanied by the survivor who escaped the killings and divulged the incident. A historical marker was placed by the National Historical Commission some years after.

18. While 1968 is generally considered the turning point, other scholars peg the date earlier, to 1965, when Ferdinand Marcos, blamed for fanning enmity, was elected to the presidency and set off the chain of events that led to the Jabidah massacre and communal violence. Larousse (*Walking Together Seeking Peace*, p. 101) chose this date. So did Abhoud Lingga, a Maguindanao scholar writing the introduction to the collection of statements and transcribed interviews of Salamat Hashim. However, Lingga put the sequence of events differently. He implied that the failure to pass a 1961 bill in congress filed by Rep. Ombra Amilbangsa of Sulu seeking the independence of Sulu led to the creation of the MIM. He wrote: "But when congressional initiative was a disappointment since the Christian majority in Congress decided to shelve Amilbangsa's bill in the archive, Datu Udtog Matalam made a bold political move" by issuing the MIM manifesto (Abhoud Syed Mansur Lingga, "The Political Thought of Salamat Hashim", MA Thesis, University of the Philippines Institute of Islamic Studies, 1995). However, some considered the bill motivated by vested interests or just nostalgia (Larousse, *Walking Together Seeking Peace*, pp. 99–100).

19. W.K. Che Man, *Muslim Separatism: The Moros of Southern Philippines and the Malays of Southern Thailand* (Quezon City: Ateneo de Manila University Press, 1990), p. 74.

20. Reuben Canoy, *Mindanao: The Quest for Independence* (Cagayan de Oro City: Mindanao Post Publishing Company, 1987), p. 101.

21. See Muslim, *The Moro Armed Struggle*, p. 93.

22. Misuari, "The Bangsa Moro People's Struggle", p. 16.

23. Jubair, *Bangsamoro, A Nation*, p. 144. Jubair is the pseudonym of Datucan Abas, who is more often known as Mohager Iqbal, a member of the Central Committee of the MILF. He chaired the MILF negotiating panel for talks with the Philippine government after Hashim Salamat died and the chair of the panel, Al Haj Ebrahim Murad, became the chair of the MILF.

24. Cited in Muslim, *The Moro Armed Struggle*, pp. 83–84.

25. For an analysis of the national-local dynamics during these decades, see Patricio N. Abinales, *Making Mindanao, Cotabato and Davao in the Formation of the Philippine Nation-State* (Quezon City: Ateneo de Manila University Press, 2000); also, Thomas M. McKenna, *Muslim Rulers and Rebels: Everyday Politics and Armed Separatism in the Philippines* (Manila: Anvil, 1998).

26. Among these were the 1951–55 Hadji Kamlon rebellion in Sulu and the uprising in Lanao led by chieftains Adbulmajid Panondiongan and Tawantawan; the short-lived Hajal Ouh (Hadjal Uh) insurrection of the 1960s for the independence of Sulu, Basilan and Zamboanga; and various skirmishes in Cotabato.

27. Jubair, *Bangsamoro, A Nation*, p. 144.

28. Misuari, "The Bangsa Moro People's Struggle", p. 32. Canoy likewise wrote that the replacement with Mindanao was made "to accommodate the Christians who wanted to join" (*Mindanao: The Quest*, p. 98).

29. This quotation and the preceding account on Matalam was taken from Canoy, ibid., pp. 96–98.

30. Ibid., p. 98.

31. Email message from the Catholic priest Eliseo Mercado to kusogmndanaw@yahoogroups.com dated 30 June 2008. Mercado opined the possibility of Majul being somehow involved through his student de los Santos. He also considered it unlikely that the draft was written by the circle of young lawyers around Matalam, among them former governor Sambaluwan, Simeon Datumanong and Salipada Pendatun. UP Professor Julkipli Wadi confirmed the role played by de los Santos, as per his conversation with de los Santos. Email message to kusogmindanaw@yahoogroups.com dated 30 June 2008 with subject title "Organizing MNLF". See also Rommel Banlaoi, "'Radical Muslim Terrorism' in the Philippines", in *Handbook on Terrorism and Insurgency in Southeast Asia*, edited by Andrew T.H. Tan (Cheltenham, UK: Elgar, 2007), p. 199.

32. Email of Patricio P. Diaz dated 30 June 2008 and of Abhoud Syed M. Lingga dated 1 July 2008 in the kusogmindanaw@yahoogroups.com with subject title "Organizing MNLF". Diaz cited as his source the late Dr Alunan C. Glang who was responsible for getting the manifesto published in *The Manila Times*. According to Glang, Buat and Pangato made up the two-man MIM secretariat who initialled documents and press statements made by MIM — with their initials 'MB' and 'HP'. Buat was a member of the MILF's negotiating panel for talks with the government during the Macapagal-Arroyo administration.

33. Muslim, *The Moro Armed Struggle*, pp. 183–84, 107. He cited a statement made in 1971 by then brig. gen. Fidel Ramos that "the armed men in black shirts were likely 'remnants of a disbanded strike force'" (p. 107).

34. Listed among its organizers were Dr Cesar Majul (chair), Macapanton Abbas (secretary), Senator Domocao Alonto, Senator Mamintal Tamano, Rep. Salipada Pendatun, Rep. Ali Dimaporo, Rep. Rashid Lucman, Datu Mama Sinsuat, Sultan Amilkadra Abubakar, Mrs Zorayda Tamano, Abdul

Karim Sidr, Musib Buat, Farouk Carpizo and Nur Misuari (Che Man, *Muslim Separatism*, pp. 76–77).

35. MNLF (1982), cited in Che Man, *Muslim Separatism*, p. 77.
36. Muslim, *The Moro Armed Struggle*, p. 113.
37. Interview with Salamat Hashim by Jose F. Lacaba, "The Bangsamoro Agenda", *Midweek*, 10 December 1986, reprinted in Salamat Hashim, *Referendum Peaceful, Civilized, Diplomatic and Democratic Means of Solving the Mindanao Conflict* (Camp Abubakre as-Siddique, Mindanao: Agency for Youth Affairs–MILF, 2002), p. 30.
38. Misuari, "The Bangsa Moro People's Struggle", p. 33.
39. Jubair, *Bangsamoro, A Nation*, p. 135.
40. Ibid.
41. Che Man, *Muslim Separatism*, p. 77.
42. Jubair, *Bangsamoro, A Nation*, p. 145.
43. Canoy, *Mindanao: The Quest*, p. 105.
44. Jubair, *Bangsamoro, A Nation*, p. 145.
45. Che Man, *Muslim Separatism*, p. 78, citing the 1982 MNLF document *The Misuari Betrayal of the Bangsa Moro Struggle* issued by the MNLF-Pundato Faction and the BMLO. Canoy, meanwhile, also credited Rep. Salipada Pendatun for teaming up with Lucman to form the BLMO (Canoy, *Mindanao: The Quest*, p. 106).
46. Canoy, *Mindanao: The Quest*, p. 106.
47. Not in Sabah, as is commonly known, but supposedly in Pulau Pangkor in the State of Perak (Jubair, *Bangsamoro, A Nation*, p. 151). This is corroborated by Canoy, who cited Commander Sali Wali as one source, an original member of the MNLF Central Committee who had surrendered to the Marcos administration. Another former MNLF commander, who became governor of Tawi-Tawi, also reported being trained and armed by Malaysian officers in Palau Bangui near Sarawak. According to Canoy, although the Malaysian government denied involvement, Philippine intelligence reports asserted the opposite. The report of government agent Capt. Solferino Titong, who served as driver of Sabah chief minister Tun Mustapha, moreover claimed that Malaysian minister for home affairs Tan Shri Ghazali bin Shaffie had a hand in creating the MNLF. The Malaysians reportedly believed an independent Mindanao could serve as a buffer state between Malaysia and the Philippines. Malaysia was disturbed by Project Merdeka, the reported attempt to invade Sabah as exposed in the aftermath of the Jabidah killings. See Canoy, *Mindanao: The Quest*, pp. 109–10; also accounts by Arnold Azurin, *Beyond the Cult of Dissidence in Southern Philippines and Wartorn Zones in the Global Village* (Quezon City:

University of Philippines Center for Integrative and Development Studies and UP Press, 1998).

48. Among the youth organizations was the "Green Guards" of Zamboanga. Canoy, *Mindanao: The Quest*, p. 109.

49. Che Man, *Muslim Separatism*, pp. 75, 78. According to Jubair there were 64 Maranaos, while 15 came from the Sulu region and 11 from Cotabato (Maguindanao). He attributed the large number of Maranaos to the fact that Lucman was a Maranao (Jubair, *Bangsamoro, A Nation*, p. 151).

50. Che Man, *Muslim Separatism*, p. 79.

51. Ibid.; Jubair, *Bangsamoro, A Nation*, pp. 152–53.

52. Che Man, *Muslim Separatism*. Jubair dated the overtures to 1975 (*Bangsamoro, A Nation*, p. 153).

53. Che Man, *Muslim Separatism*, p. 89; Jubair, *Bangsamoro, A Nation*, p. 152.

54. Sema broke ties with Nur Misuari in the late 1990s and subsequently became Cotabato City governor. In 2010, his wife Sandra, also an MILF member, sat as Cotabato City representative in the House of Representatives. Sema signed the petition in September 1977 calling for the ouster of Misuari, but he continued to identify himself as MNLF and did not join the MILF. His relatives, Ibrahim and Kabilan Sema, also signed the petition (Jubair, *Bangsamoro, A Nation*, p. 154).

55. Isnaji became the head of one of the other Misuari breakaway groups in the early 2000s.

56. Murad became the chair of the MILF in 2003 when Salamat Hashim died.

57. Jubair, *Bangsamoro, A Nation*, p. 150.

58. Jubair wrote that the three top contenders — Nur, Hashim and Dr Saleh Loong (who, like Hashim, belonged to the Cairo group) — met and resolved the issue in favour of Nur. "[Hashim] could have prolonged the process and allowed the intramural to protract while subtly maneuvering to take the post for himself. He knew that Dr. Saleh Loong, who simply cannot see eye-to-eye with Misuari, would side with him. But after intense soul-searching, Hashim opted for Misuari, for the sake of unity and in deference to what Islam teaches — that a Muslim cannot vote for himself to become a leader" (ibid., p. 150).

59. Canoy, *Mindanao: The Quest*, pp. 107–8.

60. Email message of UP professor Julkipli Wadi to kusogmindanaw@ yahoogroups.com dated 30 June 2008 with subject title "Organizing MNLF". According to Wadi's account it was Jalaluddin Santos and Abul Kayhr Alonto "who disturbed the peace of Nur here in UP and visited him several times here at Teacher's Village [a residential area near the UP Diliman campus] and enticed him to lead the Moro youth in Manila in

the aftermath of the 'Jabidah Massacre'. There were many Moro student leaders then *pero porma lang ang karamihan. Papogi!* [but they were just posturing]. Nur was challenged: the two guys' argument came almost like this. Hey! Nur you are a Tausug; *kababayan mo yung na-massacre sa Corregidor* [those massacred in Corregidor were your tribal kin], what are you doing here in UP? They pushed, cajoled and possibly even shamed him to take the cudgel. When I talked to lots of Nur's former classmates and faculty here, they were shocked by the transformation of Nur: from well-behaved, silent, smoker, fond of eating *turon* [banana wrapped in rice paper], soon-to-become Majul's heir, into a fiery revolutionary. Do you know that Nur's first course was not Political Science? It was Medicine! So he should have been Dr. Misuari not Chairman Misuari. Why should Santos and Abul Khayr get Nur? Because Nur has a hidden charisma; he is a master of words. Inside he is sheep but when he is at the peak of his usual Moro discourse, he can be like a lion that can make anyone humble themselves as if they are wet chicks. And look at his eyes!" Wadi's views are informed by his recorded interviews and talks with Jalaluddin Santos and Cesar Majul. This was confirmed by my phone interview with Abul Kayhr Alonto on 14 December 2010.

61. Canoy, *Mindanao: The Quest*, pp. 110–11.
62. While Che Man claims Misuari and the others belonged to the first batch, or the 'Top 90', other sources closer to the MILF claim this group was part of the second batch made up of three hundred trainees. See Salamat Hashim identifying Murad as part of the second batch (*Referendum Peaceful*, p. 38) and Lingga saying Alonto and Misuari were as well ("The Political Thought"). Murad succeeded Hashim as chair of the Kutawato Revolutionary Committee in the MNLF and joined him in the split from the MNLF. On the other hand, Banlaoi wrote that the Top 90 completed their military training in 1971 and Salamat Hashim joined the second batch in 1972 ("Radical Muslim Terrorism", p. 200).
63. Desdemona Tan, a political science instructor at Notre Dame University in Jolo, was arrested upon the declaration of martial law. She joined Misuari in the hills upon her release from detention, where they later married. She died in exile in Pakistan. Misuari later married her sister Rohaida, who raised the children. Hussein succeeded Misuari as governor of the Autonomous Region in Muslim Mindanao during the Macapagal Arroyo administration.
64. Canoy, *Mindanao: The Quest*, pp. 108–9. The rest of the information in this paragraph was also taken from Canoy.
65. Ibid., p. 112. Mustapha eventually lost political stature in Sabah.

66. Lucman reportedly counted on the loyalty of Maranaos trained at his secret camp in Kapai near the Lanao-Bukidnon border. Ibid., p. 111.
67. Jubair wrote that this accusation was never proven. *Bangsamoro, A Nation,* p. 152.
68. Che Man, *Muslim Separatism,* pp. 78–79.
69. Muslim thus considers the declaration of martial law as the third trigger event that followed the Jabidah massacre and the communal violence. *The Moro Armed Struggle,* pp. 104–9.
70. Prior to this, statements released in Cotabato were issued in the name of the "High Command of the Moro fighters". Jubair, *Bangsamoro, A Nation,* p. 150.
71. Muslim, *The Moro Armed Struggle,* p. 115. Jubair claims that up to early 1975 the MNLF had wrested towns and islets in Sulu, Tawi-tawi, Basilan, on the Zamboanga Peninsula and in the Cotabato provinces (*Bangsamoro, A Nation,* p.162). He explains how the stalemate was reached in 1975: MNLF offensives since 1973 had been blunted by a massive counter-offensive by the government, given that two unified commands of the AFP, the Southern Command and the Central Mindanao Command, had been deployed in Mindanao and Sulu. Given its limited logistical capability, the MNLF retreated from conventional to guerrilla warfare. The AFP, in turn, ended wide-scale campaigns and retreated into small-unit operations. In this situation, a "strategic stalemate" was reached (pp. 166–67).
72. The MNLF negotiating panel was made up of Nur Misuari and the MILF's central committee members; namely, Salamat Hashim, Abdul Bake Abubakar, Hatimil Hassan and Ahmed Asani. The government panel was made up of deputy defence minister Carmelo Barbero as chair, deputy foreign minister Pacifico Castro, Col. Eduardo Ermita, Ambassador Liningning Pangandaman and Ambassador Simeon Datumanong (Canoy, *Mindanao: The Quest,* p. 132).
73. Ibid., pp. 132, 137. Canoy noted how Imelda Marcos's meeting with Qaddafi succeeded in getting the Libyan leader's acquiescence to the compromise. He also quoted the chair of the government panel's observation that the MNLF negotiators "behaved like Libyan puppets". These reasons were more or less confirmed by Nur Misuari in a later account. See "Speech of Chairman Nur Misuari during the Opening Ceremony of the Formal Peace Talks" in 1993 in Azurin, *Beyond the Cult,* pp. 306–11.
74. See Jubair for an insider's account of these AFP operations in 1977 (*Bangsamoro, A Nation,* pp. 167–71).
75. Luwaran editorial, 13 July 2018, at http://www.luwaran.net.
76. See "The Nine-Point Proposal of the Reformist Group", dated 7 March 1983, in Che Man, *Muslim Separatism,* p. 197. Among the reform measures

proposed were a real, functional and representative (in terms of tribal affiliation) Central Committee; the creation of an Executive Committee and other committees; revitalization of all branches and organs; localization of leaders at all levels and commands in the province, with natives of the province given priority for the posts; promulgation of a "Constitution and By-Laws of the Islamic Revolution"; and forging of unity with the other factions. See also Jubair, *Bangsamoro, A Nation*, p. 156.

77. Jubair, *Bangsamoro, A Nation*, p. 157.
78. Canoy, *Mindanao: The Quest*, p. 127. Others who joined the Pundato faction were Napis Bidin and Jebre Redha.
79. Canoy, *Mindanao: The Quest*, pp. 126–28.
80. Jubair, *Bangsamoro, A Nation*, pp. 163–165. Although some just left the revolution without surrendering, Jubair had harsh words for those who succumbed to the enticement of the regime: "These 'dogs' were the hypocrites, the opportunists, the waverers, the pseudo-revolutionaries, the unbelievers, and the dregs of society, who finally realized that a revolution was not the pace and time for pleasure or for any self-serving end. The time came after 1977, when everyone became free to choose based on one's true self. Singly or in droves, they crossed over to the side of the enemy, where there was licentiousness in everything, from sex to material satisfaction."
81. Che Man, *Muslim Separatism*, pp. 82–85.
82. As part of the implementation of the 1996 agreement, an amended Organic Act for the ARMM (Republic Act 9054) was passed and ratified with five provinces (Basilan, Sulu, Tawi-tawi, Maguindanao and Lanao del Norte), and Marawi City joining the enhanced regional autonomy.
83. Che Man, *Muslim Separatism*, p. 127.
84. For his biography, see Lingga, "The Political Thought", pp. 23–31.
85. Jubair, *Bangsamoro, A Nation*, p. 154.
86. Interview with Salamat Hashim by Jose F. Lacaba, "The Bangsamoro Agenda", in Hashim, *Referendum Peaceful*, p. 30. Hashim qualified that the original idea at that time was not to take up arms but to launch reforms. He also said that he was not in any way connected to the MIM, although the founder Utdog Matalam was his uncle.
87. Lingga, "The Political Thought", p. 28.
88. Ibid.
89. Among the signatories to the petition were its author Jubair, Al Haj Murad and Ghadzali Jaafar. All the signatories, like Hashim, were from Cotabato. Jubair, *Bangsamoro, A Nation*, p. 154. See also Lingga, "The Political Thought", p. 29.
90. Jubair, *Bangsamoro, A Nation*, p. 155.

91. Canoy, *Mindanao: The Quest*, p. 126. The fifty *ulama* supposedly behind Misuari were educated in Tripoli and allegedly were given monthly stipends as missionaries by Libya.
92. Cited in Jubair, *Bangsamoro, A Nation*, p. 54.
93. Che Man, *Muslim Separatism*, pp. 84–85; Jubair, *Bangsamoro, A Nation*, p. 154.
94. Canoy, *Mindanao: The Quest*, p. 126.
95. Lingga, "The Political Thought", p. 4.
96. Ibid., 29.
97. Canoy, *Mindanao: The Quest*, p. 126.
98. Soliman Santos, Jr., *The Moro Islamic Challenge, Constitutional Rethinking for the Mindanao Peace Process* (Quezon City: University of the Philippines Press, 2001), pp. 39–41.
99. Che Man, *Muslim Separatism*, p. 195.
100. Thomas M. McKenna, *Muslim Rulers and Rebels, Everyday Politics and Armed Separatism in the Philippines* (Manila: Anvil, 1998), pp. 213, 216, 282.
101. Ibid.
102. Shamsuddin L. Taya, "The Political Strategies of the Moro Islamic Liberation Front for Self-Determination in the Philippines", *Intellectual Discourse* 15, no. 1 (2007), p. 64.
103. Ibid., p. 66.
104. Abhoud Syed Lingga, "Understanding Bangsamoro Independence as a Mode of Self-determination" (paper presented at the Forum on Mindanao Peace sponsored by the University of the Philippines in the Mindanao Department of Social Sciences, the Philippine Development Assistance Programme and the Association of Mindanao State University Alumni, Davao City, Philippines, 28 February 2002), p. iv.
105. Jubair derisively called the 1976 agreement the "new Kiram-Bates Treaty". The treaty signed by the late sultan of Sulu and Brig. Gen. John Bates in 1899, according to Jubair, deluded the sultan that it would protect his homeland, but it only gave the Americans breathing space for them to be able to concentrate on suppressing the forces of Gen. Emilio Aguinaldo. The Tripoli Agreement allowed for a cessation of hostilities with the MNLF, enabling Marcos to move his army to communist-affected areas. Like the earlier treaty, the Tripoli Agreement was thus a "mere scrap of paper" not observed faithfully by the other party. In this analogy it was the non-implementation, not the autonomy deal itself, that Jubair condemned. See Jubair, *Bangsamoro, A Nation*, pp. 181–83.
106. *Maradika* (MILF newsletter) 6 (December 1987) cited in Jubair, *Bangsamoro, A Nation*, pp. 184–85. The OIC and the Muslim World League (MWL) were facilitating the merger of the two fronts and both Misuari and

Hashim had already reportedly agreed to close ranks. President Aquino was reportedly informed by the OIC and the MWL that they would only host the negotiation if both the MNLF and the MILF were represented. As it turned out, the OIC agreed to move ahead and support the peace talks between the GRP (Government of the Republic of the Philippines) and the MNLF. In any case, the talks broke down in early 1987: the GRP and the MILF could not agree on what provinces should be placed under full autonomy, and the GRP moved ahead with the process of drafting the Organic Act for Muslim Mindanao without the MNLF's participation.

107. It refrained from further offensives after signing an informal truce with then national affairs minister Aquilino Pimentel, Jr. on 17 January 1987. The MNLF signatory was Murad Ibrahim, with Mohager Iqbal/Jubair as witness. Jubair, *Bangsamoro, A Nation*, pp. 186–87.

108. Hashim, *Referendum Peaceful*, p. 57.

109. Interview with Abhoud Syed Lingga, 5 November 2008, Cotabato City.

110. Jubair, *Bangsamoro, A Nation*, p. 187.

111. Lingga, "Understanding Bangsamoro Independence", p. iv.

112. Salamat Hashim, *The Bangsamoro Mujahid: His Objectives and Responsibilities* (Mindanao: Bangsamoro Publications, 1985), pp. 6–7.

113. Ibid., pp. 16–18.

114. Ibid., pp. 24–25.

115. Ibid., p. 57.

116. Ibid., p. 52.

117. Interview with Iqbal, 7 November 2008, MILF Compound, Crossing Simuay, Sultan Kudarat, Maguindanao.

118. Hashim even suggested how to best allocate time in a day for prayers, exercise, reading the Qu'ran, study and time with family and visitors. Care for communal property of the MILF and obedience to lawful commands were the other injunctions. The criteria for and qualities of a leader (Amir or Imam) were also spelled out, mostly having to do with moral probity. Three strengths or weapons of the mujahid were outlined: spiritual or moral, intellectual and material. He urged observance of the following: purification from non-Islamic beliefs; education against all forms of regionalism, prejudices against other tribes, family differences and other divisive factors; justice, honesty and truthfulness; avoidance of haram or forbidden deeds; constructive criticism; disowning relations with oppressors; and dedication to the cause and industry. See Hashim, *The Bangsamoro Mujahid*, pp. 32–35, 38–50, 54–56.

119. Hashim wrote against "the futility of launching a fight by a disorganized group much less by an individual struggle" (ibid., p. 25).

120. Interview with Abhoud Syed Lingga, 5 November 2008, Cotabato City.

121. Gutierrez and Gulial (1997), cited in the World Bank, Environment and Social Development Unit, East Asia and Pacific Region, *Social Assessment of Conflict-Affected Areas in Mindanao*, Philippine Post-Conflict Series #1 (2003), p. 21. The names of the camps were referenced from signed documents between the government and the MILF in February 1999.

122. Nu'ain Bin Abdulhaqq, *"We Must Win the Struggle!" by Ash-Shayk, Ash-Shaheed Salamat Hashim* (Camp Abubakre as-Siddique: Agency for Youth Affairs-MILF, 2005), pp. 120–21.

123. Ibid.

124. Ibid., "Epilogue", pp. 123–24. Abdulhaqq chairs the Agency for Youth Affairs of the MILF.

125. Al Haj Murad Ebrahim, "Foreword, Tribute to a Great Hero of the Bangsamoro and Muslim Ummah", in Abdulhaqq, *"We Must Win"*, pp. v–vii.

126. Ibid.

127. Abdulhaqq, *"We Must Win"*, p. 129. Sultan Kudarat is the Maguindanao sultan who ruled over the Cotabato empire and fought against Spanish incursions in the mid-seventeenth century.

128. The six legs of Salamat Hashim's Long March are described in the epilogue of Abdulhaqq, *"We Must Win"*, pp. 115–24. All quotes on this are from this text.

129. 'All-out war' has become part of the language of the Philippine media and civil society groups to refer to the major, sustained government offensives against the MILF that effectively broke the ceasefire. In 2003, when the Arroyo administration launched another 'all-out war' against the MILF, peace groups in Manila (myself included) launched the All-out Peace Groups (AOPG) to call for a return to the ceasefire.

130. Abdulhaqq, *"We Must Win"*, p. 125–26. The dramatic account continued: "Endangered species of birds resembling the 'Green Birds of Paradise' mysteriously flocked over the Chairman's deathbed as if singing to welcome him to the hall of the martyrs: the Jannatul Firdaws."

131. Cited by Al Haj Murad Ebrahim in Abdulhaqq, *"We Must Win"*, p. v.

132. Ibid., pp. 124–25.

133. Mimbantas died in May 2012 at the age of sixty.

134. Salah Jubair, *The Long Road to Peace: Inside the GRP-MILF Peace Process* (Cotabato City: Institute of Bangsamoro Studies, 2007), p. 40.

135. Ibid., p. 41.

136. The injunction continued: "Following the tradition of the Prophet (peace be upon him) which says: 'One who aspires for a position should not be given such position.' The leadership of the Front makes it a policy to exclude from the list of prospective appointees those who fall under the category referred to in this particular hadith" (Hashim, *The Bangsamoro Mujahid*, p. 57).

137. Jubair, *The Long Road to Peace*, p. 41. This injunction was floated, perhaps as a reminder, every time the MILF had to come up with a list of nominees; first in the Bangsamoro Transition Commission that was created in 2013 and again in 2017 to produce the draft Bangsamoro basic/organic law, and in the Bangsamoro Transition Authority in February 2019 that followed the plebiscite for the Bangsamoro Autonomous Region in Muslim Mindanao.

138. Abdulhaqq, *"We Must Win"*, p. 126.

139. Ibid., p. 126.

140. Ibid., p. 125.

141. Interview with Abhoud Syed Lingga, director of the Institute of Bangsamoro Studies in Cotabato City and secretary-general of the Bangsamoro Consultative Assembly, 5 November 2008, Cotabato City. From my own engagements with the MILF during the peace negotiations from 2010 to 2014 and the first years of implementation up to 2016, the collective decision-making and practice of consultations were sustained. In fact, several major consultations assumed a performative function and took place in the form of huge public gatherings in Camp Darapanan, headquarters of the MILF in Sultan Kudarat, Manguindanao, with several of these events attended by government officials involved in the peace process.

142. Hashim, *The Bangsamoro Mujahid*, p. 58.

3

The Cordillera Movement (1970s–2008): Building and Losing the Consensus

> "To claim a place is the birthright of every man.... For us indigenous peoples, ancestral land is literally life, our continued survival as viable communities and distinct cultures with our brand of indigenous ethnic identities."
>
> — Macli-ing Dulag[1]

Unlike in Mindanao, where the Moro population was overtaken by the influx of migrants from Luzon and the Visayas, the indigenous populations in the Cordillera remained the dominant populations in the region. Mining operations and government-led projects did lead to land-use conversion and changes in ownership in the more economically developed areas, but there was no massive resettlement of migrant populations. Relative deprivation and underdevelopment, a common context of many ethnopolitical mobilizations, are present within the region and vis-à-vis the national capital region. But several Cordillera provinces fare better in terms of income and other human development indicators than other provinces in the country. The region as a whole is better off than several other Philippine regions, especially Muslim Mindanao. The process of political and cultural differentiation also differed. Earlier initiatives of zealous Spanish friars from the Ilocos provinces failed. One Bontoc anthropologist wrote that "Christianity was established by the Spaniards on Igorot soil" only in 1893 when the first baptism was performed, but this event was allegedly never repeated under Spanish rule.[2] But unlike in Muslim Mindanao, American Protestant and European Catholic missionaries made inroads in the region in the early twentieth century. They established churches and schools and generated conversions among the natives to Christianity.[3]

Although control of the entire territory was uneven,[4] the American colonial regime succeeded in 'pacifying' and incorporating the northern mountainous region under their rule, a feat unaccomplished by the Spaniards. Finin cited several reasons for the relative absence of resistance against the American administrators. One is what he described as the paternalistic and exoticized treatment that the Americans accorded the natives. They gave the Igorots — the collective name used by colonial officialdom for the natives in the region — a privileged status that was not extended to lowlanders in Baguio. Cultural performances and traditional feasts like the *cañao* were encouraged and supported. The American regime kept their hands off the rice fields and paid wages to the locals who were hired in the public works. Although the Philippine Constabulary remained the main tool of the state for subjugating resistance, local mediators were sought to settle conflicts and other forms of pressure were applied. The American administrators also mediated some disputes. Roy Franklin Barton, the American anthropologist who studied Ifugao society in the early 1900s, claimed that the natives viewed the Americans' coercion as a "perfectly natural exercise of power".[5]

Other scholars credit the colonial practice of ethnography for the success of the United States in conquering the Cordillera. The ethnographic studies supposedly gave the American administrators more knowledge of the different ethno-communities, which enabled them to differentiate and construct ethnic boundaries. Florendo writes: "By knowing the plural psychologies of the people of the Cordillera, the Americans were able to engineer change through the inoculation of Cordillera culture and the corresponding cognitive structures."[6]

Nonetheless, under both Spanish and American colonialism, social discrimination of non-Christians was institutionalized. Census data taken by both colonial governments divided the population into Christian or civilized tribes on the one hand and non-Christian or wild-tribes on the other (with the appellate 'tribe' used for all non-foreign inhabitants on the islands). A map drawn by the Spaniards at the Jesuit Observatory and published by the US Coast and Geodetic Survey in 1900 divided the archipelago into three areas: Christian-Hispanic-Filipinos, the Moros, and the territory of the "new Christians and infieles", with the last extending northward from Nueva Vizcaya to cover today's Cordillera provinces.[7] The Americans put up the Bureau of Non-Christian Tribes, which governed the Moro and Cordillera provinces whose populations they perceived to be different and backward.

State ownership of public domain was fortified under the American regime with the passage of the Public Land Act of 1902. The Mining Act of 1905 allowed the entry of big commercial mining firms and created mining towns. Also, agricultural cash crops were introduced. The Cordillera provinces have rich mineral resources and are major agricultural producers. The provinces produced 25 per cent of the country's total ore production and 89 per cent of total gold production in 1968.[8]

The American colonial regime put in place administrative and political mechanisms that enabled it to govern the territory. The policy of public mass education and scholarship grants for the cultural minorities produced intellectual and political elites who participated in the provincial/regional and national society. In the Cordillera, as already mentioned, conversion to Christianity took place largely through the religious and educational institutions. The judicial system instituted local courts that coexisted with customary dispute resolution practices.

The American regime's Mountain Province was the precursor to the region now called the Cordillera. It was made up of seven sub-provinces: Benguet, Ifugao,[9] Bontoc, Lepanto, Amburayan,[10] Kalinga and Apayao.[11] These were later reorganized to become the five sub-provinces of Benguet, Ifugao, Kalinga, Apayao and Bontoc.[12] Bontoc was made the provincial capital. It had an American provincial governor and seven American provincial lieutenant governors. The provincial Philippine Constabulary was also headed by American officers.[13]

Unlike the Americans' Moro Province that was disbanded in 1914, the Mountain Province government unit was kept intact until 1966 when it was divided into the four provinces of Kalinga-Apayao, Ifugao, Benguet and Bontoc (Bontoc is the equivalent of present-day Mountain Province).

Finin credits this administrative grid constructed by the Americans for the development of an ethno-regional consciousness that informs the current discourse on regional autonomy. "The imposition of local government throughout the province was as subversive of traditional villagers' notions of leadership as it was important to the promotion of a pan-Cordillera outlook", he said of the seeming paradox.[14]

Direct rule exercised by the American colonial regime through the governor and lieutenant-governor and the different mechanisms that were instituted helped link communities. Finin identified these integrative institutions in his book. One comprised the Philippine Constabulary units put up in the sub-provinces. Igorots were recruited into the constabulary, which took charge of peace and order problems. Public works like trail construction between 1909 and 1912; public sector jobs such as teaching and administrative posts in the public schools and government offices; the mining industry and consequently the workers' unions pushed villagers outside of their homes and brought together different tribes in the same workplace. The missionary schools drew in the youth from all over the region and forged bonds that translated into pan-regional youth and professional organizations. In particular, Baguio City — with its numerous educational institutions, government offices and commercial establishments — became the hub for this inter-tribal bonding.[15]

Heads and boards/councils were appointed by the colonial regime until elections were gradually introduced.[16] They governed even though the traditional 'councils of elders' continued to be the key decision-making bodies in some districts.[17] The province was given political representation in the National Assembly through the congressional districts into which the provinces were divided.[18] Electorally, it was connected through the system of political parties that supported local-national political elite alliances down to the municipal levels. Finin writes: "The elective official system gained ground, encouraged by the salaries attached to the post, and copied many features of partisan lowland-style politics."[19] The introduction of the electoral system for local and provincial board candidates in the late 1940s, for the governorship in 1955, and for Baguio city officials (mayor, vice-mayor and council members) in 1959 firmly linked local politics and administration into the post-colonial national polity dominated by lowlander Filipino elites.

TABLE 3.1
Population Distribution by Religion, 1960

Pop/Prov. Religion	Benguet	Bontoc/ Mt. Province	Ifugao	Kalinga- Apayao	Total Per Religion	Percentage of Pop.[c]
Roman Catholic	112,444	31,592	24,982	59,461	228,479	53.57
Protestant	21,324	28,341	5,505	11,990	67,160	15.75
Aglipayan	3,546	1,162	301	6,116	11,125	2.61
Iglesia ni Kristo[a]	1,128	295	299	532	2,254	0.53
Muslim	9	2	—	13	24	0.01
Buddhist	247	—	4	58	309	0.07
Others	50,837	23,473	31,985	10,835	117,130	27.46
Tot Pop/Prov	183,657	85,866	63,094	89,528	426,481/ 422,145[b]	99

Notes: (a) Iglesia ni Kristo is a homegrown Philippine church, like the Aglipayan; (b) The two totals do not tally; (c) The 426,481 population total was used to compute the percentages.

Source of Data: Philippine Office of the Presidential Economic Staff, Province Profile of the Mountain Province, 1969, pp. 20–21.

As noted, religion did not become a mobilizing force against the Filipino majority. In 1960, 53.57 per cent of the population were registered as Roman Catholics and 15.75 per cent were Protestants, for a total of 69.32 per cent of the population counted as Christians (see Table 3.1). The successful overlay of Christian beliefs and practices on the indigenous 'pagans' was largely due to the work of the Christian schools and churches. Besides, even during the Spanish times, highlanders for the most part peacefully co-mingled and traded with the expanding Christianized communities in the lowlands as a matter of course, so long as they were left to their own way of life. Early writings by foreigners on Tinguian settlements in coastal, Christianized Ilocos found them well adapted to the majority Ilocano communities.[20] Christian Ilocanos were also early settlers in the town centres of Abra.[21]

In all, indigenous belief systems, practices and institutions persisted and coexisted peacefully, albeit with all the dilemmas that can arise from competing loyalties.[22] For the resistance movements — whether the CPP-NPA, whose leadership and membership base belonged to the Filipino majority, or the breakaway CPLA group composed of the native residents — religion was a non-issue. Add to this the fact that many of the leaders who joined or supported the resistance were native priests, nuns, seminarians and young people who studied in the Protestant and Catholic schools.

Unlike in Mindanao, as noted, no massive dispossession of land took place as a result of resettlement of migrant populations. Population growth in the region was relatively slow. Only 1,100 Ilocanos were recorded to have migrated in the Bontoc area from 1922 to 1928.[23] In 1960, the Mountain Province (with its five sub-provinces) reportedly had a total population of only 435,839, largely made up of "Igorotas, Ilocano and Tagalogs".[24] Growth per annum from 1948 to the 1960s averaged only 1.61 per cent, as against the national average of 3.1 per cent. In all, in 1960 the province constituted only 1.161 per cent of the country's total population of 27,410,000.[25] It is very possible, however, that census taking was unreliable because of the difficult terrain and cultural barriers between the census-takers and the local people.

Felt Discrimination

For the most part, since the 1950s, Cordilleran intellectuals who benefited from the education system felt they could find a niche in the modernizing society and polity. They felt their good educational credentials, good command of English, access to national officials in Baguio and wartime heroism against the Japanese occupation forces enabled them to pursue professional careers and become local elites in their communities.[26]

So why did resentment against the Filipino government develop, eventually providing a supportive environment for an armed resistance in the 1970s? According to Finin, Filipino leaders did not have the same "admixture of paternalism and fascination toward highlanders".[27] This supposedly made the Cordillera uplanders feel they were second-class citizens in the Philippine polity. Their representatives elected in Congress complained about government neglect and low budgetary appropriations for their provinces. One congressman filed a bill to ban the use of the derogatory term 'Igorot', but rescinded it as other (self-ascribed) Igorot intellectuals defended the term and imbued it with ethnic pride.

Needless to say, the demands of modern society and of customs and traditions created peculiar economic demands on the traditional community. *Kedot*, a pop song written in Ibalaoi by Roy Basatan of Benguet, illustrates this tension. It expresses the various pressures the writer's family faced upon the death of his grandmother in 1999:[28]

No wa'y mengdot jen kaidian	Oh that somebody among us will host a kedot
Say wara kay kebikatan	So that there is an occasion to attend
Pan-aamtaan, pan-aaspulan,	An opportunity to meet and to get acquainted,
Penuntunan ni nay-again.	To discover our kin and kindred.
En-ahad kita ni mamashem	We go home late in the afternoon
Ebuteng kita ma ni tafey,	Drunk with rice wine
Wara pay vatvat jen egshian	And carrying our own portions of meat
Say wara'y kanas jen inkitungtungaw.	Our consolation for sitting around.
Egto inges eshan da nontan	It was not like before
No wara'y sahit ni bakdang	When the body is sick
Shagshagos sha en-iuhatan	They immediately provide
Say wara'y man-ekan shi kaapuan.	Something to offer one's ancestors.
No bayag kono ira man-isturya	In earlier times, they say
Eshahel i eg nan-iskweda	Many have not gone to school
Ebiteg kono'y edapuan sha	Their folks were poor
So kedot da ma'y ukaten sha.	They only know how to perform the kedot
Nem karakdan may e-Kristianoan	Now many have become Christians
Mangkaumas mala ira tan	Those things are being erased
Mankesadati sigud jen ugadi	The former practices are now being changed
Eshahel mala i mankebuliwi.	Many things are changing.
Nem no wara'y esobdaan shitan,	But if somebody has more than enough
Mapmapteng ngo eshan	It is still better
No mengibingay ke'd kaasakang	That you share with your neighbours
Say so suwartem ket mamashoman.	So your luck abounds.
Satan emo'y pan-iyamanan	Perhaps that is where one can be thankful
Pengibingay ni kaidian	That he has shared with his fellows.
Saksahey i pengibunongan	To only one we pray and offer
Son Apo Shiyos met laeng jen Kabunian.	To God who is Kabunian.

Fong tells us that "Many Ibaloi and other Cordillera songs now tell us about the importance of getting an education in order to land a profitable job and to gain social acceptance. These and other new costly values have been added to a traditional lifestyle that has become expensive, despite their symbolic and social values. The natives are hard-pressed by the demands of both ideologies."[29] Fong reports that for the *kedot* (wake and burial ceremony) of the grandmother of the author-singer above, two pigs every day for three days were butchered before the funeral. Two pigs and two carabaos were killed on the funeral day, and after the funeral several chickens and one more pig were butchered for the closing ritual. In addition, nine cavans of rice (approximately 395 litres) and hundreds of bottles of gin, soft drinks and rice wine were served. It is a custom that has become more taxing because other expenses such as schooling for the children compete for one's resources. Fong writes that "[t]he integration of Cordillera villages into the global market economy demands that high prices be paid for sacrificial animals, besides the need to spend for the education of one's children, for health and other basic needs plus wants."[30] The custom is also being challenged by new values introduced by education and Christianity. At the same time, the writer "expresses a longing for somebody in the community to host a feast which has apparently become few and far between".[31] Such feasts traditionally served socializing functions that strengthened kinship and friendships.

The growth of the mining industry and commercial agriculture created new social and economic opportunities as well as problems. The Mining Act of 1905 rendered all untitled property alienable — meaning, land could be occupied, purchased and exploited by any Filipino or American citizen interested in investing in mines. This opened up the mines operated by the local families in Benguet to acquisition by American capitalists,[32] but it also provided more jobs as miners for locals. Farmers who shifted to cash crops found themselves at the mercy of traders and market forces, but they also found new earning opportunities. While the Cordillera provinces outpaced other provinces and regions in the country in economic growth, social inequalities and intraregional unevenness grew.

A decrease in the supply of indigenous fruits, vegetables, game animals and fish due to changes in the forest habitat also led to changes in the people's diet. New food like bottled milk for babies and commercial liquor, and new ways of cooking like *lugaw* (rice porridge) also reportedly contributed to changing lifestyles. Beliefs and practices with regard to health and healing also underwent transformation. Bathing regularly and Western medicine and Western-defined illnesses were introduced and addressed by Belgian missionaries in the case of the Mayoyao municipality in Ifugao.[33]

Lastly, mega-development projects of the state dislodged certain populations and drew the locals' concern. The Ambuklao-Binga Dam projects in Benguet, the biggest power generator in Asia at that time, were constructed in the late 1950s. They supplied power to industrial centres outside of the region. Hundreds of Ibaloi families were displaced by these dam projects. They complained that many of the promises that accompanied their resettlement in other areas were not met.[34]

During the American colonial regime, the Americans built Baguio City as their summer capital. The high altitude provided them with an escape from the tropical heat. Camp John Hay (695,000 hectares), the Philippine Military Academy (363 hectares) and various vacation houses for different national government offices were consequently built in Baguio.[35] Several presidential decrees issued by Marcos made the Cordillera vulnerable to outside exploitation and threatened their land security. Among these laws were Presidential Decree (PD) 705 (Revised Forestry Code), PD 410 (Ancestral Land Decree), PD 1559 (Amending PD 705), and PDs 548 and 634, which converted ancestral forest lands into forest reserves and national parks.[36] These included the 123,000 hectares of the Ambuklao-Binga Watershed Reserve; the Mt. Data National Park in Mountain Province, which totals 5,513 hectares, and the 20,000 hectares of the Balbalasang National Park in Kalinga-Apayao. These development and conservation projects served the development needs of the Philippine state and stood to benefit the majority, but they entailed loss of traditional land ownership, displacement and resettlement of the cultural communities

In effect the native was faced with way-of-life dilemmas alongside real economic pressure, but was also provided with options. There was identification with the bigger 'national', 'Christianized', 'Westernized' community and adoption of their ways. At the same time there was a nagging need to re-evaluate one's roots and traditional practices. It is argued that in the case of the small-scale mining communities in the region, the people's concept of sharing gold and working together in community projects, along with traditional resource use and ecological practices, has enabled them to adapt to environmental and social change through various strategies.[37]

This fluid self and collective negotiation with the challenges of a changing society rendered the indigenous population in the Cordillera open to new articulations of identity and programmes of action. Such identity formation reached a dynamic point in the 1970s when they encountered two powerful forces: the forces of a government imposing a developmental agenda that would lead to further modernization but also the destruction of their land and way of life; and the revolutionary forces of the Communist Party of the Philippines-New People's Army (CPP-NPA), who introduced to them a new ideology and programme that was useful in combating government intrusion.

The Beginnings

In the late 1960s, youth organizations like the Highland Activists (Hi-Act), the Kilusang Kabataan ng Kabundukan (KKK, or Highlander Youth Movement) and the local chapter of the national democratic youth organization Kabataang Makabayan (KM, or Nationalist Youth) became the vehicles for political activism of students in Baguio City or those from the Cordillera studying in Metro Manila. In 1971, during the 'Congress for National Liberation' held in Bontoc, the KKK and Hi-Act converged and formed the Kilusang Kabataan ng Kordilyera (also KKK, or Mountain Youth Movement).[38] The new KKK led a demonstration in Manila of five hundred Manila-based college students from the four Cordillera provinces on 1 October 1971. They demanded respect for civil liberties and asked that "Igorot students, unite!" to address national issues.

The imposition of martial law in September 1972 closed down these organizations.[39] Student activists with links to the underground were fielded to continue their 'mass work' in the region. They organized student groups that eventually became visible in street protests. In the second semester of 1981, the slogan of "Lansagin and Diktadurang US-Marcos!" ("Overthrow the US-Marcos dictatorship!") was the main call carried by some eight thousand student demonstrators from the different universities in Baguio.[40] These students were studying in Baguio but they came from different parts of the country. Their organizations were thus composed of different ethnolinguistic groups. Distinct organizations for Cordillera youth along the lines of the 1971 KKK were also formed. An example is the Progressive Igorot Students (PIGSA, which means strong in the Ilocano language, the lingua franca in Baguio City). It was formed in 1982 and opposed, among others, the government's tourism projects.[41]

Other cadres of the CPP were fielded to organize the NPA in the Cordillera. One pioneer returned to his hometown in Ifugao in January 1971 and formed the first guerrilla unit in the mountain range. Soon, with the help of a political elite in the town, they were able to expand their area of operation to forty-two barrios. However, the operatives were routed by the government army by the end of the year.[42] Another platoon found its way to Mayoyao, Ifugao, and in April 1972 the NPAs in Banaue and Ifugao formed what they called the first Party branch in Montañosa. Other youth activists who joined the underground helped popularize the communist movement with their mass work comprised largely of rural health and education programmes, and the punishment of petty crimes. Ifugao became the seat of the Northern Luzon Command of the NPA during these early years when growth was tenuous and slow moving. Meanwhile, in Abra the first NPA team entered in 1974, but its members were killed by government forces. The NPA re-entered Abra only in 1981, on the heels of the protest movement that had exploded in the region.

Growth of the Resistance

Unknown to the young cadres who tried to cultivate the revolution in the region in the early 1970s, a social and political upheaval was taking shape in the mid-1970s, generating a momentum that greatly benefitted the CPP-NPA project. The precipitating developments that led to this upheaval were the introduction of the multi-million Chico River Dam projects and the Cellophil Resources Corporation. With the assistance of the World Bank, in 1973 the Marcos government began feasibility studies for the construction of four hydroelectric dams — two in Mountain Province and two in Kalinga — along the Chico and Pasil Rivers. The Chico River Basin Development Program would have submerged 2,735 hectares of agricultural lands crucial to the economic and cultural survival of the people in the region.[43] A report made by the now defunct Montañosa Social Action Center in 1976 estimated that the Chico II dam in Mountain Province would directly displace 3,000 people and submerge 120 hectares of fertile rice lands, while the Chico IV in Kalinga would directly or indirectly affect 972 families or some 6,000 people.[44] Since swidden farming would be banned in the watershed areas, it was estimated that the livelihoods of at least 10,000 people would be affected.[45] The project also lacked details on the relocation of the affected population. Residents feared they would suffer the same deplorable situation of the Ibaloi, who were resettled in Nueva Vizcaya when the Ambuklao and Pantabangan dam sites were constructed in the 1950s. The resettled Ibalois found themselves farming salinated fields.[46] The disbursement of funds for the relocation was also marred by anomalies.

As in Mindanao, the state responded to opposition to the dam projects by sending in the troops. When villagers tore down two camps of survey teams in Besao, a poor municipality in Mountain Province, the government fielded military escorts to accompany the third attempt to construct a surveyors' camp. Abuses by Philippine Constabulary units against men from the local community followed.[47]

Local leaders in Bontoc and Kalinga asked to meet with government representatives in order to know more about the plans and to stop further harassment. A Kalinga elder was quoted as saying, "We are not against the dam. We are just opposed to the dam site."[48] One of the earlier petitions also expressed support for the dam so long as it would be built in another place. But in two attempts in 1974, the government agencies involved in the Chico dam projects, notably the National Power Corporation (NAPOCOR) tasked with surveying and the Presidential Assistant on National Minorities (PANAMIN), failed to come to the arranged meetings. Also in 1974, six petitions were brought to the presidential palace by tribal elders accompanied by local church representatives, to no avail. Marcos never met with them. Instead, he sent a reply by letter where he branded their arguments as sentimental and asked them "to sacrifice themselves for the sake of the nation".[49]

This "record of attempts to communicate with the agencies involved in the dam project is marked by, above all other things, the refusal, neglect — call it whatever you will — of the agencies to explain their position, to hear out the position of the Chico inhabitants, or to in any way seek full information of all aspects of the proposed project and the larger context of its possible effects".[50] Because of the government's arrogance and use of might, the opposition became a movement beyond the dam issue, harnessed to but not totally dovetailed by the CPP, to become one against the state at large. From mobilizing only affected villages, it spread to other villages, tribes and provinces in the Cordillera mountain range.

In 1975 a church-sponsored conference in Manila attended by 150 villagers from Bontoc and Kalinga led to the forging of a multilateral 'peace pact'. The peace pact drew inspiration from local practices of forging a shared penal code between tribes, promising no harm to the other, and taking responsibility in case violence is committed by a villager against a member of the other tribe. This practice of pact-making is called *bodong* among the Kalingas and *pechen* among the Bontocs. The multilateral 'peace pact' adopted but modified the practice in light of the pan-tribal nature of the threat coming from the state. As Hilhorst noted, the peace pact forged in Manila differed from the traditional practice in two respects: first, the signatories were not just two villages but a greater number of *ili* (villages) and participants, including outsiders who were extending solidarity; second, the pact aimed not only to regulate relations among the villages but to also unite them against the government.[51] Among the stipulations were sanctions against those who cooperated with the NAPOCOR, and exemptions from revenge or retribution should a villager be killed by another tribe for working with the NAPOCOR.[52]

Shortly after, Marcos ordered the NAPOCOR survey teams to be pulled out from Mountain Province. However, later the same year, in October 1975, survey work in Tomiangan, Kalinga (Chico IV) began. The PANAMIN worked to secure the support of the Kalingas through gifts and also by pitting warring villages against the other. But the villagers continued to attack the NAPOCOR camps. By 1978 they did so with the help of the New People's Army (NPA) band that had found its way to Kalinga. The harassment of villagers by soldiers, including the detention of a hundred villagers allegedly involved in one of the attacks on the NAPOCOR camp in 1976, drew the attention and support of groups in Manila.[53] On 24 April 1980, prominent Kalinga tribal leader Macli-ing Dulag from the town of Bugnay was killed by government soldiers and became the martyr of the Cordillera revolution. His stirring words in defence of their land were widely quoted, and international support for the struggle poured in.[54]

Plans for Chico 1 (Sabangan) were suspended because of protests along the Chico River by Bontoc villagers, but also supposedly because of questions about the feasibility of the project.[55] Chico III (Basao) was suspended allegedly as early as 1975, but its cancellation was publicly announced only on 19 July 1978.[56] Although the construction of Chico II (Anabel-Tucucan) was scheduled to start in 1978 and end in 1982, by October 1981 both the Chico II and Chico IV (Tomiangan) projects were also scrapped because of local and international protests.[57]

The 1975 pan-*ili* (Kalinga-Bontok) peace pact gathering mediated by the church marked the beginning of a common pan-Chico Valley response by villages against these government incursions. In December 1983, tribal elders from twenty-three Kalinga and Bontoc villages formally coalesced into the Kalinga-Bontoc Peace Pact Holders Association.[58] In December 1985, as membership expanded to include *pangats* (peace pact holders) from other provinces, it was renamed the Cordillera Bodong Association (CBA). Combined with the influence of the CPP-NPA units that had arrived in the area around 1978,[59] the protest movement assumed a region-wide and mono-ethnic character that was distilled in the notion of a 'Cordillera people'. Their heroic defiance of the dictatorship's programmes made the issue one of national significance. Consequently, the notion of a unitary 'Cordillera' captured the national imagination.

At about the same time as the Chico dam surveys took place, the Cellophil Resources Corporation (CRC) acquired a 200,000-hectare logging concession for paper and pulp manufacturing in the Abra portion of the Cordillera range. The CRC was owned by Herminio Disini, an in-law and businessman crony of the Marcoses who secured funding from a consortium of European banks and a Japanese corporation. Military and local government officials were used to force the native Tingguian residents to sell their lands. Those who refused were driven out of their communities. In view of the cases of harassment, church and community leaders began mobilizing against the CRC. Four indigenous Roman Catholic priests from Abra who actively campaigned against the CRC received death threats. Consequently, they joined the NPA.[60]

The concurrent mobilizations that were taking place in Kalinga, Bontoc and Abra created the conditions for the eventual integration of Abra in the notion of a Cordillera region. Agbayani wrote of these events: "With the development of a self-consciousness, a pan-Cordillera consciousness and movement were also developing. This was a qualitative shift in the movement. The largely spontaneous features of the early movement led by the elders in the barrios were giving way to a movement of planned and unified actions led by sectoral and people's organizations with a broader character."[61]

Harnessing the Mass Movement

The NPA as the armed component of the popular resistance grew, especially in Kalinga, as government militarization intensified. Conflict-related deaths by 1980 were estimated at a hundred, mostly among the government troops, local collaborators and the NAPOCOR personnel who were implementing the Chico dam projects.[62] Also, the NPA became an important mechanism that facilitated linkages of the different *ili* or villages at the provincial level.

At this point the CPP-NPA's narratives had broadened to include ethnicity, discrimination, national oppression and class issues. However, the appreciation of the particularities of the Cordillera region among leading CPP cadres differed. Leading local cadres adapted to local conditions and tapped and tweaked local structures like the clan or tribe and the peace pacts as organizational mechanisms.[63] Theoretically, the CPP regional committee acknowledged the particularities of the Cordillera:

> Neither feudal nor semi-feudal exploitation could become dominant in the Cordillera interior … [the main problem is the] state perpetuating the marginal state of their production and subsistence. The anti-feudal orientation cannot serve as our key link in the village and district levels for immediately arousing, organizing and mobilizing the peasant masses here.[64]

Along this line, the local cadres debated with the CPP leadership on the correct strategies and tactics to employ in the Cordillera. Those operating in Ifugao in the early 1970s proposed to form the Federation of Igorot Tribes for Liberation and the Igorot Liberation Army to highlight Igorot ethnicity and draw broad unity from the shared identity.

The CPP leadership however saw this as a "narrow political line" and that, "being localist, it tended to gloss over nationalist concerns".[65] Moreover, stressing the ethnic character of the Cordillera struggle was deemed detrimental to the revolution's class character. The proposal was also seen as divisive, since lowlanders would be excluded from the formation.[66] In 1979, NPA cadres in Kalinga proposed to establish a broad coalition of anti-dam activists to be called the Anti-Dam Democratic Alliance (ADDA), with the NPA as its army. The anti-dam focus would effectively harness the local groundswell that an organizing platform founded on anti-feudalism could not. The same cadres argued that neither feudalism nor semi-feudalism defined the property regimes or land ownership patterns in the region.[67] But the regional CPP leadership disapproved of the proposal, arguing that the ADDA might replace the party organization, and that the dam issue is but a manifestation of the ills of feudalism (the landlord purportedly was the government laying claim to peasant lands).[68] The CPP leadership preferred harnessing politicized recruits into the CPP-led organizations, namely the National Democratic Front (NDF) and the NPA for the underground, complemented by a broader-based organization operating as the open campaign machinery.

In effect the CPP formula for developing organs of political power by building a national democratic front prevailed. In 1981, plans for setting up an underground alliance as the advanced front that would draw more people from the Cordillera to the national democratic revolution began. In the CPP's revolutionary schema, therefore, the underground movement would take the form of the Cordillera People's Democratic Front (CPDF) as the 'sectoral organization' representing the Cordillera in the NDF. CPDF spokesperson Andres Fernandez described the essential relationship between member organizations like the CPDF with the NDF thus:

> In essence, the CPDF is just like the NDF in the Cordillera. First, because it is composed of democratic sectors and with people from these sectors agreeing on the program along the ND [national democratic] line and pursuing the Cordillera people's particular interests. Second, as a front for the struggle and a political center ... The CPDF as a revolutionary organization has to bind itself to or align itself with the entire revolutionary effort.[69]

TABLE 3.2
Revolutionary Member-Organizations of the NDF (2003)

Communist Party of the Philippines
New People's Army
Revolutionary Council of Trade Unions
Pambansang Katipunan ng Mga Magbubukid (National Association of Peasants)
Kabataang Makabayan (Patriotic Youth)
Makabayang Kilusan ng Bagong Kababaihan (MAKIBAKA, Patriotic Movement of New Women)
Cordillera People's Democratic Front (CPDF)
Christians for National Liberation (CNL)
Katipunan ng mga Gurong Makabayan (KAGUMA, Association of Patriotic Teachers)
Katipunan ng mga Samahang Manggagawa (Federation of Labor Unions)
Lupon ng mga Manananggol para sa Bayan (LUMABAN, Council of Lawyers for the People)
Artista at Manunulat ng Sambayanan (ARMAS, Artists and Writers of the People)
Makabayang Kawaning Pilipino (Patriotic Government Employees)
Makabayang Samahang Pangkalusugan (Patriotic Health Association)
Liga ng Agham para sa Sambayanan (LAB, League of Science for the People)
Moro Revolutionary Organizations (MORO)
Revolutionary Organization of Lumads (indigenous peoples)

Source: NDF Website, http:/www.philippinerevolution.org/ (accessed 18 August 2005).

All other NDF member organizations are structured along sectoral and class lines (see Table 3.2), but the CPDF is distinguished as the only firmly territorially constructed NDF member organization. According to CPDF spokesperson Andres Fernandez, "The CPDF, while being a sectoral organization, is in essence also a mass organization because we have individuals as members, and *because we organize the CPDF on a territorial basis, the Cordillera region, to represent the Cordillera people in the NDF.*"[70] This particularity of the resistance that developed in a 'national minority' territory turned out to be the greatest challenge posed to the CPP's orthodoxy from within.

The proposed structure for the CPDF somewhat mechanically operationalized 'minority' representation and merely mimicked that of the NDF. For example, a separate Cordillera youth organization called the Demokratiko a Timpuyong Dagiti Agtutubo ti Kordilyera (DATAKO, or "Democratic Movement of the Cordillera Youth") was formed as the youth arm of the CPDF, whereas those Ilocano, Tagalog and Pangasinenses in the Cordillera were kept under the national Kabataang Makabayan (KM).[71]

The CPP-NPA cadres in the region also organized the Cordillera People's Guerilla Forces (CPGF), made up of 'seasonal Red fighters' or local people who served as part-time guerrillas. They were tasked with guarding their respective villages and were occasionally mobilized in NPA operations.[72] As the 1980s progressed, party imperatives, notably the goal to reach the stage of 'strategic counter-offensive' and therefore the need to intensify military operations, prevailed. The NPA regularized its guerrilla units into company- and battalion-sized formations and the Cordillera terrain was utilized for the training of guerrillas destined for other areas.

Hilhorst analyses the merging of local resistance with the CPP-NPA's national democratic movement as follows: "We can conclude that the involvement of the CPP/NPA in the local struggle against the dams was the result of blending of different interests. For local villagers, the NPA represented a resource that could be mobilized for their local struggle. For the CPP/NPA, on the other hand, the controversy over the dams in the Chico river provided the political opportunity to gain a foothold in the area, in order to further their revolutionary struggle."[73]

Alongside building the underground front in support of the armed struggle, in 1984 the Cordillera Peoples Alliance (CPA) was formed.[74] The CPA was the umbrella organization of twenty-seven new 'aboveground' or 'open' organizations. According to its official narrative its founders were "mainly indigenous leaders and activists who spearheaded the widespread and successful opposition to the World Bank–funded Chico dams project and the commercial logging operations of the Cellophil Resources Corporation".[75] Its icon was Macli-ing Dulag, the highly esteemed tribal leader. It was during this period under the

Marcos dictatorship that the need "to strengthen the mass movement of indigenous peoples in the Cordillera to work for the promotion, recognition and defense of indigenous peoples (IP rights) and human rights arose, and the CPA answered this need".[76]

The number of member organizations of the CPA was said to have reached about 60 at the time of the alliance's second congress in 1985, among them village organizations; NGOs; professional organizations; clans; tribes; and workers, miners and anti-dictatorship groups in urban areas. The CPA claimed to be the "leading group and organized expression of the Cordillera people's aspiration for self-determination".[77] In 1986 the CPA lobbied for a regional autonomous region in the Cordillera. In 1987 it facilitated the formation of the electoral party named Partido Kordilyera (PK). The regional party was affiliated with the Partido ng Bayan, which unsuccessfully fielded CPP-NPA and NDF personalities in the 1987 senatorial elections. In 2005 the CPA claimed to have expanded to 120 community organizations, with three provincial chapters, in the Mountain Province, Kalinga and Abra; an urban multi-sectoral chapter in Baguio city; a municipal chapter in Itogon, Benguet; and sectoral federations of youth, women, elders, peasant and cultural workers.[78]

At the time that the CPA was being formed in 1984, a smaller group of activists who were critical of the CPP trajectory in the Cordillera had formed the Montañosa National Solidarity (MNS). According to one of its founders, Abrino Aydinan, the CPP hastened the formation of the CPA as a reaction to MNS organizing.[79] But the CPP infrastructure was definitely more established in the region. The CPA was thus more successful in implementing large campaigns with an organizational machinery.[80]

The Split

The CPDF finally held its first congress on 17 January 1987 in Sagada, Mountain Province. There the CPDF's Eight-Point Program was presented. The CPDF boasted control or influence over four hundred of a thousand barrios in the Cordillera.[81] It claimed to be a revolutionary force numbering several hundred thousand, of whom a few thousands were armed men and women. However, by this time the CPDF was facing a serious split in its ranks. The leadership of a new faction called the Cordillera People's Liberation Army (CPLA) was already negotiating peace with the Corazon Aquino administration.[82] Not surprisingly, the first CPDF Congress became an anti-CPLA event.

The CPLA represents what the late anthropologist-activist Agbayani called the "indigenist trend" in the CPDF — a line of thinking already articulated in the debates among CPP-NPA-CPDF cadres in the 1970s. Agbayani explained his use of the term: "I derived the term 'indigenist' from Indigenismo, the ideology of some of the leaders of the South American Indian (indigenous peoples) movement. For me, the term captures the essence of the CPLA political line. Just like some of the South American leaders, they view themselves as separate from the majority people. They see their interests as separate, if not diametrically opposed, to the interests of the majority people. And they view the majority people as one of the reasons for their current problems."[83]

How did the split happen? Commanders of the Lumbaya Company[84] led by Mailed Molina, an ethnic Tingguian from Abra in Northern Luzon, also known as Ka Wanas, reportedly formed the nine-man military commission in November 1985 in Tinglayan, Kalinga province.[85] This body became the CPLA core. CPDF spokesperson Andres Fernandez on the other hand dated the covert formation of the CPLA as early as 1984.[86] These alleged early secret activities were among the charges made by the CPP-NPA leadership against the dissenters later on.

According to Aydinan, the decision to secede was finally made on 25 February 1986. Even then they were supposedly willing to remain under the guidance of the CPP.[87] A similar reconstruction of the events co-written by ex-CPLA officer Fernando Bahatan recounted that the CPLA leaders resigned before the party committee and reportedly tried to negotiate an alliance between them and the NPA, to no avail.[88]

Agbayani, on the other hand, provided another angle supplied by an unnamed CPDF source. According to this source, Conrado Balweg took advantage of the fact that the commanding officer (CO) of the Lumbaya Company was on leave. The vice-CO in charge was his cousin, Ka Wanas. Balweg reportedly convinced Ka Wanas that there was a plot against his life. Ka Wanas thus called on his troops and convinced them to split from the NPA based on their own 'Cordillera line'.[89]

These accounts differ in slant but they share basic facts — namely, the existence of a group in the Lumbaya command leadership disenchanted with the CPP leadership; the temporary suspension of Lumbaya CO Ka Sungar for an offence, which elevated Ka Wanas to the strategic position of acting CO; and the failed attempts of the faction to achieve an amicable settlement or peaceful coexistence with the CPP.

Balweg, the popular Tingguian former priest who led the struggle against the Cellophil Resources in Abra and subsequently joined the NPA and became a media figure, dated the formation of the CPLA to March 1986.[90] But it was in April 1986 when, reportedly joined by some sixty combatants, the group formally broke away from the CPP-NPA and formed the CPLA.[91] President Corazon Aquino had made overtures to open peace negotiations in that month, and the Lumbaya group decided to take advantage of the offer.[92] Balweg became the CPLA's de facto chair. He was joined by his former fellow-priest Bruno Ortega.[93] By this time the CPLA reportedly numbered about two hundred armed men, operating along the Abra-Bontoc-Kalinga border alongside CPDF forces.[94]

The CPLA explained in one press release that the "Party's failure to understand and accommodate differences between the Cordillera and lowland society" was the reason for the split.[95] The CPDF acknowledged these differences. Its spokesperson said that while organizational issues were involved, "the primary aspect boiled down to the analysis of the Cordillera society", with the CPLA wanting "the Cordillera to become a nation".[96] The CPDF accused the military and the United States of exploiting the split within the party.[97]

In our interview with him in 1987, Balweg further distinguished the thrust of the CPLA in this manner: "It [the Cordillera resistance] started from spontaneous mass movements which revolved mainly around tribal interests, not sectoral or class interests. It's more on people's interests unlike in the majority Filipinos' context wherein [the] political line is defined in terms of classes and sectors. The movement of our struggle was that of one people in the context of their relation to their land."[98] The threat to their lands brought the different tribes together as one people, and "there developed a political line for the struggle for self-determination".[99]

Balweg and the Lumbaya Company allegedly wanted to concentrate on developing the *bodong* system in order to thwart 'lowland rule' (referring to the CPP-NPA) in the Cordillera, which subordinated the Cordillera struggle to the national struggle. They also raised charges of ethnic discrimination inside the party organization. They claimed that the CPP members who belonged to the ethnic minority were allocated less support and resources by the party hierarchy and that non-ethnics monopolized the party leadership in the region.[100] Indeed, Cordillera remained a subsection of the Northern Luzon party leadership, and most of the cadres in the subsection came from Cagayan Valley.[101] Moreover, after President Ferdinand Marcos was overthrown in February 1986, the CPLA disagreed with the CPP-NDF's unchanged policy to continue the armed struggle against the new government.

The CPP, in turn, charged Balweg and his group with organizational misconduct, including sexual and financial opportunism.[102] Among the charges detailed in a May 1986 document entitled "The CPLA: Our Investigation and Policy" issued by the Northern Luzon Commission of the CPP were: spreading the lie that the CPP practised ethnic discrimination within the party; magnifying criticisms raised by ethnic comrades against non-ethnic party members; and branding the CPDF as an "instrument of the lowlanders" for taking over the wealth of the Cordillera and destroying its socio-political system.[103]

In March 1986 the contentious division among the underground armed forces surfaced in the break-up of the peace-pact holders' organization, the Cordillera Bodong Association (CBA). The CPLA faction later adopted the name Cordillera Bodong Administration (CBAd) for the members who went to its side. The CBAd was formed by then CBA chair Mario Yag-ao and three other officers.[104] It appears however that many more from the CBA stayed in the CPA, the national democratic coalition. The CPA claimed that only 4 of the 13 CBA officers and only 16 of 200 *pangat* (or peace pact holders) joined the CPLA.[105]

The CPLA and CBAd were joined by Aydinan of the MNS and the Filipino Socialist Movement, which advocated a federal system. Aydinan was reportedly requested by Ka Wanas of the Lumbaya Company to help the CPLA draft its programme and head its negotiating panel in the talks with the government.[106]

In its 28 November to 2 December 1986 Fourth Congress, the CPLA's CBA faction ratified the *Manabo Pagta*, the constitution of the Cordillera Bodong (Nation). The document called for the establishment of the confederation of tribal groups to be called the Cordillera Bodong. With this, the word *bodong* or 'peace pact' was transposed to stand for 'nation'.

Reacting to these developments, the CPDF passed a resolution during its First Political Congress held in January 1987. The resolution blamed the "American imperialist, the Aquino government and the fascist armed forces" for successfully engineering the break up with the Balweg faction and for supporting the CPLA and the CBAd, thereby causing disunity among the Cordilleran member tribes.[107] The CPDF resolved to "expose" and "isolate" all of these forces and mete out punishment to those found guilty of "misdeeds and crimes against the people and the revolution".

Subsequently, several leaders in each camp became victims of retaliation from the other side. In June 1987, eight CPLA and CBAd officers were ambushed by the NPA in Baay-Licuan, Abra; in turn, Daniel Ngayaan, an anti-dam leader allied with the CPA, was killed by the CPLA.[108] In December 1999 Balweg was killed by an NPA team that allegedly included his own brother.[109] In all, about a hundred people were killed in these retaliatory attacks between the two camps.

CPLA Negotiations with the Government

The CPLA sought to dislodge the Cordillera peoples'[110] struggle for land, development and self-determination from the CPP-led struggle. In the post-Marcos period, it saw the peaceful, negotiated and parliamentary route to the creation of regional autonomy within a federal set-up as the appropriate strategy to advance the right to self-determination. On 19 May 1986, Balweg wrote a letter to President Aquino expressing the CPLA's willingness to enter into peace negotiations. A meeting with the president's brother-in-law, Agapito 'Butz' Aquino, was arranged on 15 June in Sagada, Mountain Province. Shortly after, on 13 September 1986, the CPLA, CBAd and MNS exchanged tokens with the Aquino government to mark the cessation of hostilities. They forged what became known as the Mt. Data Accord.

However, the drafting of the details of the ceasefire by the joint CPLA and Armed Forces of the Philippines (AFP) Ceasefire Committee was contentious and took several months. The CPLA guerrillas who had wanted to be transformed into the regional security force were merely integrated into the AFP as militias. Their participation in military operations in the region made relations with the CPP-NPA-CPDF even more antagonistic.

A draft executive order creating an Interim Cordillera Autonomous Region (ICAR) with an Interim Cordillera Regional Administration was penned by the CPLA and CBAd in February 1987. President Aquino issued Executive Order 220 only on 15 July 1987, creating the Cordillera Administrative Region (CAR). The terms of Executive Order 220 were much less than the CPLA had wanted. The CBAd was relegated to the status of a commission within the ICAR instead of serving as the interim government, and the responsibility for peace and order was retained by the national government.[111] To achieve some gains, the CPLA settled for it. The CAR was governed by the Cordillera Regional Assembly, with more than 200 members, and the 29-member Cordillera Executive Board (CEB). These bodies however were given a budget of a measly five million peso to undertake their programmes, and, moreover, they were encumbered by unclear guidelines for implementation and the slow release of funds.[112]

The privileging of the CPLA in the political process was met with consternation by the other political forces. The CPA had also made overtures to the Aquino government. Around the same time that Balweg wrote to the president, a group of CPA leaders sought and got an audience in Malacanang, where they lobbied for an autonomous government and the appointment of their two nominees in the Constitutional Commission (ConCom) tasked to draft a new constitution.[113] Their nominations were rebuffed, although the ConCom did eventually write into the constitution the creation of an autonomous region in the Cordillera and Muslim Mindanao. As for the peace talks, the CPA refused to join the Cordillera panel, believing that doing so would have been "a compromise of our democratic principles and misrepresentation of the views of many Igorot people".[114] The Cordillera Broad Coalition organized by the BIBAK Professionals Association had two seats in the Cordillera panel, but it also pulled out from the process when, in March 1987, their proposal for a Cordillera Regional Development Council (that was earlier adopted by the government) and the Cordillera panels were waylaid with the formation of the ICAR.[115] By the latter part of 1987 the CPA and the CBC were part of a coalition that called for disarming and disbanding the CPLA; moreover, the CBC also filed a petition in the Supreme Court questioning the constitutionality of E.O. 220.[116] Disdaining the CBAd's dominance in the set-up and the absence of any role for them, legislators from the region also objected to the proposed ICAR and to the idea that the CPLA would serve as the peacekeeping force in the region. When the CAR was formed, the six legislators from the Cordillera region filed a House Bill in September 1987 seeking to abolish the regional assembly and executive board and proposing to revert the set-up to a "simple administrative region" to be governed by a Cordillera Development Council.[117]

Within the CPLA forces and among its allies, tensions also brewed. Leadership issues and disagreements over joint ventures entered into by Balweg through the Cordillera Executive Board created friction among them. The CPLA and the MNS eventually parted ways. Aydinan's MNS reportedly left the CPLA panel in October 1987 when the CPLA killed Daniel Ngaya-an, who had headed the CBA faction that sided with the CPA.[118] The CPLA fighters also disagreed over whether to settle for integration into the Philippine army, mainly as citizens' auxiliary forces, instead of being formed into a regional security force. Balweg insisted on the Cordillera Regional Security Force, but CPLA commander Sawatang wanted to accept the integration offer in order to provide a needed source of income to the former guerrillas.[119] In 1993, Sawatang broke away from Balweg and pushed for the integration of his men. In 1997, CPLA stalwart Mailed Molina also broke ties with Balweg. Molina likewise wanted to pursue the integration effort in order to help former cadres. To force the government to respond, the pro-integration bloc returned to the government the *sipat* (peace token) exchanged during the signing of the Mt. Data Accord.[120] In customary practice, the return of the *sipat* was tantamount to a declaration of war. This forced the government to take notice and to act on their demands. In 1999, then president Estrada finally approved an integration scheme, but he was forced to step down from the presidency in January 2001. The next president, Gloria Macapagal Arroyo, signed Administrative Order 18 to finally put into effect an integration programme.

By this time, Balweg had been killed by the NPA. His loyalists and the Molina-Sawatang factions reportedly reunited in 2002.[121] In October 2008, Molina was elected chair of the CPLA, and Bon-as, who belonged to the Balweg camp, became the chief of staff. Allied forces in the CBAd tried to reconstitute the CBAd. A peace congress held in November 2008 elected a new set of officers led by engineer Andres Ngao-i, secretary-general of the Kalinga Bodong Congress and holder of several peace pacts for his tribe in Kalinga.[122] But it was evident that the CPLA-CBAd had become an aging force with weak leverage vis-à-vis the government. Some of its commanders instead pursued elected government posts in localities where they wielded influence.

Failed Autonomy Project

In June 1988, Congress passed Republic Act No. 6658 that created the Cordillera Regional Consultative Commission (CRCC). The CRCC was to assist Congress in drafting the Organic Act of the Cordillera Autonomous Region. Aydinan, who by then had dissociated himself from the CPLA, was appointed by Aquino to head the CRCC. The national democratic CPA-CBA criticized the choice of twenty-nine commissioners appointed by President Aquino as allegedly a mixture of non-Cordillera residents, Cordillerans discredited in their own provinces, people who had been opposed to autonomy, people representing multinational and big business interests, and people associated with the previous regime.[123]

The CRCC finished its draft Organic Act in December 1988 and submitted it to Congress. The national legislature further diluted the draft of autonomy powers, thus also earning the opposition of the CRCC to the Organic Act that the Congress eventually passed. Among the points of contention over the Organic Act were the degree to which laws governing ancestral domains and natural resource use should be subjected to national law; the revenue-sharing among the constituents of the region; whether or not to have a parliamentary form of government in the Autonomous Region, to directly elect the regional officials, or to rotate the top posts among the provincial governors, as in the case of the Metro Manila Development Authority; who would have control over the police in the region; and the territorial coverage of the region.[124]

Republic Act 6766 or the Organic Act for its creation was passed in 1989 and amended as Republic Act 8438 in 1998. Two plebiscites have been held to ratify the two laws and to determine the area of coverage of the Autonomous Region. In both cases, only in one province did a majority vote in favour of inclusion: Ifugao in 1990 and Apayao in 1998. After the 1990 plebiscite, the Supreme Court ruled that a single province could not constitute a region.[125] The Cordillera Administrative Region was retained pending amendments to the Organic Act and another referendum that was hoped would result in the coverage in at least two, if not all, of the five provinces in the Gran Cordillera mountain range and of Baguio City. But this did not happen in 1998. Critical of the anomalous situation and the failure to institute a regular autonomous government, the Senate finance sub-committee chaired by Senator Aquilino Pimentel at one point had refused to provide funding for the CAR.

In all, the factionalism within and between the pro-autonomy, non-state actors (represented by the CPLA and the CPDF and their respective allies) weakened the bargaining strength of the progressive, non-government camp vis-à-vis the state and traditional political elites in the region. Political and military interests that were threatened by the granting of autonomy subverted the initial intentions of the Aquino government to grant substantial autonomy. The military establishment, for one, did not look kindly on the recognition of another armed force not directly under its command. Similarly, the traditional politicians and elites in the region were wary of rearranging the patronage structures and power bases that they had re-established upon the restoration of regular elections. The administration of President Corazon Aquino was unable to bring together all these disparate groups and interests.

To date, the stipulation in the 1987 Constitution for the establishment of a regional autonomous government in the Cordillera has not been implemented, given that the two organic laws passed in 1991 and 1998 were not ratified by the Cordillera voters. Ifugao Representative Teodoro Baguilat rounded up a host of reasons for this failure, including the negative campaign of the Catholic hierarchy that autonomy would only add another layer of corruption, and parochial concerns like fears by government employees that they would suffer pay cuts. "Then there were tribes that rejected the organic act simply because they did not want politicians identified with the autonomy drive to lord it over the region as corrupt kings", wrote Baguilat.[126]

From a discourse analytic frame, Casambre wrote: "The rejection of R.A. 8438 has been interpreted in various ways — the result of ignorance, indifference, skepticism, or disagreement with the law — and all of these are in part valid."[127] However, a crucial factor was the substance of the autonomy that the law provided; namely, its failure to grasp the anthropological complexity of the region.[128] According to Casambre, autonomy was mainly articulated by 'outsiders': the CPP, which was made up of and led by lowlanders; and Balweg, who came from Abra, which while part of the Cordillera mountain range is outside the more conventional territorial delineation made up of the provinces of Benguet, Ifugao, Bontoc, Apayao and Kalinga.[129] The dialogues for autonomy were subsequently dominated by bureaucrats, lawyers and politicians and the mechanics were found to be constricting. The resultant draft laws were effectively sanitized of local attributes; for example, the second proposed Organic Act did not even mention the *ili*, or the traditional villages.[130] The state also continued to work on the premise that there is a pan-Cordilleran regional identity when in fact there is a variety of sub-regional/provincial identities with their respective indigenous land ownership and resource management systems and conflict resolution mechanisms.[131] Casambre called for a more authentic discourse — "one that is 'anthropologically' rather than 'ideologically' or 'bureaucratic-legalistically' determined or 'politically' driven".[132]

Equally detrimental was the absence of a broad consensus and the differing lines of action among the 'motive forces'. Consequently, the autonomy movement was orphaned and left mainly in the hands of the legislators. The CPA did not reject regional autonomy but it rejected the "CPLA and its crimes against the people, the collusion of the central government and the CPLA-CEB-CRA-CBAd to coopt the earlier gains and derail the mass movement, the infighting and corruption of traditional politicians and opportunists who had jockeyed themselves into position in the new Cordillera bureaucracy, and the insincerity of government to substantially recognize indigenous people's rights".[133] They felt a sense of betrayal — "tayo ang nag-tanim, nag-ani, nagbayo at nagluto, tapos iba ang kumain".[134]

In the late 1980s to early 1990s, moreover, the organized bases of the NPA in the Cordillera suffered the brunt of the counter-insurgency operations by the AFP and the burden of supporting a large army. The CPP became muddled in internal party debates, first on the Cordillera question then over the admitted 'tactical error' of the leadership in deciding to boycott the snap election that led to the overthrow of the Marcos regime, which other critical cadres saw as a strategic blunder. The national democratic forces were left in the cold as the new coalition government of Corazon Aquino was formed. Questions over strategy and tactics, on the handling of the peace negotiations, the relationship with the Aquino government, the viability and correctness of armed struggle as the primary form of struggle in contrast to the insurrectionist line propagated by leading cadres in Mindanao and Metro Manila regional committees, organizational democracy, etc., rocked the CPP. In 1992, CPP chair Amado Guerrero settled the internal party debates by affirming the CPP's orthodox strategy.[135] Military losses were blamed on the untenable company-sized formations of guerrillas. Cadres were called to revert to basic mass work and to small guerrilla formations. Remaining CPDF forces thus returned to their political work. Although unable to reach the same level of strength in the Cordillera mountain range, they were able to recover some ground and managed to expand to new areas. But, like the CPLA, the CPDF had lost the momentum generated by the upheaval of the 1970s.

And while the CPA has not given up on the struggle for "genuine regional autonomy as the form of self-determination in the Cordillera",[136] in subsequent decades the disjuncture between the more visible 'ancestral domain' campaigns and the dispersed 'regional autonomy' movement became more evident. The latter is being left behind. Up until the early 1990s, ancestral domain was equated with regional autonomy, as can be gleaned from this statement: "Ancestral domain must assume regional autonomy, which, without the former, is merely a slogan."[137] Today there is a return to the more primordial essence of ancestral domain along the lines articulated by an anthropologist: "The issue of land rights is inseparable from the question of survival."[138] The title of the CPA's 2008 collection of articles, *Ti Daga ket Biag* ("Land is Life"), indicates the saliency of the land issue first and regional autonomy second. This essence is pre-eminent, no matter the unit of autonomy (local, provincial, regional, federal state) being discussed.[139]

That the advocacy for regional autonomy in the Cordillera has taken a retreat about a generation later is affirmed in a 2009 comment by Dr Ed Bagtang, president of the Kalinga Agricultural State College. According to him, a wider information dissemination drive on autonomy for the Cordillera is necessary because most of the people in the region today belong to the younger generation who are no longer aware of the history of the struggle for autonomy.[140]

Subsequent attempts by legislators from the region to pass a new autonomy law some twenty years after the second law was enacted but not ratified by the region's voters have not moved beyond refiling and committee hearings in succeeding Congresses.[141] Fairclough wrote: "A new discourse may come into an institution or organization without being enacted or inculcated. It may be enacted, yet never be fully inculcated."[142] Despite its momentous revolutionary origins, "enacted but not fully inculcated" seems to apply very well to the Cordillera autonomy discourse.

Notes

1. Revered Kalinga chieftain Macli-ing Dulag was murdered by government troops in 1980. Cited in Rizal G. Buendia, "The Cordillera Autonomy and the Quest for Nation-Building: Prospects in the Philippines", *Philippine Journal of Public Administration* 34, no. 4 (October 1991), p. 357.
2. Carmencita Cawed, *The Culture of the Bontoc Igorot* (Manila: Communication Foundation for Asia, 1981), p. 2. I am thankful to the daughter of Cawed, Maryanne Trono, for lending me a copy of this rare book.
3. Belgian priests arrived in 1904 in Bontoc; in 1911, Belgian missionary sisters came as well and opened up schools for girls, as only boys were taught in the schools established earlier (ibid., pp. 4–5). Missions were also set up by Protestant Episcopalian/Anglicans, Presbyterians and Lutheran churches.
4. Administrative oversight was strongest in Benguet; there was very little in Apayao. The elders retained authority in so-called unorganized municipal districts, although American-appointed presidents may have acted as executive figureheads. Gerard Finin, *The Making of the Igorot: Contours of Cordillera Consciousness* (Quezon City: Ateneo de Manila University Press, 2005), p. 109.
5. Cited in ibid., pp. 48, 51, 55, 73, 101–3.
6. Maria Nela B. Florendo, "The Movement for Regional Autonomy in the Cordillera", in *Advancing Regional Autonomy in the Cordillera: A Source Book*, edited by Arturo C. Boquiren (Baguio City: Cordillera Studies Center, University of the Philippines; Manila: Friedrich Ebert Stiftung, 1994). Notably, the Americans restricted the use of the label *Igorot* to the inhabitants in the southern Cordillera, whom they considered the "more civilized" cultural group compared to the Kalinga and the Apayao/Isneg in the east (ibid.).
7. Finin, *The Making*, p. 23.
8. Philippine Office of the Presidential Economic Staff, *Province Profile of the Mountain Province* (1969), p. 55.
9. From 1902 to 1908, Ifugao was part of the Nueva Viscaya province. In 1908, Ifugao was carved from Nueva Vizcaya province to become the sub-province for the 'Ifugao tribe' in the newly created Mountain Province.
10. Also in 1902, Lepanto and Bontoc were merged and their boundary was extended to cover Tagudin in the Ilocos coast. The Lepanto-Bontoc province

had three sub-provinces: Amburayan, Lepanto and Bontoc. In 1908 the three sub-provinces were incorporated into the Mountain Province. Other tracts count 'Bontoc-Lepanto' as one of therefore only six sub-provinces of the former Mountain Province and date the latter's formation to 1907. See, for example, Cawed, *The Culture*, p. 4.

11. In 1966, Kalinga and Apayao became the single Kalinga-Apayao province. They became separate provinces again in 1995.

12. In 1920, Amburayan and Lepanto were abolished as sub-provinces and its villages were distributed to Ilocos Sur, La Union or the sub-provinces of Mountain Province like Benguet and Bontoc. The boundaries (and names) of these sub-provinces have their respective histories as well. Benguet up to the 1850s was made up of the present Trinidad Valley only; Tabuk and Lubuagan became incorporated in Kalinga only in the 1890s; and the name Bontok in the 1850s referred to a Spanish military district. William Henry Scott, *Of Igorots and Independence, Two Essays* (Baguio City: Era, 1993), pp. 58. The first written record on Ifugao is traced to a 1739 Dominican manuscript, and a study made by Father Lambrech hypothesizes that the present Ifugao province was a resettlement site of Ifugaos who escaped Spanish incursions in the upper Magat River valley (ibid., p. 12).

13. Finin, *The Making*, p. 42.

14. Ibid., pp. 17, 139.

15. Ibid.

16. Municipal districts headed by appointed local municipal presidents were created in the province by clustering scattered hamlets into villages based on "geographic and ethnic" factors. In the mid-1920s the Bureau of Non-Christian Tribes introduced an informal system for municipal elections by popular vote, starting in Benguet and parts of the Bontoc sub-province. The secret ballot was introduced in some areas, later modified into a "semisecret ballot" process using coloured paper corresponding to candidates, due to low literacy. In the early 1930s, one seat in the Provincial Board was reserved for "mountaineers"; this was increased a few years later to two seats won by votes among district and sub-province officials. See ibid., pp. 108–15.

17. Ibid., pp. 109–10.

18. Previously, the Mountain Province and Moro Province shared the seats allocated for areas under the Bureau of Non-Christian Tribes. In 1935, three legislative seats in the National Assembly were given to the Mountain Province. Ibid., p. 115.

19. Ibid., pp. 111–12.

20. One such author was Merton Miller, writing in the 1900s. Cited in ibid., p. 39.

21. An official 1888 report on Abra divided the province among three races: the Ilocanos, who were Christians; the pagan Tingguians, who lived in municipal districts near town centres; and the Igorots, who lived in the interior. Finin, *The Making*, p. 289, citing Antonio Alagao (1987).
22. For example, an indigenous couple would get married in church garbed in Western or Filipiniana-style dress, but they would celebrate the wedding by hosting a huge traditional feast or *cañao* lasting for two days or more, with the compulsory ritualistic slaying of animals.
23. Cawed, *The Culture*, 5.
24. Philippine Office of the Presidential Economic Staff, *Province Profile of the Mountain Province* (1969), p. 16.
25. Ibid.
26. Finin, *The Making*, p. 185.
27. Ibid., p. 132.
28. Documented and translated by Jimmy Fong in "Change and Identity in Ibaloi Pop Songs", in *Towards Understanding Peoples of the Cordillera: A Review of Research on History, Governance, Resources, Institution and Living Traditions*, vol. 1 (Baguio City: Cordillera Studies Center, University of the Philippines Baguio, 2001), pp. 219–20.
29. Ibid., p. 220.
30. Ibid. Fong cited another song by Lourdes Fangki and Amy Guesdan that "bewail[s] the dilemma of the people: whether to give in to tradition, or to save some for education and other modern expenses." He commented: "Certainly, it is ironic that these thoughts are being expressed in songs which have also become market commodities."
31. Ibid., p. 224.
32. Ed Maranan, "Development and Minoritization", *Diliman Review* 35, nos. 5–6 (1987): 11.
33. See Leah Enkiwe-Abayao, "Apfu-ab chi Chokoh: Mayoyao's Ethnomedicine in a Changing Cultural Context", in *Towards Understanding Peoples of the Cordillera: A Review of Research on History, Governance, Resources, Institution and Living Traditions*, vol. 1 (Baguio City: Cordillera Studies Center, University of the Philippines Baguio, 2001), pp. 182–97.
34. Francisco A. Suling, "Once More to the Breach: More Destructive Dams in Kalinga-Apayao", mimeographed (n.d.) (accessed at the UP Baguio library), p. 2.
35. Rizal G. Buendia, "The Cordillera Autonomy and the Quest for Nation-Building: Prospects in the Philippines", *Philippine Journal of Public Administration* 34, no. 4 (October 1991): 359. The heirs of the Ibaloi tribal leader Mateo Carino, who had ownership rights over the land seized by

the American colonial regime for Camp John Hay, asked that the camp be renamed after the tribal leader to rectify the historical injustice, and that unused portions be allocated to the Ibaloi clans. Carino's ownership over the land was upheld by the American Supreme Court in a decision dated 4 June 1908, but the land was never returned. See Desiree Caluza, "Kin of Ibaloi Leader Want John Hay Named after Him", *Philippine Daily Inquirer*, 2 September 2008, p. A15.

36. Buendia, "The Cordillera Autonomy", pp. 356–57.
37. See Evelyn Caballero, "Strategies of Survival for a Community of Traditional Small-Scale Miners", in *Towards Understanding Peoples of the Cordillera: A Review of Research on History, Governance, Resources, Institutions and Living Traditions*, vol. 1 (Baguio City: Cordillera Studies Center, University of the Philippines Baguio, 2001), pp. 171–81.
38. Rene Agbayani, "The Political Movement in the Cordillera", *Diliman Review* 35, nos. 5–6 (1987), p. 15.
39. The KM was subsequently revived as the underground youth organization affiliated with the CPP-led National Democratic Front.
40. Nestor Castro, "Ang Kilusang Komunista sa Kordilyera: Pagtatagpo ng taal at katutubong kultura", *Philippine Social Science Review, Special Issue on Ang Kilusang Masa sa Kasaysayang Pilipino 1900–1992* (January–December 1994): 205.
41. Agbayani, "The Political Movement", p. 18.
42. Most of the information in this paragraph was sourced from ibid., p. 16.
43. Suling, "Once More", p. 1.
44. Cited in Carol H.M. Brady-de Raedt, "To Know the Meaning of the Chico Project", mimeographed (n.d.). Carino (1980) claimed Chico IV would submerge six barrios with a total of 670–1,000 families. Cited in Dorothea Hilhorst, *The Real World of NGOs: Discourses, Diversity and Development* (Quezon City: Ateneo de Manila Press, 2003), p. 37.
45. Brady-de Raedt, "To Know".
46. Ibid. The government succeeded in convincing some families to relocate. For example, twenty families from Tanglag village relocated. They returned, however, when the promised government benefits did not materialize. Hilhorst, *The Real World*, p. 36.
47. Hilhorst, *The Real World*, p. 36.
48. Cited in Brady-de Raedt, "To Know".
49. Cited in Hilhorst, *The Real World*, p. 34. See also Agbayani, "The Political Movement", p. 16.
50. Brady-de Raedt, "To Know".
51. Hilhorst, *The Real World*, pp. 36–37.

52. Ibid.

53. Francisco A. Suling, "Chronology of Events and Military Activities and Harassments in the Chico Dam Area from January to April 1980", mimeographed (n.d.) (accessed at the UP Baguio library); Hilhorst, *The Real World*, p. 38.

54. I joined the international delegation that went to Kalinga in May 1980 as a show of opposition to the killing of the respected tribal leader. The expedition entailed scaling mountain trails and crossing the mighty Chico River. Every year thereafter, Macli-ing's death has been commemorated with events that draw local and foreign participants to the Cordillera. Pedro Dungoc, Macli-ing's son-in-law who survived the assassination plot became the new spokesperson. He joined the NPA in 1983. He died after being pinned down by a fallen tree in a thunderstorm in Kalinga in 1985.

55. Brady-de Raedt, "To Know".

56. Ibid.

57. Agbayani, "The Political Movement", p. 16.

58. Buendia, "The Cordillera Autonomy", p. 346. Other sources peg the year at 1982.

59. In 1978, one unit of the NPA that was fleeing the hot pursuit of government forces in Isabela province reached Tanudan, Kalinga. This group fortuitously linked up with the growing indigenous opposition to the Chico River dams in Tinglayan, Kalinga. By 1979 the NPA fighters numbered thirty-three, as villages sent their youth to join the armed group. This account and other details are in Castro, "Ang Kilusang Komunista sa Kordilyera", pp. 191–238. The marriage of Ka Sungar, the NPA commander, to a local Kalinga woman was also cited as an important factor for the effective integration of the NPA team in the local political and social landscape. See Hilhorst, *The Real World*, p. 40. However, Agbayani pegs the entry of the NPA squad from Isabela, Cagayan Valley to 1976, not 1978. See Agabayani, "The Political Movement", p. 16.

60. Agbayani, "The Political Movement", p. 17. The four priests were Nilo Valerio, Conrado Balweg, and cousins Bruno and Cirilio Ortega. They belonged to the Missionary of the Divine World, which has a seminary in Bangued, the capital town of Abra.

61. Ibid., p. 17.

62. Carino (1980) cited in Hilhorst, *The Real World*, p. 40.

63. Castro noted that although the CPP-NPA used traditional forms in Kalinga, such as warfare and the *bodong*, it introduced new elements. These were accepting women into the guerrilla force (warfare was traditionally assigned to men) and, as in the 1975 Manila peace pact, converting the bilateral *bodong* into a multilateral instrument. Castro, "Ang Kilusang Komunista sa Kordilyera", p. 202.

64. CPP-Northwestern Luzon Regional Party Committee (1981) cited in Castro, "Ang Kilusang Komunista sa Kordilyera", p. 206.

65. CPDF statement cited in Agbayani, "The Political Movement", p. 19.

66. Recalling the disagreement, Abrino Aydinan, then the youngest of the NPA field commanders in the Cordillera before his arrest in November 1971, said that the CPP insisted on ignoring the "primitive formations" in Philippine society: "Kami, hindi lang naming kinikilala yun, kundi yun ang basis nung particular struggle namin sa Cordillera. Sa CPP, that cannot be allowed kasi it will only divide the Filipino nation. Sa amin naman, what Filipino nation? Wala pang Filipino nation." (We didn't only recognize the "primitive formations" but considered it as the basis of our particular struggle in the Cordillera. The CPP said that cannot be allowed because it will only divide the Filipino nation.... As for us, what Filipino nation? There is no Filipino nation yet.). This is a direct quotation from my interview with Abrino Aydinan, 20 October 2008, in Quezon City. Aydinan was the first CPP cadre sent to Ifugao, his home province. He was in prison at the time the ILF (Igorot Liberation Front) proposal was discussed, deliberated and disapproved of by the CPP Central Committee, but he said he was in touch with the forces. He worked on this slant with another colleague who was also in jail and another comrade who eventually backtracked and became the first chair of the CPDF. Aydinan was working with the Department of Agrarian Reform at the time of the interview. See also Nestor T. Castro, "The Zigzag Route to Self-determination", *Diliman Review* 35, nos. 5–6 (1987) for an account of the party debates during this period.

67. Social scientists concur with this position. Cawed, for instance, wrote: "Landlords and tenants do not exist in Bontoc. Each terrace along the Chico River and in the slopes of the mountains is a piece of private property owned by those who cultivate it." The mountains, forests, hills and pastureland are communal properties. Cawed, *The Culture*, p. 40. Across and within tribal groups, several property regimes coexist, including individual, communal and corporate/family types. See Cordillera Schools Group, Inc., *Ethnography of the Major Ethnolinguistic Groups in the Cordillera* (Quezon City: New Day, 2003).

68. Castro, "The Zigzag Route", p. 29; Hilhorst, *The Real World*, p. 43.

69. "Forum: Interview with Andres Fernandez, CPDF Spokesperson", *Diliman Review* 35, nos. 5–6 (1987), p. 46.

70. Ibid. (italics mine).

71. In the March 1989 regional congress organized by the CPDF Preparatory Commission, the CPDF was fully launched as the NDF chapter in the Cordillera. This time, the KM chapters and other sectoral groups in the region were put under the CPDF umbrella, thereby transforming it fully into a multisectoral organization. The CPP-led CPDF Congress approved

a constitution and a revised programme. See Castro, "The Zigzag Route", pp. 206, 210.

72. Agbayani, "The Political Movement", p. 25.

73. Hilhorst, *The Real World*, p. 40.

74. The CPA initially spelled out its name as "People's", but it shifted eventually to "Peoples". For consistency, I use the current spelling.

75. CPA, "About the Cordillera Peoples Alliance", http://www.cpaphils.org/aboutus.htm (accessed 26 November 2005).

76. Ibid.

77. Agbayani, "The Political Movement", p. 18.

78. CPA, "About the Cordillera Peoples Alliance".

79. Interview with Abrino Aydinan, 20 October 2008, Quezon City.

80. As with the cadres who set up the CPA, MNS members were former university students recruited into the CPP-led national democratic movement. Among the personalities in the MNS were the early cadres of the CPP in the Cordillera who advocated a different approach and eventually distanced themselves from the CPP. Some were former political detainees based in Metro Manila, but they continued to engage with other activist groups in the opposition to martial law and in charting a different course for the Cordillera.

81. Agbayani, "The Political Movement", pp. 18, 20, 23.

82. Signed and official documents relating to the CPLA up to 2015 used "People's" in its name, but other publications have used the plural "Peoples" as well. For consistency, I have used the spelling used in official documents.

83. Agbayani, "The Political Movement", p. 25.

84. The company was named after anti-dam tribal leader and *pangat* (peace pact holder) Ama Lumbaya, also of the Butbut tribe, the tribe of Macli-ing Dulag. He joined the NPA and he died in June 1985 due to illness at a time when a military blockade prevented the entry of food and medicine. The Lumbaya Company was the first full-time NPA guerrilla unit in the Kalinga-Bontoc-Abra border area. See ibid., pp. 25, 21.

85. Fernando D. Bahatan, Jr. and Gabino P. Ganggangan, "Struggle for a Cordillera Nation (CBA-CPLA Struggle for a New Socio-economic Political Order in the Cordillera)", unpublished manuscript, May 2004 version. The paper is part of a collection of studies on peace building in the Cordillera commissioned by the United Nations Development Program in the Philippines.

86. *Diliman Review*, "Forum: Interview with Andres Fernandez", p. 49.

87. Interview with Abrino Aydinan, 20 October 2008, Quezon City.

88. Bahatan and Ganggangan, "Struggle for a Cordillera Nation".

89. Agbayani, "The Political Movement", pp. 21, 25.
90. Interview with Conrado Balweg on 16 June 1986 by Gerard Finin, quoted in Gerard A. Finin, "'Igorotism', Rebellion, and Regional Autonomy in the Cordillera", in *Brokering a Revolution: Cadres in a Philippines Insurgency*, edited by Rosanne Rutten (Quezon City: Ateneo de Manila University Press, 2008), pp. 109–10. According to Balweg, they had agreed that fighters who decide to join either side may bring their arms, and communication and coordination were to be maintained to avoid misunderstanding.
91. Bahatan and Ganggangan, "Struggle for a Cordillera Nation". This accords with Agbayani's account, which dates the transformation of the Lumbaya Company into the CPLA to 7 April 1986. Agbayani, "The Political Movement", pp. 21–22.
92. Interview with Abrino Aydinan, 20 October 2008, Quezon City.
93. The other SVD priest, Cirilo Ortega, remained with the CPDF, while Nilo Valerio died in the hands of the Philippine Constabulary in Central Benguet in August 1985. Agbayani, "The Political Movement", p. 25.
94. Ibid., p. 22
95. Cited in Hilhorst, *The Real World*, p. 46.
96. "Forum: Interview with Andres Fernandez", *Diliman Review*, p. 49.
97. Ibid.
98. "Forum: Interview with Conrado Balweg", *Diliman Review* 35, nos. 5–6 (1987), p. 42. I was then a member of the *Diliman Review*'s editorial team. The interview was held in Baguio City together with colleague Antoinette Raquiza.
99. Ibid.
100. Agbayani, "The Political Movement", p. 21.
101. Castro, "The Zigzag Route", p. 206.
102. At the time of the split, Balweg was already under disciplinary action for alleged extramarital relations with Ka Tina, a young female NPA cadre. The punishment was handed down by the District Party Committee, where Balweg was the secretary. The disciplinary action consisted of a one-year suspension from the party, the severance of relations with the woman, and self-criticism before the woman's community. Agbayani, "The Political Movement", p. 21.
103. Cited in Ed Maranan, "Development and Minoritization", p. 10.
104. Bahatan and Ganggangan, "Struggle for a Cordillera Nation".
105. Agbayani, "The Political Movement", pp. 21–22. The CBA was apparently strong in the Mountain Province, Abra and Kalinga-Apayao, but not in Ifugao and Benguet (based on *Diliman Review*, "Forum: Interview with Conrado Balweg", p. 43). According to Buendia, the CBAd was organized to serve as the administrative arm of the envisioned Cordillera Autonomous

Government, whereas the CBA was intended as an instrument to unite the peace pact holders. Buendia, "The Cordillera Autonomy", p. 346.

106. Interview with Aydinan, 20 October 2008, Quezon City. He was already working as a journalist in the now defunct *Business Day* at the time he joined the panel. His long-time friends in the MNS, Cameron Odsasey and Greg Tagiba, both from Bontoc, joined him in drafting the CPLA programme and in the negotiating panel.

107. Cordillera People's Democratic Front, "Resolution against Reactionary Reformism and Counter-revolution" (paper presented at the First Political Congress of the CPDF, Sagada, Mountain Province, 17 January 1987).

108. Buendia, "The Cordillera Autonomy", p. 347.

109. Balweg had accused the CPP of having already ordered him to be killed as early as 1985/1986 at the time of the disciplinary action against him. Agbayani, "The Political Movement", p. 23.

110. I use the plural "peoples" to reflect the multiplicity of tribes/ethnic groupings that are ascribed to the Cordillera identity label, unless used in the singular in quoted texts.

111. Buendia, "The Cordillera Autonomy", p. 348.

112. Ibid., p. 348.

113. Athena Lydia Casambre, *Discourses on Cordillera Autonomy* (Baguio City: Cordillera Studies Center, University of the Philippines Baguio, 2010), p. 20.

114. Ibid., p. 22.

115. Ibid., p. 23.

116. Ibid., p. 23.

117. Ibid., p. 24.

118. See Buendia, "The Cordillera Autonomy", pp. 347, 349. Despite the distancing during the negotiation, Aydinan continued to help the CPLA pursue the implementation of the terms of the agreement.

119. Separate interviews with Kalinga *bodong* holder and engineer Andres Ngao-i on 7 November 2008 and Juanita Chulsi, then deputy chief of the CPLA, on 8 November 2008 in Tabuk, Kalinga. According to Ngao-i, "Many of the CPLA cadres are family men. They want to send their children to school. That led them to decide to accept the integration offer of the government.... The debate lasted for a long time; the forces were fatigued. They were tired [of waiting]. As the head, Ambo [nom de guerre of Balweg] didn't want it. If the armed forces are integrated into the army, where will he go? He will be nothing. He didn't want to be integrated because he didn't want to be a military man. But what about his men?"

120. Interview with Ngao-i, 7 November 2008, Tabuk, Kalinga.

121. Bahatan and Ganggangan, "Struggle for a Cordillera Nation". The authors claimed that the reunified CPLA maintained four brigades and thirteen battalions at that time, but they were made up mostly of unarmed troops.

122. I attended the two-day conference held at the Pastoral Center in Tabuk, Kalinga on 7–8 November 2008 under the auspices of the Peacemakers Movement (a civil society organization led by Tabuk Bishop Andaya and Ngao-i) and the Cordillera Bodong Administration.

123. Cited by Buendia, "The Cordillera Autonomy", pp. 348–49.

124. Cited by Maria Nela B. Florendo, "The Movement for Regional Autonomy in the Cordillera", in Arturo C. Boquiren, *Advancing Regional Autonomy in the Cordillera: A Source Book* (Baguio City: Cordillera Studies Center, University of the Philippines; Manila: Friedrich Ebert Stiftung, October 1994), p. 47; "Basic Principles and Concepts", handout by CEB director Robert Fanagayen, cited in Boquiren, *Advancing Regional Autonomy*, p. 85. These same issues confounded the negotiations between the government and the MILF.

125. Ordillo vs. COMELEC 192 SCRA100-110.

126. Teodoro Baguilat, "Do the Cordillerans Really Want Autonomy?", Inquirer. net, 16 July 2013, https://newsinfo.inquirer.net/446367/do-cordillerans-really-want-autonomy#ixzz5fbXv7xYb.

127. Casambre, *Discourses on Cordillera Autonomy*, pp. 85–86, 99.

128. Ibid., pp. 95–103.

129. This contradicts the assertion by the Kalinga Andres Ngao-i about the closeness of the indigenous Tingguian with the Kalingan, culturally and geographically, although Abra itself may have been separated administratively for the most part.

130. Casambre, *Discourses on Cordillera Autonomy*.

131. Casambre, Athena Lydia, "The Failure of Autonomy for the Cordillera Region, Northern Luzon, Philippines", in *Towards Understanding Peoples of the Cordilleras: A Review of Research on History, Governance, Resources, Institutions and Living Traditions*, vol. 1 (Baguio City: Cordillera Studies Center, 2001), pp. 21–26.

132. Casambre, *The Failure of Autonomy*.

133. Joanna K. Carino, "Cordillera Indigenous Peoples' Struggles in Defense of Life, Land, Livelihood and Resources", in *Ti Daga Ket Biag, Land is Life: Selected Papers from Three Cordillera Multisectoral Land Congresses (1983, 1994 and 2001)* (Baguio City: Cordillera Peoples Alliance, 2009), p. 223.

134. Carino, "Cordillera Indigenous Peoples' Struggles", p. 224. Translation: "We planted, harvested, pounded and cooked the rice, then others ate it."

135. For a summary of the debates, see Miriam Coronel Ferrer, "The Communist Insurgency", in *A Handbook of Terrorism and Insurgency in Southeast Asia*, edited by Andrew T.H. Tan (Cheltenham, UK: Elgar, 2007), pp. 405–36. For an in-depth view, see Dominique Caouette, "Persevering Revolutionaries — Armed Struggle in the 21st Century, Exploring the Revolution of the Communist Party of the Philippines" (PhD dissertation, Cornell University, 2004).

136. Carino, "Cordillera Indigenous Peoples' Struggles", p. 223.

137. Zenaida Hamada Pawid (1991) cited in Minerva M. Chaloping, "Recognizing and Protecting Rights to Ancestral Domain: A Core Element of Cordillera Regional Autonomy", in *Building Local Administrative Capability for Regional Autonomy in the Cordillera: Some Implementing Guidelines*, edited by Lorelei Crisologo Mendoza (Baguio City: Cordillera Studies Center, University of the Philippines, Baguio; Manila: Friedrich Ebert Stiftung, December 1992), pp. 49–50. Pawid is a long-time activist active in indigenous peoples' and peace campaigns. She was a member of the Cordillera Executive Board. In 2010, President Benigno Aquino, Jr. appointed her commissioner of the National Commission for Indigenous Peoples.

138. June Prill-Brett (1988) cited in Mendoza, *Building Local*, p. 50.

139. By its own account, the CPA's role in the regional autonomy campaign was limited to pushing for its inclusion in the 1987 Constitution and rejecting the Organic Act because, it claimed, the act did not embody the CPA's true aspirations. It concluded that "the struggle for genuine regional autonomy could not be achieved, unless there is truly a democratic and sovereign national government that will recognize the collective rights of indigenous peoples for self-determination and governance". See "CPA Through the Years" at http://www.cpaphils.org/campaigns.

140. "Cordillera SCUs Push Info Drive on Autonomy", *Manila Bulletin*, 1 March 2009, http://www.mb.com.ph.

141. House Bill 5595 was filed under the 15th Congress in 2012 and refiled again as House Bill 4649 in 2014 during the 16th Congress by Representative Nicasio M. Aliping, Jr. (Lone District, Baguio City), Rep. Manuel S. Agyao (Lone District, Kalinga), Rep. Teddy Brawner Baguilat, Jr. (Lone District, Ifugao), Rep. Eleanor Bulut-Begtang (Lone District, Apayao), Rep. Maria Jocelyn V. Bernos (Lone District, Abra), Rep. Ronald M. Cosalan (Lone District, Benguet) and Rep. Maximo B. Dalog (Lone District, Mountain Province). House Bill 5343, which was filed in 2017 during the 17th Congress, did not fare any better.

142. Norman Fairclough, *Analysing Discourse: Textual Analysis for Social Research* (London: Routledge, 2003), p. 208.

4

Nation, Homeland and Ancestral Domain: Intertextuality in the Moro Discourse

This analysis of the discursive practice of the Moro resistance movement uses the notion of intertextuality to illuminate discursive change as affected by and in turn affecting the social condition and politics of the Philippines. Intertextuality refers to how a text draws on other texts, such as by combining elements from different discourses. Such concrete language use "can change the individual discourses and thereby, also, the social and cultural world. By analyzing intertextuality, one can investigate both the reproduction of discourse whereby no new elements are introduced, and discursive change through new combinations of discourse."[1]

There are several ways to discern this intertextuality as practised by text producers-interpreters. Bakhtin differentiates between horizontal and vertical intertextuality. Of interest here is vertical intertextuality, which refers to intertextual relations between a text and other texts within it as they are historically linked within various timescales and along various parameters.[2] In this regard, Fairclough introduced the related notion of interdiscursivity. In interdiscursivity, elements of orders of discourse, and not just other texts, are combined, resulting in heterogeneous texts. Heterogeneous texts may vary in the extent of their integration or accentuation of other discursive formations and practices.[3] Consequently, intertextuality can be the source of much ambivalence in the texts.[4] Such ambivalence has allowed our resistance entrepreneurs in this study to survive decades of protracted conflict and to overcome new global and domestic challenges and contexts.

Significantly, the producers of the resistance texts that will be examined here were part of a "chain of speech communication" or an "intertextual chain".[5] The "[d]iscourses and the texts which occur within them have histories, they belong to historical series."[6] They drew from existing discourses/texts and were influenced by dominant and alternative ideologies, paradigms and ideas that prevailed during their time, locally and globally. As competitors for leadership in the Moro ethnopolitical movement, they engaged each other and the state directly and indirectly in a power struggle, including the power to interpret and change social reality. They were interpreting and weaving texts as they simultaneously engaged in the acts of discourse production, membership base-building, and armed struggle. Put another way, their movement entrepreneurs used multiple positioning within their discourses to negotiate power relations.[7] This dynamic process reflects the basic notion of critical discourse analysis that discourse is constituted by the social condition, as well as constitutive of society and its politics. The relationship between discourse and socio-political change is dialectical. That is why discourse is a site of and is also at stake in the power struggle that the resistance organizations examined here have been waging against the state, and also with each other, as competitors in the resistance project.

This essay will focus on how the Moro National Liberation Front (MNLF) and the Moro Islamic Liberation Front (MILF) tapped various global discourses to build their claims to nationhood and homeland. In particular, I will examine the strands of the global discourses that emerged from the 1960s onwards that influenced the discursive practices under study. The first set includes the secular discourses on the right to self-determination and the rights of minorities and indigenous peoples, including the right to an ancestral domain — all part of the 'third-generation' rights that developed internationally and were gradually institutionalized in the United Nations. This set drew resources from academic scholarship and social movements and generated new perspectives that penetrated multilateral institutions like the United Nations and the World Bank, which in turn helped promote their currency. The second set of discourses is that of Islamic revivalism, which largely influenced the MILF's discursive practice.

The Right of/to Self-Determination[8]

The right to self-determination was already an established principle in the 1960s when Moro movement articulators began their political activism. Although decolonization processes peaked in Europe at the end of World War I, the period after World War II saw many more new states liberated from Western colonial rule in Asia and Africa.[9] The UN Charter, drawn up in 1945, provided mechanisms to protect the rights and promote the development and self-government "of territories whose peoples have not yet attained a full measure of self-government".[10] This recognition at the international level boosted aspirations for independence that achieved fruition in the succeeding decades. As Ronen noted, "The recognition of self-determination as a human right by the international community encouraged decolonization in Africa and Asia both directly and indirectly."[11]

Stronger impetus was provided by the Declaration on the Granting of Independence to Colonial Countries and Peoples, or UN General Assembly Resolution 1514 (XV), adopted on 14 December 1960, which reaffirmed the right to independence of former colonized states in Asia and Africa.[12] By the 1960s, therefore, the dominant use of the principle of the right to self-determination was in the context of the decolonization of African and Asian peoples, or the so-called Third World. In this context, it was interpreted to apply to 'whole peoples' of colonial territories and not (yet) to ethnic components.[13] Alongside decolonization struggles, however, renewed ethnonationalist stirrings became manifest. "This potentially separatist role of ethnic identity was born in the second half of the 1960s", wrote Ronen.[14]

The MNLF was conceived in the context of these distinct but converging discourses on the decolonization of Third World states and ethnonationalist sentiments brewing within newly independent states. The two discourses carried with them the related concepts of independence and separatism, respectively. Given the nature of the Moro claims, the MNLF could anchor its cause to both national and ethnic self-determination. However, between the two, decolonization was the more internationally established basis to claim the right to independence.

Mainly, the MNLF built its claim to independence on the Moros' status as a 'whole people' or a nation, a collective entity with a shared identity. "Today our people are five million. They share a common past and look up to a common future. They constitute one single nation, endowed with a common culture and a common religion. And as such they are occupying well-defined territory of their own", MNLF founding chair Nur Misuari wrote in 1973.[15] They are distinct from the Filipinos: "The Bangsa Moro (Moro Nation) people had always been a separate nation. They were not Filipinos, for they were never for a single moment subject of the Spanish Crown."[16] As a nation, the Bangsa Moro (spelled then as two words) is imbued with sovereignty. That sovereignty, in turn, is immutable. "Despite the extent of Filipino success in carrying out their pernicious colonial design against our people, homeland and Islam, still one thing remains unsullied and undiminished — that the Bangsa Moro people are one and [a] distinct nation endowed with sovereignty, which is one, indivisible, inalienable, and imprescriptible. As such it is at once immutable and valid for all time."[17] Along the lines of the right to self-determination of colonized states, the MNLF called for a separate "Bangsa Moro Republik".

Minority Rights

In addition to the right to self-determination of colonized peoples, the rights of ethnic, religious, and linguistic minorities were laid down in Article 27 of the International Covenant on Civil and Political Rights in 1966.[18] In 1992, minority rights were codified in the Declaration on the Rights of Persons Belonging to National or Ethnic, Religious and Linguistic Minorities. However, the dominant interpretation of international law reserved the right of self-determination for *peoples* and not for *minorities*. The distinction was entrenched in this Commentary of the Working Group on Minorities to the United Nations Declaration on the Rights of Persons Belonging to National, or Cultural, Religious and Ethnic Minorities, which was adopted in 2004:

> The rights of persons belonging to minorities differ from the rights of peoples to self-determination. The rights of persons belonging to minorities are individual rights, even if they in most cases can only be

enjoyed in community with others. The rights of peoples, on the other hand, are collective rights. While the right of peoples to self-determination is well established under international law, in particular by common Article 1 of the two International Covenants on Human Rights,[19] it does not apply to persons belonging to minorities. This does not exclude the possibility that persons belonging to an ethnic or national group may in some contexts legitimately make claims based on minority rights and, in another context, when acting as a group, can make claims based on the right of a people to self-determination.[20]

The commentary further clarified the issue of minorities claiming the right to self-determination:

> If the group claims a right to self-determination and challenges the territorial integrity of the State, it would have to claim to be a people, and that claim would have to be based on article 1 common to the Covenants and would therefore fall outside the Declaration on Minorities since the Declaration on Minorities neither limits nor extends the right to self-determination that peoples have under other parts of international law, and group rights to self-determination do not fall under the ambit of the Declaration.[21]

Despite the denial of sovereign rights to national minorities in the obtaining international legal regime, the MNLF still tapped the minorities discourse, perhaps because it needed to summon all related arguments to build its claim. It may also have been oblivious to the distinction made between the entitlements of *whole peoples* as against *minorities*. It is also possible that from the beginning it was open to the autonomy framework (to which states were more amenable since the territorial integrity of existing states would not be directly challenged), with independence as a last resort or reserve option.

In any case, among the many categories of minorities, the MNLF wisely hinged its ethnicity-based claim on the category of *national minorities*. *National minorities* was a new term added in the 1992 Declaration on Minorities. It was not a category in the 1966 Article 27 of the International Covenant on Civil and Political Rights. Compared to religious or ethnic minorities, the prevalent thinking is that national minorities have a firmer basis to claim 'national identity'. It also converges more neatly with the 'people' frame because the struggle for liberation is for the Bangsa Moro[22] as a national minority and not just for Muslims (a religious identity) in the Philippines.

Even then, as noted, the right to self-determination under the declaration did not apply to minorities.[23] Still, the principle is powerful in itself. Not surprisingly it found itself woven into the MNLF resistance text. As Ronen pointed out: "Neither written words nor official interpretations ... motivate people to seek self-determination; they are merely instrumental in spreading it. When a political leader speaks of the right to self-determination for his 'people,' he refers not to the legal term but to the *idea* of an 'inalienable right' to freedom from 'them.' The idea lies at the root of the struggle."[24]

After breaking with the MNLF, the MILF continued this two-pronged argumentation whereby it claimed the right to independence as a people and also explored attaining entitlements within the sovereignty of the Philippine state as a nation within a nation. Within the latter frame, the basis of the defunct Memorandum of Agreement on Ancestral Domain Aspect of the GRP-MILF Tripoli Agreement in Peace of 2001, or the MOA-AD,[25] was fortified with the added concept of the Bangsamoro as "the First Nation". It was obviously inspired by the First Nations appellation of some aboriginal groups in Canada in the 1980s.[26] Self-identification as First Nations reinforced the demands of Canada's aboriginal groups for entitlements from the Canadian government. One can surmise that MILF thinkers found it useful as a rhetorical tool because the word *First* encapsulated their assertion of a nationhood that preceded the Filipino nation.[27]

In addition, the MILF drew on an unrelated line of argument in buttressing claims to the right to self-determination. MILF leader Salamat Hashim said that "all our endeavors and efforts to defend our religion, the dignity of the Bangsamoro people, and to regain our legitimate rights to self-determination fall squarely within the category of Jihad in the Way of Allah deserving great rewards from Almighty God".[28] We will discuss the influence of the Islamic discourse on the MILF in a later section. But it is important to note that Islam did not replace the secular-rights discourse entirely. It supplemented it and made for effective multiple positioning in the MILF's discursive practice. All in all, the MILF carried over much of the MNLF's secular analysis on Bangsa Moro/Bangsamoro statehood and nationhood. The basic tenets of the original Bangsa Moro ideal as developed in the late 1960s have therefore achieved the status of a 'master frame' or 'valorized version'. In this manner, the MILF cannot be said to be completely ideologically distinct or different from the MNLF.

Indigenous Peoples and Ancestral Domain

As the United Nations continued to problematize minorities, a new momentum took shape in the 1980s around the category of indigenous peoples (IPs). The campaigns and discourse on the latter have now superseded those on the former in terms of vibrancy and visibility. In fact, the term *minorities* is sometimes considered politically incorrect.[29] The International Labour Organization (ILO) can be considered the pioneer in adopting the word *indigenous* and in addressing global concerns with special interest in these populations. In the 1930s it used the term *indigenous workers* to discuss and address some of the labour issues manifested in Latin America.[30] In 1957 it passed the first international legal document on tribal and indigenous populations, the "Convention concerning the Protection and Integration of Indigenous and Other Tribal and Semi-Tribal Populations in Independent Countries". The well-meaning document was notably couched in the dominant 'integrationist' policy approach of its time.[31]

The UN began adopting the term *indigenous* only in the 1970s. In 1972 the United Nations Economic and Social Council (ECOSOC) appointed Jose Cabo as special rapporteur mandated to conduct a study "on the problem of discrimination against indigenous populations". In 1981 the UN established the Working Group on Indigenous Populations (WGIP) with the mandate to develop standards pertaining to the rights of indigenous populations. This set off a global process in which IP activists actively participated, engaged officialdom and raised the standards of group rights.[32] In 1988 the WGIP dropped *populations* in favour of *peoples* to become the popular name we use today — Indigenous Peoples — commonly shortened in the Philippines simply to IP.

When the UN began its work, the integrationist, paternalistic approach towards tribes was still the dominant operative frame in most institutions.[33] As the UN process progressed with IP representatives in attendance, the question of the application of the right to self-determination for IPs could not be skirted. The 1989 Report of the

International Meeting of Experts on Further Study of the Rights of Peoples convened by the United Nations Educational, Scientific and Cultural Organization (UNESCO) in Paris expressed the view that minorities also partake of the right to self-determination since they belong to a people as a whole. In 1992 the recognition of the right to self-determination was included in the area of general policy of the Draft Declaration on Indigenous Peoples. The following formulation was agreed upon by the UN Working Group on Indigenous Peoples: "Indigenous peoples have the right to self-determination, in accordance with international law, by virtue of which they may freely determine their political status and institutions and freely pursue their economic, social and cultural development. An integral part of this is the right to autonomy and self-government" (para. 1). But as a precaution, perhaps more accurately as a compromise, it also cited the "Declaration on Principles of International Law concerning Friendly Relations and Cooperation among States in accordance with the Charter of the United Nations", which stressed the pre-eminence of the principle of territorial integrity of states.[34]

Compared to the MNLF, the MILF more effectively appropriated and internalized the language of IPs and the attached claim to the right to their 'ancestral domain'. MNLF leader Nur Misuari mentioned the word *homeland* seven times in his 1993 speech at the opening ceremony of formal negotiations with the Fidel Ramos administration. Misuari did not refer to ancestral land/domain at all. The whole speech remained framed in the 1960s–70s discourse. Indeed, the MNLF's negotiating stance was to seek the full implementation of the 1976 Tripoli Agreement. The 1996 Final Peace Agreement (FPA) referred to "the area of autonomy", as had the 1976 Tripoli Agreement. The terms *ancestral land* and *indigenous peoples* were not used, nor even *homeland* for that matter. The FPA vested preferential rights over the exploration, development and utilization of natural resources for "the residents in the area of autonomy", which could be commonly understood to include not only the Moros but also the Christian settlers and the non-Moro indigenous peoples (Lumad) residing in the "area of autonomy".

Having matured at a time when the discourse of indigenous peoples and ancestral domain was increasingly being adopted by both social movements and officialdom, domestically and globally, the MILF utilized the two concepts advantageously in negotiations.

On 25 February 1997, during the term of President Fidel Ramos, the MILF Technical Committee on Agenda Setting submitted a "Talking Point" document to the Philippine government stating that the Bangsamoro problem "involves a wide variety of social, cultural, economic and political issues and concerns".[35] Ancestral domain topped the non-exhaustive list of nine items that pertain to the 'Bangsamoro problem', the solution to which "will form part of the agenda in the forthcoming formal talks … with the end in view of establishing a system of life and governance suitable and acceptable to the Bangsamoro people".[36] Under President Gloria Macapagal Arroyo, who resumed the talks after the preceding president Joseph Ejército Estrada engaged the MILF in major warfare, the agenda was categorized into three aspects; namely, security, rehabilitation and ancestral domain. The relevant part reads: "On the aspect of ancestral domain, the Parties, in order to address the humanitarian and economic needs of the Bangsamoro people and preserve their social and cultural heritage and inherent rights over their ancestral domain, agree that the same be discussed further by the Parties in their next meeting."[37]

The seven years of hard talks that followed resulted in the controversial 2008 Memorandum of Agreement on Ancestral Domain (MOA-AD). Among the documents on which the MOA-AD founded its acknowledgement of the MILF's ancestral domain/lands claims were the Indigenous Peoples' Rights Act, the UN Declaration on the Rights of Indigenous Peoples, the older Universal Declaration of Human Rights, the principles of International Humanitarian Law, and international human rights instruments. All these indicate how the MILF successfully utilized legitimized, officialized global discourses that enriched its discursive practice and buttressed its demands. In turn, the Philippine government, a signatory to these conventions, acknowledged its international commitments.

How then did the MOA-AD distinguish and reconcile the concept of ancestral domain with the older concept of homeland and the equally contested territory of the envisioned Bangsamoro Juridical Entity (BJE)?[38] Or did it? Item No. 3 under the section on "Concepts and Principles" of the MOA-AD stated that ancestral domain "does not form part of the public domain but encompasses ancestral, communal and customary lands, maritime, fluvial and alluvial domains as well as natural resources therein".[39] The Bangsamoro ancestral domain and ancestral lands are "those held under claim of ownership, occupied or possessed, by themselves or through the ancestors of the Bangsamoro people, communally or individually since time immemorial continuously to the present, except when prevented by war, civil disturbance, force majeure or other forms of possible usurpation or displacement".[40] These provisions explicitly vest ownership rights to the claimants. At the same time, the BJE was to have political and administrative authority over these lands.[41]

Similarly, Item No. 2 on the Bangsamoro homeland states that "Ownership of the homeland is vested exclusively in them [the Bangsamoro people] by virtue of their prior rights of occupation that had inhered in them as sizeable bodies of people, delimited by their ancestors since time immemorial, and being the first politically organized dominant occupants".[42] Going by this provision, homeland and ancestral domain are virtually the same, and ownership of the two are vested in the Bangsamoro people. Indeed, as former government negotiator and historian Rudy Rodil wrote: "By the current Bangsamoro understanding of ancestral domain it means the combination of tribal ethnolinguistic homeland and the political domains of the sultanates and *pat a pongampong ko ranaw*."[43]

Meanwhile, in the section on "Territory", the same features were reconfigured and collapsed into the "Bangsamoro homeland and historic territory", referring not only to the landmass but also to "the maritime, terrestrial, fluvial and alluvial domains, and the aerial domain, the atmospheric space about it, embracing the Mindanao-Sulu-Palawan geographic regions".[44] However, the actual territorial scope is delimited by the categories and schedules provided. The section on "Territory" was replete with detail as to coverage based on existing local government units. These confusing overlaps in the definitions and scopes of the three distinct political concepts (homeland, ancestral domain, and juridical territorial units/local government units) and between ownership and jurisdiction created ambiguities and fears that complicated political negotiations and clouded the public, as well as the MILF's own, discourse.[45]

Expectedly, the appropriation of the ancestral domain language put the MILF in direct conflict with other IPs who are likewise ancestral domain claimants *within* the territorial/homeland claims of the Bangsamoro. The 2001 Agreement in Tripoli and the MOA-AD was not oblivious to this problem. One of the paragraphs in its preamble recognized that the peace negotiation "is for the advancement of the general interest of the Bangsamoro people *and other indigenous people*" (italics mine).[46] The MOA-AD included, albeit very briefly, a provision respecting "vested property rights"[47] — which may signify an acknowledgement that other IPs are vested with the same rights to 'native title' as the Moro IPs.

In his 2007 book, Jubair also addressed this concern of competing land claims between the Moros and IPs, saying that "the 'traditional boundaries' between Moros and IPs set by their ancestors will be more or less followed, subject to some new but just arrangements reflective of the present ground situation".[48] According to Jubair, the Moros will do justice to the IPs because they understand the mental psyche, cultures and traditions, the historical experiences and expectations of the IPs, and vice-versa, as proven by their generally good and symbiotic relationship over time. The MILF also pledged to respect the rights of legitimate settlers as well.[49]

These assurances did not assuage the fears of Moro takeover and tyranny among the non-Moro IPs, several of whom expressed concern in petitions and various fora.[50] The perceived privileging of Bangsamoro ancestral domain claims over those who did not self-identity as Moros was one of the major reasons for the vocal opposition to a peace deal with the MILF. Negative public reaction on this and other concerns such as a lack of transparency and consultation eventually led the Gloria Arroyo administration to cancel the signing of the MOA-AD, even before the Supreme Court ruled against its constitutionality on some other, but related, grounds. This shows that while the new discourse on ancestral domain and IPs buttressed Moro homeland claims, they were likewise contested by other stakeholders who were equal bearers of the discourse and its promised welfare and benefits. At the same time, titled land owners among the settlers (migrants or descendants of migrants from other regions) were equally threatened, although they cannot claim the same prior or historically vested rights as the other IPs in Mindanao.

Consequently, the ancestral domain agenda as stipulated in the 2001 Tripoli Agreement was leapfrogged when talks resumed in 2010 under President Simeon Benigno Aquino III. The Framework Agreement on the Bangsamoro (FAB) that was signed on 15 October 2012 instead laid down the general principle of creating a "new political entity"

and provided a partial list of the proposed allocation of powers. The
FAB, which now forms part of the 2014 Comprehensive Agreement
on the Bangsamoro (CAB), avoided the contested overlaps among
ancestral domain, territory and homeland. There was no reference
to ownership of homeland and no definition of ancestral domain,
especially one that vests possession, occupation and ownership on the
Bangsamoro or their ancestors. Rather, political-administrative units like
provinces, cities, municipalities, barangays, and the yet unlegislated
but constitutionally introduced notion of *geographic areas* were used to
refer to potential constituent units of the new political entity.[51] Instead
of *homeland* the agreement stuck to the more neutral term of *territory*
to refer to "the land mass as well as the maritime, terrestrial, fluvial
and alluvial domains, and the aerial domains and the atmospheric
space above it".[52] These two provisions were followed, respectively,
by the qualifications that "[t]he authority to regulate on its own
responsibility the affairs of constituent units is guaranteed within the
limit of the Bangsamoro Basic Law",[53] and that "[g]overnance shall be
as agreed upon by the parties in this agreement and in the sections
on wealth and power sharing."[54]

The Annex on Power Sharing signed on 8 December 2012 did list
jurisdiction over ancestral domain and natural resources among the
"exclusive powers" that the autonomous government shall exercise within
the Bangsamoro.[55] This was consistent with what the 1987 Constitution
gave as powers to autonomous regions. The government negotiating
panel had insisted on *ancestral domains* (plural, instead of singular) to
imply several ancestral domains and not a singular, collective Bangsamoro
ancestral domain, and to more clearly distinguish ancestral lands/domain
(ownership) rights from the territorial jurisdiction or governance of the
autonomous government. But because Article X of the 1987 Philippine
Constitution listed *ancestral domain* (singular) among the powers vested
in the autonomous regions, the MILF did not concede to use the plural.
In any case, the MOA-AD provision that "vested property rights shall
be respected" was carried on to the FAB/CAB with the intention to
lock in the proprietary rights of owners of lands that were legally
acquired and titled under the national land laws, as well as the same
ancestral domain rights of other, non-Moro IPs as provided for in the
constitution and national law, particularly the Indigenous Peoples'
Rights Act. In addition the FAB provided that "[t]he customary rights

and traditions of indigenous peoples shall be taken into consideration in the formation of the Bangsamoro justice system."[56] Eventually, as a result of the strong lobby of IP groups and their NGO supporters, more guarantees were put in place in the 2014 draft Bangsamoro Basic Law and the different House and Senate versions that followed, many of which were incorporated in the Bangsamoro Organic Law (BOL) that was finally passed by Congress in August 2018.

The MILF's practice of intertextuality, as can be seen from this recounting, advanced or elevated their cause by weaving into it the internationally acknowledged rights of IPs to their ancestral domains. However, the perceived exclusiveness of their Bangsamoro ancestral domain claim put them at loggerheads with other IP claimants who were equally entitled to the right. As 'minorities among minorities' in the prospective Bangsamoro autonomous region, the latter earned the sympathy of interlocutors, resulting in legislation that put in place more guarantees to protect the non-Moro indigenous populations.

International Humanitarian Law

Compared to the MNLF, the MILF also more assiduously incorporated human rights and international humanitarian law (IHL) into its discourse from the 1990s onwards. The MNLF intellectuals of the 1960s, as traced earlier, did adopt the language of human rights. The 1974 Manifesto of the MNLF committed to adhere to the UN Charter and the Universal Declaration of Human Rights. However, neither human rights nor IHL were put on the agenda in its negotiations with the government in the 1970s and the 1990s. In contrast, the MILF's Technical Working Group papers issued in the early 2000s had specific sections on violations of human rights and IHL, including the issue of reparation and recourse to world courts — a campaign that slowly peaked in the early 2000s with the forging of the Rome Statute of the International Criminal Court as a significant landmark. The first two substantial agreements between the government and the MILF that followed the framework-setting Tripoli Agreement of 2001 specifically applied to human rights and IHL. In this vein the non-Marxist MILF could be said to have hewed closer to the CPP-led discourse on human rights and IHL violations than did the MNLF.[57]

Santos noted that the charges of genocide against the Philippine state in the 1970s, which earned the indignation of Muslim-majority states and earned the MNLF an observer status in the Organization of the Islamic Conference (OIC), "appears to be used more in a generic rather than an international legal sense".[58] The chosen reference in what appears to be the only MNLF tract on rules of war was Islamic teachings, not the secular discourse of IHL. Misuari's injunction to his fighters cautioned them "not to go beyond the limit prescribed for Mujahideen in the Holy Qu'ran, the Hadith or the sacred traditions. Do not hit innocent civilians, especially children, women, old people, the infirm, etc. Do not destroy the properties of the civilians...".[59]

The MILF's avowed adherence to IHL was supported by its exposure to global campaigns. An early influence came from other non-state groups like the Philippine Campaign to Ban Landmines (PCBL), which pioneered in securing MILF compliance to the ban on landmines and in exposing its members to the international arena in which humanitarian law was discussed.[60] The MILF also committed to demobilize children in its armed forces and signed up to an action plan with UNICEF to this end in 2009, several years before the CPP-National Democratic Front did. As of 2011, UNICEF reported that some six hundred children in situations of armed conflict in MILF-influenced areas have been provided with education and health services that would "prevent recruitment".[61] At the same time the UN Secretary General Special Representative on Children and Armed Conflict called on the MILF to enforce compliance with the plan and to come up with accountability measures and complaints procedures.[62]

A major development was the post-9/11 constriction on Islamic movements. Wary of being listed as a terrorist organization, the MILF took pains in various statements and shows of goodwill to pledge respect for IHL.[63] The one slogan posted during these years on its website, www.luwaran.com, was "No to Terrorism!" At the height of US president George W. Bush's 'global war on terrorism' that unduly vilified all Islamic movements and increased US military presence in the southern parts of the Philippines affected by the Abu Sayyaf Group (ASG) and Jemaah Islamiyah (JI), Hashim Salamat sent a letter to the US president through the US Ambassador in Manila, who was quoted as saying during a forum with the foreign correspondents that the United States wanted to know how the Bangsamoro problem would be solved. In this 20 January 2001 letter, Hashim recounted diplomatically the events under American colonial rule that led to the Bangsamoro's incorporation into the Philippines. "In view of the current global developments and regional security concerns in Southeast Asia, it is our desire to accelerate the just and peaceful negotiated political settlement of the Mindanao conflict, particularly the present colonial situation in which the Bangsamoro find themselves", Hashim wrote, inviting in turn the United States to participate in the process. In response the US government issued a statement offering US diplomatic and financial support to a renewed peace process "provided that the MILF renounce terror". This prompted the MILF to respond through another letter dated 20 May 2003 stating that "The MILF as a liberation organization has repeatedly renounced terrorism publicly as a means of attaining its political ends."[64]

Before these global secular norms were manifested in its discourse, MILF founder Hashim Salamat not surprisingly referenced these normative declarations in Islamic teachings. However, as noted by Santos, "under the second and current Chairman Al-Haj Murad Ebrahim, who comes from a secular and professional elite background, there is now more of what may be described as a fusion in orientation with international law".[65] A prime example is the MILF's printed 2005 Code of Conduct for its armed wing, the BIAF (Bangsamoro Islamic Armed Forces), which referenced an Islamic source (e.g., Al-Hadith, Al Insan) for each and every entry relating to troop behaviour, civilians, surrendered combatants, prisoners of war, medical or distinctive signs. All of the entries were elements of the secular regime of IHL. Reinforced with Islamic cross-citations, the interdiscursivity in the MILF's practice was shown in full play.

In the next section, I shall make a fuller examination of the Islamic content in the MILF's discursive practice.

Islamic Discourse

Elements of an Islamic order of discourse were already present in the 1960s rhetoric of Moro nationalists. Both the Mindanao Independence Movement (MIM) and the MNLF tapped Islamic forms of salutation and the notion of jihad in their statements to enhance their demands for independence. Islam and the fact of being Muslim were major signifiers of the asserted identity that differentiated them from the Filipino majority. Even then, many analysts consider that the influence of global Islam and Islamic countries in giving birth to the resistance was nil. Macapado Muslim, for example, argued that "the struggle was not caused by 'international Islam' or some radical Muslim countries as some analysts have opined. Certainly, Malaysia or Libya did not cause the war.... [T]he provoked Moro resistance efforts in the last quarter of 1972 and the early part of 1973 were largely localized and uncoordinated...".[66]

Indeed, in the 1960s there was no Islamic revivalist movement making inroads among the populace. According to a 1954 Congressional Committee Report, 80 per cent of Muslims were "ignorant" of their religion and only 10 per cent could read the Qu'ran.[67] At best there was only the beginnings of a small-scale proselytization process, attributed to some fifty imams sent by Egypt to teach in Mindanao and the building of more mosques and *madrasahs* by local Muslim groups receiving financial assistance from foreign countries. Although they "aroused religious fervor and aligned local religious practices along normative Islamic lines", they were supposedly a small and dispersed group.[68] The more than two hundred Filipinos offered scholarships in Al Azhar University in Cairo were just returning in trickles. McKenna wrote of this 1950s situation: "What is evidenced ... is not an expansion of Islamic observance among Philippine Muslims as a whole, but rather an amplification among political elites of an ethnic identity as Muslim Filipinos" or "a strengthening of ethnoreligious identity on the part of prominent Muslims".[69]

The MNLF-led national liberation movement, with its secular foundation and young, mostly secularly educated Moro leaders, overtook whatever Islamic movement potential there was in the 1950s. Proof of this is the privileging of Moro as key identity signifier over the religious signifier, Muslim. While the MILF insiders and sympathizers who (in the late 1980s and 1990s) reconstructed the evolution of Salamat Hashim as a revolutionary leader highlighted the influence of Middle East Islamic revivalism in the 1950s, it was the 1980s global context of Islamic resurgence that firmed up and elevated the Islamic discourse to a higher status in the MILF. The pre-eminence given to Islam during this period, and the drive to promote and enforce Islamic ways among guerrillas and in society, are best reflected in Hashim's tract written in 1985, the *Bangsamoro Mujahid*.

The 1980s–90s global Islamic revitalization — also referred to as resurgence, awakening, reassertion, rebirth, renewal, fundamentalism, militancy, reformism, activism, and millenarianism[70] — is said to have been supported by several developments. These events include the successful Islamic revolution that overthrew the Shah of Iran in 1979 and provided a new set of ideals for Muslims; the Soviet invasion of Muslim Afghanistan, where several Moro and other Southeast Asian guerrillas received exposure and military training; the intensification of the Arab-Israeli conflict; and the exercise of political and economic leverage in international politics by Gulf states flush with oil power.[71] Within Muslim societies in the Arab world, the dominant global order and their own modernization processes facilitated the emergence of new social classes and the marginalization of traditional groups and structures such as those founded in Islam (schools, courts); the spread of Westernization and secularization among the elites consequently widened the gap between elites and masses and diminished the former's political and intellectual legitimacy.[72] Moreover, the collapse of the Soviet Union in 1989 fed the belief that Islam had become the only counter-ideology with a global potential.[73]

The aim of revivalist movements in the second half of the twentieth century supposedly remained the establishment of a transnational Islamic caliphate, although, in fact, the rise of local movements reflected local needs and ideas.[74] Indeed, contemporary Islamic groups are diverse in formation and methods.[75] They all see a need for change in Muslim society, but they disagree on what these changes should be and how and how fast they can be achieved. In all, Islamic revivalism is basically concerned about internal regeneration, given the perceived weakness and subjugation of the Muslim world.[76] "Common to all reform movements has been the call to return to pristine Islam, the Islam of the Prophet's society and the normative period of his rightly guided succession", wrote Ayoub.[77]

In Southeast Asia the phenomenon is manifested in the return of an increasing number of followers of the faith to the mosques and *surat* for prayers and religious classes; the donning of dress and accessories such as the *songkok*, *jiihab*, *telekong-mini* and *purdah* that identify the wearer as Muslim; the use of the Islamic way of greeting in lieu of the modern "hello"; the flourishing of missionary activities (the *'da'wah* phenomenon' — although these groups are neither monolithic

nor unilinear), and the many forums and seminars on Islam.[78] In the
Philippines the 1980s Islamic renewal was said to have been led by a
generation of local *ustadz* who were relatively free from the influence
of the traditional elite (*datu*) or from military harassment and — unlike
the reform-minded, Middle East–educated clerics who were immediately
engulfed in the armed conflict upon their return to the country in the
1960s — enjoyed an environment relatively free of fighting.[79]

While remaining an 'anti-colonial' or national liberation movement,
the MILF located itself in this movement that was establishing a
foothold in the Islamic world, including Muslim Mindanao. Julkipli
Wadi, writing on this reconfiguration or accommodation, incorporation
or crystallization of the phenomenon, said: "As the [Islamic] dissent
spread beyond the Middle East and Asia, this inevitably trickle[d]
down through 'linkage politics' to other countries and minorities like
the Moros of the Philippines and shaped the domestic confluence of
the Moro rebellion. Thus the supposedly local characteristic of the
Moro rebellion was reconfigured and inevitably crystallized [into a]
new ideological dimension, new vision, new strategy and method."[80]

The MILF's discourse as reflected in Hashim's *Bangsamoro
Mujahidin* and Salah Jubair's *A Nation under Endless Tyranny* exhibits
the characteristics of Islamic revivalism in Southeast Asia. As outlined
by Mutalib, these are: (a) greater eagerness and confidence in viewing
Islam or practising the faith as a total, all-encompassing way of life; (b)
the tendency to view Muslims in different parts of the world within
the framework of a global Muslim community or *ummah*; (c) vigour
or assertiveness in espousing Islamic fundamentalist values, ideals,
and solutions in their home countries; and (d) the establishment of
movement-type bodies and organizations aimed at making Muslims more
organized in addressing their problems and plight.[81] This reconfiguring
allows the MILF to view itself, and to be viewed by others, like Wadi,
"as part of [the] challenge against the current world order".[82]

Nonetheless, for both the MNLF and the MILF, Islam is a basic
ingredient of their ideology and practice. That it served a pragmatic
purpose for both Moro fronts can be gleaned from this description by
Che Man of Moro recruitment efforts: "Recruitment into fighting units
often involved the manipulation of religious and nationalist sentiments.
Potential recruits were reminded of their religious duty to participate in
the jihad.... They were also normally advised of their *maratabat* [honour]

by a warning that 'a man who has lost his *bangsa* [identification with ancestors] has no *maratabat'*...".[83]

Of his 1985 visit to the MILF's Camp Busrah in Lanao, Che Man observed: "They believe that the strength of the Moro struggle is basically proportional to the degree of Islamic consciousness of the Moro people."[84] The MNLF also tapped into this Islamic discourse for mobilization. Che Man wrote: "All Moro liberation forces, except the MORO,[85] are founded on a similar basis of ideology — Islam. For there is no social system outside of Islam for which Muslims are allowed to die.... [It] is the most powerful symbolic means of mobilizing support and of legitimizing actions for revolutionary action."[86] Similarly, Muslim noted that "religion is involved as one of the motivations to fight"; in Islam, fighting an oppressor is a duty.[87]

Some observers have argued that the highlighting of Islam was mainly intended to fortify the distinction between the MNLF and the MILF.[88] Indeed, Hashim himself underplayed the ideological difference in a series of interviews in February 1999. He claimed that the split with the MNLF was only a "tactical move ...[in] that when the MNLF was negotiating with the Philippine government, we [were] not very sure of the negotiations and prefer[ed] to split and let the other front negotiate with the Philippine government to find out what really will happen".[89] He said the same in an interview with news anchor Noli de Castro a few days earlier, but qualified that "it was not intentionally done but it so happened like that".[90] He repeated the same to Jiji Press: "We did not split with them because we quarrelled, not because we don't like each other, we split with them for tactical purposes. We let them try the offer of government and we found out that this tactic is very useful. It was proven now that if all of us accepted the offer of government, then all of us were trapped."[91] Furthermore, in a March 1999 interview after a historic meeting with Misuari, he said, "As far as our belief is concerned, we do not have any difference. But we have difference in the means of achieving our objective.... I think we will continue to go to the same direction in different ways."[92] This apparent inconsistency, even denial of an ideological reason for the breakup, reflects the hybridity in the MILF's discourse.

On the other hand, it is also claimed that the ideological difference was there from the beginning, even before the formation of the MILF in 1962, when Hashim and his Moro cohorts formed a Muslim student organization in Cairo. Jubair, in reconstructing a Moro narrative from an MILF member's perspective, points to Hashim's 1973 letter to the OIC explaining why they were breaking up with Misuari, notably the part that reads: "The MNLF was being manipulated away from Islamic basis, methodologies and objectives and fast revolving towards Marxist-Maoist orientations."[93]

At the leadership level, we can see that this Islamic slant has emerged as the key ideological line dividing the MNLF's Misuari and the MILF's Salamat. Given the personal inclination on his part, Hashim more than Misuari eagerly embraced and more successfully appropriated Islamic revivalism in the 1980s. Hashim's background as a scholar of Islam and one who was more directly exposed to political activism among Islamic youth in the Middle East made him different from most of the MNLF and MILF founders. Born in 1942, he lived and studied in Saudi Arabia for a year and stayed for more than ten years as a student in Cairo. He returned to the Philippines in 1970 and left again in 1973 on a mission for the MNLF, returning only in 1987. He was in Pakistan for ten years and there learned to speak Urdu. He was said to be more fluent in Arabic than English.[94] Two political thinkers who allegedly greatly influenced him were Syed Qutb of the Al-Ikhwan al-Muslimun and Syed Abul A'la Mawdudi of Jamaati Islami; and he supposedly read Syed Qutb's book *Milestone* several times, and, like the Al-Ikhwan al-Muslimun, adopted the twin methods of jihad and *da'wah* to pursue the goal of establishing an Islamic government.[95] Writing in the 1980s–90s, Jubair, having loyally followed the ways of Hashim, adhered to the Islamic line. Although secularly educated, there was a decidedly strong Islamic flavour to Jubair's writings at this time.[96]

The pragmatic and ideological functionality of Islamic revivalism as incorporated in the discourse that was promoted and developed by the intellectuals[97] of the movement supported the growth of the MILF in the 1980s to the 1990s, making it a more formidable revolutionary organization than the other two Moro resistance entrepreneurs — the MNLF and the CPP-led MORO. In mid-1980, Hashim claimed that, "[a]ll factors being considered, it can be safely said that to date the single and unequalled group of fighters advocating [the] Islamic line and performing Jihad in Southern Philippines is the MILF."[98] It should be noted that he made this claim at a time when the so-called Abu Sayyaf

Group (ASG), under its founder Abdulrajak Abubakar Janjalani, was the emergent Islamic fundamentalist group that posed a more radical alternative to the MNLF and the MILF. However, this grouping remained relatively small (that is, in the hundreds) and eventually deteriorated and metastasized into banditry when its founder was killed, save for some segments led by Islamic ideologues like Isnaji Hapilon on Basilan island. Thus, Hashim's claim in the mid-1980s remained basically true in the first two decades of the twenty-first century. New groups like the Bangsamoro Islamic Freedom Fighters sprang up around 2010[99] and the so-called 'Maute Group' or the Daulat Ul Islamiyah[100] emerged around 2015. The Abu Sayyaf faction led by Isnaji Hapilon,[101] the Maute Group and smaller violent extremist groupings coalesced in the siege of Marawi City in 2017. Routed after several months of heavy bombardment but not fully extinguished, they have yet to reach the organizational size of the MILF.

Religion and Moro Nationhood

If religion was not only the glue but also the distinguishing feature of Moro nationhood, does that mean that the Bangsamoro is a nation only of and for Muslims? While movement entrepreneurs tended towards this track, they remained ambivalent and flexible in their boundary-setting. Overall, their discourse is marked by a recognized need for a more inclusive framing that would include non-Muslims in the claimed homeland in order for the project to gain wider acceptability.

Reading through MNLF founder Nur Misuari's speeches and writings of the 1970s, one gleans this ambivalence, or perhaps acknowledgement of the fact of the existence of non-Moro groups indigenous to the territory and the presence of Christian settlers from Luzon and the Visayas.

By 1975 the percentage share of Islamized groups in the total population had been significantly reduced (see Table 4.1). There was a similar and more serious decline in the Lumad's share of the population, down to 6.86 per cent of Mindanao's population. In contrast, the population share of settlers grew considerably. It is apparent that Misuari, writing in the mid-1970s, had already realized that an exclusivist claim to the territory in favour of the Islamized groups would be difficult to uphold. But instead of abandoning altogether an irredentist claim to the

TABLE 4.1
Percentage of Islamized and Lumad Population in Mindanao, Sulu and Palawan, 1903–75

Census Year	Total Population	Islamized Population	Percentage of Total	Lumad Population	Percentage of Total	Islamized & Lumad	Percentage of Total
1903	706,539	277,547	39.29	156,255	22.11	433,802	61.31
1918	1,175,212	378,152	32.17	115,456	9.9	494,608	42.08
1939	2,338,094	751,172	32.12	341,888	14.62	1,093,060	46.75
1948	3,049,593	905,812	29.70	250,819	8.22	1,156,631	37.92
1960	5,546,833	1,307,339	23.56	411,431	7.21	1,718,770	30.98
1970	6,831,120	1,629,730	23.85	437,991	6.41	2,067,721	30.26
1975	8,916,959	1,798,911	20.17	612,227	6.86	2,4411,138	27.03

Source: B.R. Rodil, *The Minoritization of the Indigenous Communities of Mindanao and the Sulu Archipelago,* revised 2004 Philippine edition (Davao City: Alternate Forum for Research in Mindanao, 2004), p. 122, based on census data.

homeland, he instead broadened and made the notion of the Bangsa Moro more inclusive. For example, in this excerpt, Misuari explicitly qualified that the Bangsa Moro people include not only the Muslims:

> The Bangsa Moro people, though majority of them are Muslims, yet there are some, particularly among the indigenous inhabitants who belong to other religions, including animistic religion, Christianity, etc. Some of them are paganistic. Nevertheless, they are part of us, part of the Bangsa Moro. In fact, many of our Muslim people trace their origin to them. Besides, their cultural and social practices are very akin to those of the Muslims. As such, they are an integral part of the Bangsa Moro people and are generally sympathetic to the Bangsa Moro Revolution. As a matter of act, not a few of them are actually heroically fighting side-by-side with the Muslim freedom fighters.[102]

Similarly, he nuanced his reference to the Bangsa Moro with qualifying clauses like "the Bangsa Moro people, particularly the Muslims" or "The Bangsa Moro people, the Muslims particularly".[103] However, he also sometimes made Islamic precepts encompass the supposedly diverse populace, as in this statement: "The Bangsa Moro people, the Muslims in particular, understand only Hao'ullah and the concept of amanah in Islam which hold the view that property holding in Islam is fiduciary in character."[104] In this truth-claim, a supposed attribute of Muslims was universalized.

The fact of being Muslim as the more important distinguishing marker of Moro identity is similarly reiterated by Jubair, despite stating that the people who are now called Moros supposedly already possessed the essence of a nation before the coming of Islam to the islands. In this regard, Jubair views their conversion to Islam as an important factor in advancing nation-formation. Islamic laws and leaders helped create a new society, governance framework and trading networks.

Islam is also credited for providing coherence to Moro resistance to Western colonialism. It was Islam that "gave them direction, spirit and cohesiveness, hence securing for them their homeland.... It was Islam which taught them that war with Spain was a sacred obligation, with an assured place in heaven as a reward."[105] All Moros shared, "though in varying roles, in the defense of the faith, people and homeland".[106]

Although religion was the glue that fortified resistance to Spanish rule, Jubair lamented how subsequent developments have weakened the faith. The main threat came from the secularist and materialist world view and lifestyle that the United States imposed through its educational policies.[107] He harshly criticized the betrayal of the Moros who had drifted towards this secularist and materialist world view. "These elements, fawning on their masters, went to the length of despising their own people and institutions, and in many ways, religious zeal was snuffed out for worldly pleasures and other mundane matters."[108] Fast forward to the Moro resistance, where such secularized Moros became dominant among the Moro student-activists in the 1960s. To them, this rebuke: "All were Moros, but although they were all Muslims by upbringing, they were enrolled in secular universities and colleges and not all followed a purely Islamic way of thinking. Others adopted a nationalist line. This confusion remained even after the battle scene shifted from the streets to the frontlines in Mindanao and Sulu."[109]

In effect, for Jubair the true Moro is one who has remained a true Muslim. In defence of the Moro against the saying "The only good Moro is a dead Moro" — coined during the American colonial period — he wrote: "The Moro could be as sincere and trustworthy as any one, or perhaps more, because he believes in God, prays five times a day, fasts for one whole month every year, gives the poor's due diligently, and believes in the Day of Judgment when God rewards the good and punishes the evil."[110] All the attributes he ascribed in this quotation to the Moro are those of devout Muslims.

Surveying the Moro activists of the 1960s–70s, he came up with three types of Moros. The first were those who "assumed a risk-less but dishonorable stance of acquiescence and [left] everything to 'fate.'… [They] were the slaves of the insatiable self and remained in the cities; many married Christians and raised their families outside the moral realm of Islam." They left the struggle in its early stages. The second type were those who adopted a collaborationist line and whose only weapon was lip service; they shone in the heyday of student activism, especially in Manila, but were nowhere to be found when the going got rough. The third type were the "best of creations", who had the relative capability to make or unmake their own destiny. They assumed supporting roles in the parliament of the streets, but later became leaders of the revolution.[111]

Jubair's truism that the true Moro is a true Muslim sees him collapsing Moro and Muslim into a single discourse. In this paragraph the subject glided from the Moros to the Muslims: "The Moros believed that 'integration,' in essence, would lead inevitably to the abandonment of their beliefs, mores and racial or cultural traits, in favor of the system professed by the state that is suffused with Christian ideology. The essential result would be a situation where one could not distinguish Muslims from the Christians, and vice-versa. For a real Muslim, this was absolutely unacceptable. It would be incompatible with Islam."[112]

In another section of the book he begins with Muslims as the reference point and ends up with the Moros: "If the Muslims are looking back to the past, it is because the past represents the best of their lives.... The Christians' best world view is now, in the present and in the future, because, as successors of the colonizers, they now run the whole show. They control everything, have the power, access to state funds and resources, and greater opportunities; and above all, they decide and predetermine the destiny of the Moros."[113]

On the relationship between Islam and the nation, he argued there should be no conflict in loyalty between the two because Islam should always be given supremacy and it should prevail as the basis of right and wrong. Nationalism is a value in so far as it "bonds together a community of Muslims who live by the teaching of Islam"; it is not an end in itself among the Moros: "If the Moros fought for anything related to their perceived racial distinctness, it was no doubt a peripheral issue; the main point always was religion.... A Moro has so developed in himself that defense mechanism for Islam that he freely, consciously or unconsciously, instinctively rushes forward whenever dared."[114]

This Islamic identity over other social and political concerns, for Jubair, is the deeper source of their aspirations for separate nationhood. In the epilogue of the 1999 edition of his book, he wrote: "The issue before us now is deeper than, say, a matter of land, autonomy or development. To the Moros, the issue is no less than how they [will] be able to please their Lord and prepare for the everlasting Day Hereafter, an eternal life of 'all-good-and-no-bad' [Paradise] for the righteous and 'all-bad-and-no-good' [Hell] for the unbelievers."[115]

And consistent with Islamic beliefs, the way of life and the system of government should follow from Islamic teachings: "In brief, the Moros want to live — and die — in accordance with Islam. To them and every believing Muslim, Muslim in not only a religion, a way of life, but a system of government. It is a be-it-all [sic] system or ideology that guides every Muslim's needs and deed."[116]

However, the MILF also had to contend with the claims of non-Moro indigenous groups. As such, one approach taken by the MILF was to embrace them in the 'Bangsamoro' identity. In an interview in 1986, Hashim Salamat said that "Moro was the only term that could embrace all the different Moro tribes in the area."[117] But not all of these tribes were Muslims. The Tiruray/Teduray and Manobos, he said, are also called Moros. But whether the Teduray and Manobos agree to this ascription by an outsider is contestable.

In any case, even if the Moro are decidedly Muslim (and therefore the true Moro is the true Muslim) and the non-Muslim Lumad do not consider themselves Moros, the historical and future Bangsamoro (Moro Nation) itself shall not be constituted solely by Moros/Muslims. Thus, it is in the concept of the 'Bangsamoro' rather than in 'Moro' that a more inclusive coverage of the people has been made possible.

Fast forward to the peace negotiations in the first decades of the twenty-first century. In the MILF's Technical Working Group Position Papers, the Bangsamoro people (not the Moro people) were defined, albeit tautologically, as the "native inhabitants composed of Islamized ethnic groups, highlanders, Lumads, and other non-Muslims with Bangsamoro ancestry and those who have been born, raised and educated in the Bangsamoro homeland, signifying and declaring legally their being Bangsamoro members."[118]

The MILF argued that the non-Moro IPs, together with the Moros, belong to the 'First Nation' and as such have absolute birthright to Mindanao. Jubair wrote: "As the original inhabitants [in parts of Mindanao], necessarily all their territorial areas, traditional and ancestral domains constitute their natural wealth and patrimony which represent their pride."[119]

In buttressing this oneness with the IP, the contrast is made between the Moro-IP groups and Christians. Jubair wrote: "The Christian settlers from Luzon and the Visayas are another story. They started to arrive only in 1912 at the instance of the American colonial powers, but more than one half of their entire population came only in the 1960s during the regime of President Ferdinand Marcos." The IPs were recognized as "relatively weaker compared to their Islamized counterparts. However, both of them are victims of the neo-colonial presence or wars in Mindanao.... They are subsumed by the prevailing political system and marginalized to this day and on the brink of extinction."[120] In dialogues with the IPs where the IPs expressed concern over being incorporated in a Bangsamoro entity, the MILF sought unity by asking, "Now who owns the most lands in these districts, Moros or settlers?" — implying that the settlers have usurped most of the lands in Mindanao. Historical facts are also summoned: the original Moro Province created in 1903 and covering the undivided territories of Zambaonga, Lanao, Cotabato, Davao and Sulu was made up of 90 per cent Moros and IPs.[121]

On the whole the identity entrepreneurs of the MNLF and the MILF veered towards "the Moro is Muslim" precept. This is fairly consistent with the valorized history of resistance to colonial rule and religious conversion of their Islamicized ancestors. Their Muslim identity, moreover, bound them to the global Islamic community, from whom they secured moral and logistical support for their struggle, especially in the 1970s. As such, the OIC-mediated negotiations between the Marcos regime and the MNLF during this period produced the 1976 Tripoli Agreement, where "the Muslims in the Southern Philippines" was the appellation for the concerned population.[122] Moros as IPs who follow Islam were further entrenched in popularized academic tracts as the cluster of indigenous 'Islamicized' or 'Islamized' ethnolinguistic groups in the country; namely, the Badjao, Iranun, Jama Mapun, Kalagan, Kalibugan, Maguindanao, Maranao, Molbog, Palawanon, Sama, Sangil, Tausug and Yakan.

Given the mixed population in the claimed ancestral territory, a way out of the conundrum evolved by broadening the 'Bangsa Moro'/'Bangsamoro' construct to include all non-Moro IPs as a matter of birthright and settler populations by affinity (that is, through marriage) — regardless of religion. As the 2008 MOA-AD stipulated: "It is the birthright of all Moros and all indigenous peoples of Mindanao to identify themselves and be accepted as 'Bangsamoros.'" Settlers married to a Bangsamoro person were also classified as Bangsamoro. The 2012 FAB more or less adopted the same formulation, only distinguishing between ascription and self-ascription of the Bangsamoro identity.

Who Are the 'Bangsamoro People'?

In this turn the Bangsamoro is an identity founded on the land of one's ancestors' birth, rather than on religion. This decisively still excluded

TABLE 4.2

2008 MOA-AD	2012 FAB
"The Bangsamoro people refers to those who are natives or general inhabitants of Mindanao and its adjacent islands, including Palawan and the Sulu archipelago at the time of conquest or colonization and their descendants whether mixed or of full native blood. Spouses or descendants are classified as Bangsamoro. The freedom of choice of the indigenous peoples will be respected." *(MOA-AD, Concepts and Principles, No. 1)*	"Those who at the time of conquest and colonization were considered natives or original inhabitants of Mindanao and the Sulu archipelago and its adjacent islands including Palawan, and their descendants whether of mixed or full blood shall have the right to identify themselves as Bangsamoro by ascription or self-ascription. Spouses and their descendants are classified as Bangsamoro. The freedom of choice of other indigenous peoples shall be respected." *(FAB, Section I, Establishment of the Bangsamoro, No. 5)*

settlers (except by affinity) regardless of religion — although most settlers from other parts of the country are Christians (see Table 4.3). In one of our consultations on the peace deal with the Filipino Catholic clergy in Mindanao when I was the government peace panel chair, I was confronted by a priest based in Cotabato City. "With this definition," he said heatedly, "I will never be a Bangsamoro." I replied, "Yes, Father, unless you marry one." Of course the Catholic priest is celibate, but I reminded him that as a citizen in the prospective Bangsamoro region he has all the rights of everyone else, except to self-identify as a Bangsamoro.

Interestingly, other than the word *Moro* in the names of the MNLF and MILF, the MOA-AD referred to Moros only twice — in the quotation above and in an instance of "Moro sultanates". The FAB did not use *Moro* at all. The Power-sharing Annex of the CAB only used the term once, in "non-Moro indigenous communities", along with women, settler communities and other sectors who would have seats in the Bangsamoro assembly in addition to representation according to constituent political units.[123] Instead, the more inclusive *Bangsamoro people* was used consistently in the FAB and the annexes that made

TABLE 4.3
Total Population by Religious Affiliation, Region and Province: Mindanao, 2015

Area	Total	Islam	Non-Islam	No Religion	Not Stated
MINDANAO	24,135,775	5,646,010	18,451,813	11,105	26,847
Region IX	**3,629,783**	**603,289**	**3,019,275**	**6,815**	**404**
Zamboanga del Norte	1,011,393	66,784	937,919	6,417	273
Zamboanga del Sur	1,010,674	64,885	945,721	67	1
Zamboanga City	861,799	302,795	558,814	87	103
Zamboanga Sibugay	633,129	96,643	536,227	232	27
City of Isabela	112,788	72,182	40,594	12	—
Region X	**4,689,302**	**378,019**	**4,309,731**	**1,294**	**258**
Bukidnon	1,415,226	16,742	1,397,190	1,171	123
Camiguin	88,478	228	88,239	11	—
Lanao del Norte	676,395	298,909	377,460	—	26
Iligan City	342,618	39,319	303,219	1	79
Misamis Occidental	602,126	1,740	600,324	57	5
Misamis Oriental	888,509	6,475	881,908	14	112
Cagayan de Oro City	675,950	14,606	661,317	14	13
Regon XI	**4,893,318**	**167,879**	**4,721,292**	**516**	**3,631**
Davao del Norte	1,016,332	24,253	991,988	40	51
Davao del Sur	632,588	15,261	616,910	100	317
Davao City	1,632,991	63,127	1,566,659	279	2,926
Davao Oriental	558,958	32,324	526,630	4	—
Compostela Valley	736,107	16,726	718,996	48	337
Davao Oriental	316,342	16,188	300,109	45	—
Region XII	**4,545,276**	**1,032,824**	**3,505,354**	**598**	**6,500**
North Cotabato	1,379,747	405,686	972,867	148	1,046
Sarangani	544,261	58,182	485,922	157	—
South Cotabato	915,289	49,678	865,603	6	2
General Santos City	594,446	51,705	542,711	23	7
Sultan Kudarat	812,095	239,537	572,138	264	156
Cotabato City	299,438	228,036	66,113	—	5,289

Note: The breakdown excludes Region XIII (CARAGA, population 2,596,709) and the Autonomous Region in Muslim Mindanao (ARMM, population 3,781,397, of whom 91.28 percent are Muslims).
Source: Philippine Statistics Authority, 2015 Census of Population.

up the CAB. The 1990s agreements with the MNLF altogether skirted the problem of naming the identity/people by avoiding any reference to Moro, Bangsamoro or Muslims and used generic phrases like "the people of the concerned areas"[124] or "inhabitants (or residents) of the area of autonomy".[125]

Gender Relations[126]

Many Moro women directly joined the war as combatants, medics, couriers, fundraisers/collectors, and intelligence and auxiliary forces. Both Moro liberation fronts had women's committees/brigades in their respective armed forces. Several women in the MNLF rose to the rank of officers in State Revolutionary Committees. Nur Misuari's first and second wives, the sisters Desdemonia (deceased) and Rohaida Tan were known to have had a strong influence over him, although Misuari would have several other younger wives in his senior years. Rohaida joined Misuari in the negotiations in Indonesia in the 1990s. A few MNLF women secured slots for integration into the police force/ Philippine Army as part of the 1996 Final Peace Agreement (FPA). The women-led projects that were facilitated as part of the 'peace and development' fund that followed the signing of the FPA proved to be more sustainable. Having proven their worth both in wartime and post-agreement, several former MNLF commanders/officers became prominent in the Autonomous Region in Muslim Mindanao and the other institutions that they entered.[127]

However, given their milieu, both the MNLF and MILF betrayed an essential conservatism with regard to their fellow women-comrades. An interview with a woman involved in the post-conflict phase revealed she felt that "the male leadership of the MNLF tended to revert back to conservative Islamic cultural notions of the role of women when it came to policy agendas and assigning tasks".[128] MNLF leaders and commanders interviewed reportedly discouraged qualified women to avail of the integration programme "due to their perception that the army and police are difficult places for women, and that, in many cases, women who were offered slots were dissuaded by their parents"; consequently, only 28 slots out of 5,750 seats allotted in the army were given to females in the final round of the integration programme in 2008.[129]

In one paragraph of *The Bangsamoro Mujahid*, Hashim referred to women as "property" that may be given away to unmarried comrades. The paragraph reads: "Another example showing extraordinary degree of solidarity among the companions of the prophet has to do with giving [a]way one's wife to unmarried members of the community.... This is an extreme case of fraternal relations but lessons of cooperation and spiritual discipline following the Qur-an and the Sunnah can be derived from these examples in relation to [the] MILF mujahideen. For no property must be so precious and no love so intense which one cannot give up for the cause of Islam."[130]

Evidently, the feminist order of discourse has had great difficulty in penetrating the discursive practices of the MILF. One field study found that among some members of an MILF-affiliated NGO and of its Social Welfare Committee, there is the belief that women should take up leadership roles only among women and when doing so would not sacrifice their domestic responsibilities; moreover, livelihood programmes should primarily be intended to supplement family income and to make them better mothers.[131] MILF-affiliated women in the Bangsamoro Development Agency (BDA) assume stereotypical functions in the BDA's finance, administrative and human resource departments, but all division directors are men — a trend explained as "consistent with the Islamic beliefs guiding MILF policy, whereby leadership is seen as a male role, albeit premised on consultation with women, and taking into account their perspective".[132] Another study reported that while women's voices should be heard relating to the peace negotiations, Muslim respondents tended to believe that the ultimate leadership responsibility for the formal peace process belonged to the men.[133] Moreover, "[s]ome rebel leaders explicitly eschew discussions of gender, claiming that the issues central to their struggle are those of sovereignty, economic and political marginalization, and Bangsamoro identity."[134]

The dilemma that consequently arises among the more progressive Muslim women believing in the Bangsamoro cause is one "of wishing to be part of and therefore partake of and conserve the economic and political privilege in being a Bangsamoro and a Muslim, at the same time frustrated and rebellious of the replication and backlash of hegemonic rules and regulations of the old order that has slowly seeped into and polluted the nationalist cause in the course, one, of the local peace processes, and, two, and perhaps more significantly, the inventions of new myths and meanings in the Bangsamoro nationalists' emulation of foreign ideology packaged as Islamic knowledge."[135]

As a rule, female Moro civil society leaders and ordinary community members duly observe rituals such as not shaking hands with men and sitting in separate women-only sections. While devout Moro women observe such practices as a matter of choice or preference, others do so to conform with expectations. For example, some wear the veil during conferences even if they may ordinarily go unveiled.[136]

Some Muslim women's groups are thus wary that the Islamic revivalism will reinforce traditional gender relations and cut back whatever advances the women have gained in liberty and rights.[137] Hall and Hoare report: "Some of the Maranao MNLF women [interviewed] expressed apprehension that a Bangsamoro Government under the MILF would bring about greater control over women's morality, such as forcing women to have a male relative as an escort and to wear full *abayas* or *burkhas* when out in public."[138] An MNLF woman in the Bangsamoro Women Solidarity Forum noted the ambiguity in regard to the parameters of women's roles under the current MILF leadership "because the definition of women's rights passed down to the communities is provided by male religious scholars".[139] Barry observed that the stories by contemporary women writers in her anthology of short fiction by 'Muslim Filipinos' show the ambivalence, if not opposition, of the fictional women in the stories to "the expectations their families have for them, expectations based on ideas about 'proper' conduct of Muslim daughters and wives".[140]

Writing based on field research in the mid-1980s, McKenna had observed that while most of the behavioural reforms insisted on by *ulama* reflected a primary concern to regulate the behaviour of women, these did not "in 1986, extend to any specific attempts to prescribe either the proper dress or work activities of women".[141] The imposition of a 'proper Muslim female' dress code appears to have become pronounced by the time of the 1990s, the period of Islamic revivalism in Mindanao. A non-Muslim journalist recounted to me how at an MILF checkpoint that their vehicle passed sometime in the early 2000s she was queried as to why she was not wearing the veil.

Along this line, Muchashim Arquiza writes about her experience as a "middle class Moro woman negotiating the 'Islamic dress' as an issue of cultural [national] identity and feminine modesty [religious moral value] in her desire to meld and be part of the norms of conduct set by the Bangsamoro nationalist ideology at the same time facilitating the nascence of a new self by appropriating the same signification of identity as an act of liberation."[142]

She continued:

> [I]nstead of importing as well the progressive and characteristic 'openness' (i.e. religious pluralism and tolerance) of the new trend of Salaafism as represented by Madjid and the Muhammadiyah movement in Indonesia, the national and global islamists (i.e. MNLF, MILF, Abu Sayyaf) who have been the dominant voice in Bangsamoro political landscape have 'hijacked' the discourse of this Islamic resurgence by putting stronger emphasis and especially focusing its attention in restrictions and regulating women's agency and space as embodiment of the Islamic ideal. In this narrative, the woman's body becomes tasked to hold and guard the symbols of the Bangsamoro nation: the imagined new self — both the inner and external, and the physical (i.e. home and workplace) as well as the spiritual world to be recreated.[143]

A suggestion from an outsider interlocutor to include a woman member in the MILF negotiating panel was, reportedly, deliberated seriously in the MILF, but the traditional *ulama* perspective was that it would be hard for a woman to keep up with the pace and to travel abroad for the peace talks.[144] Only in 2011 did a woman join the MILF delegation in the talks in Kuala Lumpur, after much prodding from domestic and international civil society organizations. The first woman to join the MILF delegation in the talks, Raisa Jajurie, a human rights lawyer, had to be accompanied by a male relative for the negotiations in Kuala Lumpur — until another woman joined and the requirement was waived. My appointment in November 2012 as chair of the government panel for the talks with the MILF — the first woman to serve in the post — was met with initial opposition from the MILF panel, which expressed uncertainty as to how to deal with a woman counterpart.

Non-discrimination on the basis of gender are mentioned in agreements signed by the two fronts with the government.[145] The increased participation of women in the negotiating room and the accompaniment of women's organizations and civil society in the talks with the MILF in the second decade of the twenty-first century led to enhanced articulation of women's rights in the Comprehensive

Agreement on the Bangsamoro.[146] They built on the earlier success of UNICEF, which in 2007 signed a Joint Communiqué with the MILF stating that both parties agree "that the rights of children and women should be upheld at all times and that all essential services to them should always be provided."[147]

On the whole, proving themselves worthy as combatants, community organizers, development workers and peace builders, and having experienced greater mobility due to the abnormal conditions of armed conflict,[148] many Moro women have pursued roles that challenge the traditional perceptions that have placed them in subordinated roles in society. The growth of women's organizations networked with other groups outside of the Bangsamoro communities has seen an increasing number of women becoming involved in public affairs. At the community level, many women have earned respect as effective mediators imbued with integrity.[149]

Recently, somehow, the MILF leaders have manifested pragmatic openness to women's activism and appreciation of their contributions to peace building.[150] In fact, many of their daughters are active in the civil society organizations that multiplied during the drawn out period of ceasefire and peace talks, and which is now in the implementation phase.[151] In speeches, one can hear some MILF leaders greeting their Muslim or Bangsamoro "brothers and sisters" instead of just extending salutations to their "brothers", which was so typical up to the 1990s. Indeed, one could say that these small but significant progressive manifestations indicate that the gendered discourse in the twenty-first century has permeated Bangsamoro advocacy, but it has not yet been absorbed. Dwyer and Cagoco-Guiam describe the ongoing dynamics thus: "To the extent that there has been some conflict-related transformation in traditional gender roles, there is also frequently a profound struggle taking place both within communities and among external agents about whether, and how, partial or significant gains in transforming gender roles can be maintained or even nurtured."[152]

Other Ambiguities: Folk Beliefs and Class

Among Moro/Muslim communities there are also emerging tensions around the issue of how much value should be given to folk beliefs and practices in the context of a revolution-backed Islamization movement in which law and justice, dress and decorum, governance practices and civil relations are being defined according to Shariah law and other Islamic tenets. Some imams have negotiated the totalizing inroads of purist *ulama* (both independent and 'inside' the rebel organization) by distinguishing between un-Islamic and anti-Islam, arguing that most traditional practices do not fall under the latter.[153]

Questions are also being raised about the pre-eminence given to the role of the sultanate (as against autonomous *datus* and councils of elders) in defining the evolution of Bangsa-hood. Other voices are coming out to emphasize the diversity among Moro ethnic groups in light of a perceived tendency to view local Muslim histories and practices (and even those of non-Moro indigenous groups) as a non-variegated strand of a singular Bangsamoro history largely drawn from the dominant Moro ethnic groups (Tausug, Maguindanao and Maranao). Arquiza elaborates on this diversity and the resultant tension over the homogenizing claims of the Bangsamoro revolutionaries:

> [The] Sama Dilaut still practice their traditional ancestral worship and pantheistic spirituality and tend to be the least Islamized. The Tausugs are supposed to have considerably mainstreamed and fully imbibed the Muslim values especially the teachings coming from Arabian shores, values that have become the basis of the political, economic and social ideology of the traditional sultanate system. The Sama and Yakan, on the other hand, whose folk beliefs, pantheism and syncretic forms of spirituality still flavor their practice of Islam appear to be in the median.
>
> Having been traditionally autonomous from the centralized sultanate system, the 'commoner' social status and the combined factors of ethnicity and economic class maintained … somewhat fluid Islamized communities among the Sama Dilaut, Sama and Yakan allowing [the] practice of [a] more tolerant kind of Islam that is deeply embedded within indigenous culture. This is apparent in the extant practice of religious syncretism (i.e. folk Islam) and the prevailing *a'dat* or customary traditions that rule the day-to-day conduct of life [while] the Tausug, being the dominant ethnic community and the politically privileged class to comprise the Sultanate and the datu class have assumed a more rigid adherence to Islamic *fiqh* (jurisprudence) and *shari'a* (corpus of rules/laws).[154]

Finally, even within Moro society, the absence of any class element in MILF and MNLF discourse is being questioned. The matter of class, according to Aijaz, is a touchy issue: "Much of the Muslim intelligentsia conjures myths of communal land ownership and egalitarian classlessness within Moro society. From this they draw a strategic perspective that directs the revolutionary struggle solely against Christian 'colonialism', and seeks to preserve and reproduce the existing social structure of the Moros."[155] Class cleavages are also manifested among the thirteen Islamized ethnolinguistic groups that have become the standard coverage of the Moro people. The dominant communities of the Tausug, Maguindanao and Maranao are differentiated from the subordinated groups (Badjao, Yakan, Samal and others), not only by being more populous but also by "territorial and hierarchical division and varied specializations in actual economic production. The Samal and Badjao for example are sea faring peoples. Without any stake in the agrarian economy and occupying a subordinate position in the ethnic hierarchy, they have played no role in the war led by the Moro National Liberation Front (MNLF) whose leading cadres are characteristically drawn from the three dominant groups."[156]

Arquiza — informed by "the spirit of the 400 years struggle of the Bangsamoro for national liberation and firm in faith that it is in Islam and by the will of Allah *subhanahu wa taala* that real liberative powers emanate" — questioned the MILF's silence on the accumulation of wealth and power of religious and political elites, and its uncritical stance on *ulama* justifying social inequality.[157] She wrote: "The tendencies for exclusivism, at the same time, homogenizing remain fore-shadowed in the nationalists' defensiveness in immediately dismissing as isolationist, tribalist and divisive, at best, and, at worst, stigmatizing as un-Islamic and communistic (i.e. Marxists) those who insist on the analysis of contradiction in class interests among majority and minoritized Bangsamoro ethnic communities."[158]

These critical commentaries — while still downplayed in the euphoric period of signing the CAB, passing and ratifying the Bangsamoro Organic Law and instituting the Bangsamoro Transition Authority, all within the continuing narrative of the Moro/Bangsamoro master frame — may eventually gain more saliency as the intellectual bearers of the identity encounter new socio-political tensions arising from the process of living out the right to self-determination embodied in the Bangsamoro autonomy framework.

Conclusion

In all, the Bangsamoro 'master frame' as initially constructed by the MNLF[159] and developed by the MILF has achieved a coherence[160] founded on universal rights and Islam and the historical antecedents that buttress claims to prior statehood and nationhood. It has assumed an ideological, valorized status such that believers and supporters defend it passionately — that is, they respond in 'naturalized' ways to it and the truth that it claims. They build and fortify self-identities, write fiction and poetry, engage each other via emails and blogs, organize campaigns and coalitions around it and, until recently, waged armed struggle in its name. Fairclough refers to this as the important part of the ideological work of texts and discourse — when interpretative principles operate in a naturalized way, resting upon assumptions of an ideological sort.[161]

We have already noted how the MILF more effectively incorporated other orders of discourse into the master frame. It tapped and internalized the new language of IP and ancestral domain, human rights and international humanitarian law in its discourse. The rich interdiscursivity practised by the MILF throughout the decades has helped it build strength against adversity from one administration and global context to another. It weathered the change from martial rule to the restored, still Manila-centric, elite democracy or oligarchic rule. The latter nonetheless paved the way for the protracted peace negotiations, the new terrain that the MILF cautiously but determinedly pursued. Whether in the jungle, marshland or in exile, the MILF lived through the end of the Cold War period and the hostile global environment engendered by the Bush administration. It followed through the emerging discourses in the United Nations with a clear sense of the 'internationalized' nature of its revolution.[162]

The borrowings and weavings of the MILF's discourse had not been devoid of inconsistency or ambiguity. There was ambivalence with regard to Hashim Salamat's vision of an independent Islamic state, on the one hand, and its acceptance of secular autonomous arrangements within the Philippine nation-state, on the other. While it was up to the Moros to decide their future, at the same time "the system of government to be established is pre-determined by Qur'anic principles and the traditions of Prophet Muhammad (peace be upon him). Hence, the matter of selecting a system of government for the community is completely beyond the scope of the people's will and prerogatives."[163] In the end the MILF signed up in 2014 to the CAB's promise of a decidedly secular autonomous political entity. And, as examined in an earlier section, the Moro is Muslim, but the Bangsamoro and the MILF are not exclusively for Muslims, and non-Moro identities may be subsumed under the Bangsamoro identity. The MILF still falls short of sorting out the ancestral domain issue contested by non-Moro IPs. Its qualifications for projecting a more inclusive discourse are stymied by an inherently demarcated identity based on birth, marriage and/ or ancestral origins. While it basically advocates the same right to self-determination espoused by the MNLF, it still has irreconcilable personality and organizational differences with Nur Misuari's MNLF faction. As a counter-elite, it is deemed a threat to the established political dynasties in the region, with their respective municipal and provincial turfs. All these dividing lines — plus the historical biases and prejudice of many Filipinos against Muslims/Moros and their armed groups — have continued to block the full attainment of the MILF's hegemonic Bangsamoro claims.

From within its own communities, there remains resistance to what this composite Moro ideological struggle has advanced.[164] It has yet to weave into a more inclusive frame the identities, welfare and interests of other claimants to Mindanao and the Philippines, which it must do to gain more discursive power within its own variegated society and the larger Philippine society within which it remains lodged. These claimants include non-Moro indigenous peoples, the smaller Moro ethnic groups, the lower classes in Moro society subjugated by their own elites, the settlers, the business groups, and the politicians and other self-appointed guardians of national territory and sovereignty. They also include the nascent groups espousing violent extremism and privileging Islamic identity over nationhood.

Beyond these discursive tracks are the emerging discourses of Moro women and sympathetic feminists, of other Moros and Filipinos who have transcended ethnoreligious identities in favour of 'Filipino' or universal humanity, and of the Mindanaoan advocates of 'a new/ our own Mindanao' or the bigger frame of a 'tri-people Mindanao'. These discourses provide the resources for the continuing contestation on the ground, in the mass media and in decision-making institutions such as the presidency, the courts and congress. At the same time, they serve as material for synthesis and for weaving into the dominant threads of the master frames constructed in the twentieth century by the pioneering Moro identity intellectuals.

Notes

1. Louise Phillips and Marianne W. Jorgensen, *Discourse Analysis as Theory and Method* (London: Sage, 2002), p. 7.
2. Cited in Norman Fairclough, *Discourse and Social Change* (Cambridge: Polity Press, 1992), p. 103. Horizontal intertextuality refers to the dialogical ('speaking in turns') relation between a text and those that preceded it, as one may find in an exchange of letters, conversations and polemical statements.
3. Ibid, pp. 102, 104.
4. Ibid., p. 105.
5. Ibid., p. 79.
6. Norman Fairclough, *Language and Power* (London: Longman, 1989), p. 152.
7. Ian Parker and Erica Burman, "Against Discursive Imperialism, Empiricism and Constructionism: Thirty-two Problems with Discourse Analysis", in *Discourse Analytic Research*, edited by Erica Burman and Ian Parker (London: Routledge, 1993), p. 167.
8. International usage of *to* in the phrase "right to self-determination" seems to have overtaken the traditional use of *of*. We will use the more current form of *to* for consistency.
9. European states granted independence after World War I were Czechoslovakia, Hungary, Poland, Yugoslavia, Armenia, Finland, Estonia, Latvia and Lithuania. Britain gave independence to Australia, Canada and New Zealand in 1931. By 1955, ten new states were born in Asia, and a succession of new African states followed from 1957. The Asian states were Pakistan, India, Ceylon, the Philippines, Vietnam, Cambodia, Laos, Burma, Korea and Indonesia. See Dov Ronen, *The Quest for Self-Determination* (New Haven: Yale University Press, 1979), p. 4–5.
10. See Chapter XI: Declaration Regarding Non-Self-Governing Territories, Charter of the United Nations. See also Chapters XI and XII on the International Trusteeship System.
11. Ronen, *The Quest*, pp. 37, 40.
12. "All peoples have the right of self-determination, by virtue of that right, they freely determine their political status and freely pursue their economic, social and cultural development", point number 2 of the adopted UN Resolution stated. This statement was adopted entirely to become

Art. 1.1 of the International Covenant on Civil and Political Rights passed in 1966. The 1960 UN Resolution also asked that all repressive measures on dependent people be stopped to allow them to peacefully and freely exercise the right.

13. Patrick Thornberry, "The UN Declaration on the Rights of Persons Belonging to National or Ethnic, Religious and Linguistic Minorities: Background, Analysis, Observations and an Update", in *Universal Minority Rights*, edited by Alan Phillips and Allan Rosas (Turku/Abo and London: Abo Akademi University Institute for Human Rights and Minority Rights Group, 1995), p. 17–18.

14. Ronen, *The Quest*, p. 40.

15. Nur Misuari, "Appeal to Islamic World for Support of the Moro People in Southern Philippines", *Philippine Development Forum* 6, no. 2 (1992): 61. The appeal was read during the 23 January 1973 session of the Jeddah Negotiations.

16. Ibid., pp. 79–80.

17. Ibid.

18. "In those states in which ethnic, religious or linguistic minorities exist, persons belonging to such minorities shall not be denied the right, in community with the other members of their group, to enjoy their own culture, to profess and practice their own religion, or to use their own language" (Article 27, International Covenant on Civil and Political Rights). The ICCPR was adopted by the General Assembly in 1966 and entered into force in 1976.

19. The two covenants are the International Covenant on Civil and Political Rights and the International Covenant on Economic, Social and Cultural Rights. Common Article 1 reads in full:

"1.1.   All peoples have the right of self-determination, by virtue of that right, they freely determine their political status and freely pursue their economic, social and cultural development.

1.2.   All peoples may, for their own ends, freely dispose of their natural wealth and resources without prejudice to any obligations arising out of international economic co-operation, based upon the principle of mutual benefit, and in international law. In no case may a people be deprived of its own means of subsistence.

1.3   The State Parties to the Covenant, including those having responsibility for the administration of Non-Self-Governing Territories and Trust Territories, shall promote the realization of the right of self-determination, and shall respect that right, in conformity with the provisions of the Charter of the United Nations."

Like the ICCPR, the ICESCR was adopted by the UN General Assembly in 1966. It entered into force in January 1976, a few months ahead of the ICCPR.

20. Commentary of the Working Group on Minorities to the United Nations Declaration on the Rights of Persons Belonging to National, or Cultural, Religious and Ethnic Minorities, point number 15. The United Nations Working Group on Minorities was formed in 1977. It adopted the Commentary at its tenth session in 2004. The document was originally drawn up in 1998 by former WG chair Absjorn Eide. After receiving feedback from governments, experts and international government and non-governmental bodies, it was revised, contained in document E/CN.4/AC.5/2001/2 and passed as a commentary of the group as a whole. The WG on Minorities is under the Sub-Commission on the Promotion and Protection of Human Rights of the UN Commission on Human Rights.

21. Ibid., point numbers 19 and 20.

22. In its written texts, the MILF combined the two words to become one ("Bangsamoro"). The pre-eminence of the MILF in public discourse relative to the MNLF in the second decade of the twenty-first century has made the singular term more popular. Notably, the 2014 peace agreement with the MILF was called the Comprehensive Agreement on the Bangsamoro, while the last agreement in 1996 with the MNLF was simply called the GRP-MNLF Final Peace Agreement. By the second decade of the twenty-first century, reference to the populace as *Moro* has increasingly been replaced by *Bangsamoro*.

23. The thinking that national minorities have stronger rights was duly noted by the Working Group on the Declaration on Minorities when it wrote: "That addition does not extend the overall scope of application beyond the groups already covered by Article 27 [of the ICCPR]. There is hardly any national minority, however defined, that is not also an ethnic or linguistic minority. A relevant question, however, would be whether the title indicates that the Declaration covers four different categories of minorities, whose rights have somewhat different content and strength. Persons belonging to groups defined solely as religious minorities might be held to have only those special minority rights which relate to the profession and practice of their religion. Persons belonging to groups solely defined as linguistic minorities might similarly be held to have only those special minority rights which are related to education and use of their language. Persons who belong to groups defined as ethnic would have more extensive rights relating to the preservation and development of other aspects of their culture also, since ethnicity is generally defined

by a broad conception of culture, including a way of life. The category of national minority would then have still stronger rights relating not only to their culture but to the preservation and development of their national identity." To this question on different entitlements, the Working Group clarified that the declaration does not make substantive distinctions as to the rights enjoyed across categories, and realizing that the concept of "national minorities" is used differently in different contexts, in which case relevant factors would differ, what is required is to ensure good governance and appropriate rights to each group. See Commentary of the Working Group on Minorities to the United Nations Declaration on the Rights of Persons Belonging to National, or Cultural, Religious and Ethnic Minorities, point number 6.

24. Ronen, *The Quest*, p. 6.
25. The MOA-AD was embargoed until 5 August 2008, the scheduled but cancelled date of its signing in Malaysia. The signing was cancelled when the Supreme Court issued a temporary restraining order. See "Memorandum of Agreement on the Ancestral Domain Aspect of GRP-MILF Tripoli Agreement on Peace of 2001" in MILF Peace Panel Secretariat, *Journey to the Bangsamoro, Third Party Facilitation Phase (2001–2008)*, vol. 2 (2015), pp. 94–159.
26. The labels *Aboriginal, Native* and *First* apply to, "among others, the ancient and contemporary nations of the Innu, Mi'kmaq, Maliseet, Cree, Montagnais, Anishinabek, Haudenosaunee, Dakota, Lakota, Nakota, Assinaboine, Saulteaux, Blackfoot, Secwepemec, Nlha'kapmx, Salish, Kwakwaka'wakw, Haida, Tsimshian, Gitksan, Tahltan, Gwich'in, Dene, Inuit, Metis, etc." John Borrows, "Indigenous Legal Traditions in Canada", *Washington University Journal of Law and Policy* 19 (January 2005): 175.
27. *First Nation* was used under item number 4 on the right to self-governance based on an acknowledged prior system of government in a defined territory. Part of the paragraph reads: "The Moro sultanates were states or karajaan/kadatuan resembling a body politic endowed with all the elements of nation-state in the modern sense. As a domestic community distinct from the rest of the national communities, they have a definite historic homeland. They are the 'First Nation' with defined territory a system of government...". MOA-AD, in MILF Peace Panel Secretariat, *Journey to the Bangsamoro*, p. 95.
28. Hashim Salamat, *The Bangsamoro Mujahid: His Objectives and Responsibilities* (Mindanao: Bangsamoro Publications, 1985), p. 3.
29. For an interesting commentary on political correctness from a discourse-analytic perspective, see Norman Fairclough, "'Political Correctness': The Politics of Culture and Change", *Discourse and Society* 14, no. 1 (2003): 17–28.

30. Ian Brownlie, *Treaties and Indigenous Populations, The Robb Lectures* (Oxford: Oxford University Press, 1992), p. 56. In 1953 the ILO published *Indigenous Peoples* as part of the ILO-led Andean Indigenous Programme that it jointly carried out with the UN, the Food and Agriculture Organization, UNICEF and the World Health Organization. The ILO also used the terms *tribal* and *semi-tribal*. See also Lee Sweptson and Manuela Tomei, "The International Labor Organisation and Convention 169", in *Indigenous Peoples and International Organizations*, edited by Lydia Van de Fliert (Nottingham: Spokesman, 1994), p. 58.

31. The convention defined tribal and semi-tribal populations as those "whose social and economic conditions are at a less advanced stage". Semi-tribal populations "are those groups and persons who, although they are in danger of losing their characteristics, are not yet integrated in the national community". Those who are indigenous are so regarded on "account of their descent from the populations" which inhabited the country or parts of it at the time of conquest or colonization. Another criterion is that their ways of life conform more with the institutions of their time than that of the nation to which they belong (Convention 107, or the Convention Concerning the Protection and Integration of Indigenous and Other Tribal and Semi-Tribal Populations in Independent Countries, art. 1.1).

32. In 1985 the UN put up the Fund for Indigenous Populations to pay for travel and related expenses incurred by IP representatives in attending the annual meetings of the WGIP. Cordillera activists Joji Carino and Vicky Tauli-Corpuz played significant roles in this process. Corpuz subsequently chaired the UN Permanent Forum on Indigenous Issues.

33. For example, in 1982 the World Bank came out with a brief operational policy statement outlining its procedures to ensure the protection of rights of tribal people in Bank-financed development projects. Certainly, their negative experience with the aborted Chico River Dam projects was part of the impetus for this new policy, but it took another decade to broaden and deepen the rights-based approach to these communities. See The World Bank, Operational Manual Statement (OMS) 2.34 issued in February 1982 under the title "Tribal People in Bank-Financed Projects", cited in Selton H. Davis, "The World Bank and Operational Directive 4.20", in *Indigenous Peoples and International Organisations*, edited by Lydia Van de Fliert (Nottingham: Spokesman, 1994), p. 75. The World Bank defined tribal peoples as those ethnic groups that "have stable, low-energy, sustained-yield economic systems; exhibit in varying degrees the following characteristics: a) geographically isolated or semi-isolated; b) unacculturated or only partially acculturated into the societal norms of the dominant society; c) non-monetized or only partially monetized, production largely

from subsistence and independent of the national economy; d) ethnically distinct from the national society; e) nonliterate and without a written language; f) linguistically distinct from the wider society; h) having an economic lifestyle largely dependent on the specific natural environment; i) possessing indigenous leadership but little or no national representation; j) having loose tenure over their traditional lands, which for most parts is not accepted by the dominant society nor accommodated by its courts, and having weak enforcement capabilities against encroachers, even when tribal areas have been delineated". Cited in Davis, "The World Bank", p. 75–77.

34. Julian Burger, "United Nations Working Group on Indigenous Peoples", in Van de Fliert, *Indigenous Peoples*, p. 93.

35. MILF Peace Panel Secretariat, *Journey to the Bangsamoro, Domestic Negotiation Phase (1997–2000)*, vol. 1 (2015), p. 6. The other items were: displaced and landless Bangsamoro; war victims and destruction of properties; human rights issues; social and cultural discrimination; corruption of the mind and moral fibre; economic inequities and widespread poverty; exploitation of natural resources; and agrarian-related issues.

36. Ibid., p. 7.

37. "Agreement on Peace between the Government of the Republic of the Philippines and the Moro Islamic Liberation Front", signed 22 June 2001 in Tripoli, Libya. For a copy of the document, see MILF Peace Panel Secretariat, *Journey to the Bangsamoro, Third Party Facilitation Phase (2001–2008)*, vol. 2 (2015), pp. 5–8.

38. *BJE* was the term used to refer to the envisioned political arrangement. Although a legally appropriate term, its unfamiliarity caused it to be viewed suspiciously, even by contrarian legislators. Consequently it was publicly maligned. The members of the new negotiating team that took over the process in 2010 (myself included) refrained from using the term, so as to avoid the negativism. The term used instead was *new political entity*, abbreviated in texts as *NPE*.

39. MOA-AD, in MILF Peace Panel Secretariat, *Journey to the Bangsamoro*, p. 95.

40. Ibid.

41. The provision states: "The Bangsamoro Juridical Entity (BJE) shall have the authority and jurisdiction over the Ancestral Domain and Ancestral lands, including alienable and non-alienable lands encompassed within their homeland and ancestral territory, as well as the delineation of ancestral domains/lands of the Bangsamoro located therein." MOA-AD, in MILF Peace Panel Secretariat, *Journey to the Bangsamoro*, p. 96.

42. Ibid.

43. Rudy Buhay Rodil, "What Does the MILF Mean by Ancestral Domain as Territory?", blog post, 7 February 2014, http://iag.org.ph/index.

php/editor-s-picks/1205-what-does-the-milf-mean-by-ancestral-domain-as-territory. The *pongampong ko Ranaw* refers to the four principalities of Ranao/Lanao under Islamic chiefs. The two sultanates were in Sulu and Maguindanao, which rose in the fifteenth and seventeenth centuries, respectively.

44. Ibid., p. 96.
45. I elaborated on this matter in "Forging a Peace Settlement for the Bangsamoro: Compromises and Challenges", in *Mindanao: The Long Journey to Peace and Prosperity*, edited by Paul D. Hutchcroft (Mandaluyong City: Anvil, 2016), pp. 121–24.
46. "Agreement on Peace between the Government of the Republic of the Philippines and the Moro Islamic Liberation Front", in MILF Peace Panel Secretariat, *Journey to the Bangsamoro*, p. 6.
47. MOA-AD, in MILF Peace Panel Secretariat, *Journey to the Bangsamoro*, p. 96.
48. Ibid., p. 168.
49. Salah Jubair, *The Long Road to Peace: Inside the GRP-MILF Peace Process* (Cotabato City: Institute of Bangsamoro Studies, 2007), pp. 167–68.
50. See, for example, the 17 August 2008 statement given to the MILF by a group of Teduray, Lambangian and Dulangan Manobo in Upi, Shariff Kabunsuan, calling themselves the "Lumad-ARMM"; the Cagayan de Oro Declaration passed in September 2008 by Mindanao IP groups; and interviews with the more sympathetic Kusog sa Katawhang Lumad sa Mindanao (Kalumaran). All were cited in Ma. Cecilia L. Rodriguez, "Are Lumads Left Out in the Quest for Peace in Mindanao?", posted 18 September 2008 at http://www.rightsreportning.net, the website of the Philippine Human Rights Reporting Project. In addition, one Lumad network was divided between those who supported and those who were against the MOA, eventually leading to an organizational schism. More petitions/statements followed in the course of the negotiations from 2010 to 2014.
51. Framework Agreement on the Bangsamoro (FAB), Section I (Establishment of the Bangsamoro), item 3.
52. FAB, Section V (Territory), item 5.
53. FAB, Section I, item 3.
54. FAB, Section V, item 5.
55. Annex on Power sharing, Section III, item 29.
56. FAB, Section III (Powers), item 6.
57. The CPP-led National Democratic Front declared its adherence to IHL in 1991, noting in particular Common Article 3 of the 1949 Geneva Conventions and Protocol 2, although it claimed applicability of Protocol 1, instead of Protocol 2, to itself five years later. See Soliman M. Santos, Jr., "Jihad and International Humanitarian Law: The Case of Three Moro Rebel Groups in

the Philippines", unpublished paper dated 6 May 2018 (PDF copy emailed to me on 28 December 2018).

58. Santos, Jr., "Jihad and International Humanitarian Law". See also Soliman M. Santos, Jr., *Constructively Engaging Non-State Armed Groups in Asia: Minding the Gaps, Harnessing Southern Perspectives*, South-South Network for Non-State Armed Group Engagement (SSN) monograph no. 1, March 2010.

59. General Instructions to the Bangsa Moro Army issued by Nur Misuari on 18 June 1977, cited in Santos, "Jihad and International Humanitarian Law".

60. Together with lawyer Soliman Santos, Jr., I was co-coordinator of the Philippine Campaign to Ban Landmines and co-chair of the International Campaign to Ban Landmines Non-State Actors Working Group when we organized, in 2000, a pioneering conference in Geneva on "Engaging Non-State Actors on a Landmine Ban", attended by MILF lawyer Ali Lanang. In April 2002, Santos and I visited an MILF camp to get the signature of the MILF, represented by then vice-chair Ebrahim Murad and Central Committee member Mohager Igbal/Salah Jubair, on a Geneva Call "Deed of Commitment" banning the use, production and trading of anti-personnel mines. See "Report of the Geneva Call Mission to the Moro Islamic Liberation Front", 2002, http://www.genevacall.org/resources/test-publications/gc-03may02-milf.pdf/. It should be noted that MILF support for a mine ban also drew inspiration from the Taliban's similar commitment to the goal of banning and clearing mines, a copy of which was shown to the MILF by the PCBL.

61. Office of the Special Representative of the Secretary General for Children and Armed Conflict and UNICEF, "National Democratic Front of the Philippines Agrees to an Action Plan with the UN to Ensure That No Children are among Their Ranks", media release, 9 April 2011.

62. Ibid.

63. For example, the MILF enthusiastically pushed for the creation of a joint mechanism for cooperation in addressing criminality in areas where it operated. On 6 May 2002, the two parties issued the Joint Communiqué creating the Ad-Hoc Joint Action Group (AHJAG). The MILF subsequently pushed key ASG and Jemaah Islamiyah operatives out of their areas of influence in Central Mindanao, forcing the latter to move back to the islands of Sulu and Basilan. The ASG's head, Khadaffy Janjalani, was killed shortly after in Basilan province.

64. These letters are collected in MILF Peace Panel, *Journey to the Bangsamoro*, pp. 162–65. See also responses from State Department officials and a congratulatory letter to then president-elect Barack Hussein Obama in November 2008 (ibid., pp. 166–71). In the May 2003 letter, the MILF also

denied involvement in a series of bomb attacks in Davao City and decried the warning of then president Gloria Macapagal Arroyo to declare it a terrorist organization

65. Santos, "Jihad and International Humanitarian Law".

66. Macapado Abaton Muslim, *The Moro Armed Struggle in the Philippines: The Non-Violent Autonomy Alternative* (Marawi City: Mindanao State University, 1994), p. 160.

67. Cited in William Larousse, *Walking Together Seeking Peace: The Local Church of Mindanao-Sulu Journeying in Dialogue with the Muslim Community (1965–2000)* (Quezon City: Claretian, 2001), p. 98.

68. Gowing, *Muslim Filipinos*, p. 70, cited in Larousse, *Walking Together*, p. 99.

69. Thomas M. McKenna, *Muslim Rulers and Rebels: Everyday Politics and Armed Separatism in the Philippines* (Manila: Anvil, 1998), p. 133.

70. Omar Farouk Bajunid, "Islamic Revitalization in ASEAN: A Survey of Source Materials", in *Islamic Revitalization in ASEAN Countries: Proceedings of the Third ASEAN Forum for Muslim Social Scientists*, held at the University of the Philippines Asian Institute of Tourism, Quezon City and Mindanao State University, Marawi City, 25–30 September 1989. The author duly noted that there are subtle differences in meaning — and we may add bias — among these terms.

71. Hussin Mutalib, "Islamic Revitalization in ASEAN: The Political Dimension", in *Islamic Revitalization in ASEAN Countries: Proceedings of the Third ASEAN Forum for Muslim Social Scientists*, held at the University of the Philippines Asian Institute of Tourism, Quezon City and Mindanao State University, Marawi City, 25–30 September 1989.

72. Abubaker A. Bagader, "Contemporary Islamic Movements in the Arab world", in *Islam, Globalization and Postmodernity*, edited by Akbar S. Ahmed and Hasting S. Donnan (London: Routledge, 1994), p. 118.

73. Fred Halliday, "The Politics of Islamic Fundamentalism: Iran, Tunisia and the Challenge to the Secular State", in *Islam, Globalization and Postmodernity*, edited by Akbar S. Ahmed and Hasting S. Donnan (London: Routledge, 1994), p. 91.

74. Mahmoud M. Ayoub, *Islam, Faith and History* (Oxford: Oneworld, 2004), p. 210.

75. Ahmed and Donnan outlined six varieties in the Arab world. These are the (a) spiritualist groups who are focused on spiritual concerns, are Sufi-oriented and folklorist or rooted in cultural traditions, and are found usually among the urban poor and peasantry; (b) ritualistic groups that emphasize modest dressing and stress moral issues and social conduct but are often unconcerned about political and economic issues; (c) revolutionary or radical groups who demand immediate and fundamental

change in Muslim society through violence and extreme confrontation; (d) various Muslim Brothers' groups who succeeded in getting political power in Sudan, won in a general election in Algeria, or play the role of opposition in Tunisia and that of a moral and political authority in Egypt; (e) intellectual groups who are rejected by the traditional Islamic leaderships, and who may be nationalists and leftists; and (f) traditional leadership groups made up of muftis, jurists and professors of Islamic studies in Muslim universities. Akbar S. Ahmed and Hasting S. Donnan, *Islam, Globalization and Postmodernity* (London: Routledge, 1994), pp. 118–20.

76. Halliday, "Politics of Islamic Fundamentalism", pp. 92–93.
77. Ayoub, *Islam, Faith and History*, p. 199.
78. Mutalib, "Islamic Revitalization in ASEAN", p. 48.
79. McKenna, *Muslim Rulers and Rebels*, p. 206.
80. Julkipli Wadi, "Strategic Intelligence Analysis of Philippine National Security, Muslim Secessionism and Fundamentalism", paper presented at the Strategy and Conflict Studies of the Command and General Staff College Training and Doctrine Command, Philippine Army, Makati City, 14 June 2000.
81. Mutalib, "Islamic Revitalization in ASEAN", pp. 46–47.
82. Wadi, "Strategic Intelligence Analysis". Wadi is associate professor at the UP Institute of Islamic Studies.
83. W.K. Che Man, *Muslim Separatism: The Moros of Southern Philippines and the Malays of Southern Thailand* (Quezon City: Ateneo de Manila University Press), p. 84.
84. Ibid., p. 92.
85. *MORO* stands for Moro Revolutionary Organization, an underground organization formed by the Communist Party of the Philippines and a member organization of the National Democratic Front.
86. Che Man, *Muslim Separatism*, pp. 86–87.
87. Ibid., p. 161.
88. McKenna claims that the change from "Moro National" to "Moro Islamic" Liberation Front was only a political move on the part of Hashim. McKenna, *Muslim Rulers and Rebels*, p. 208.
89. Exclusive interview granted by Chairman Salamat Hashim to Reuters, Camp Abubakre as-Siddique, 19 February 1999, in Salamat Hashim, *Referendum: Peaceful, Civilized, Diplomatic and Democratic Means of Solving the Mindanao Conflict* (Mindanao, Bangsamoro Darul Jihad: Agency for Youth Affairs-MILF, 2002), pp. 81–82.
90. Television interview granted by Chairman Salamat Hashim to Noli de Castro of "Magandang Gabi, Bayan" of ABS-CBN, Camp Abubakre as-Siddique, 16 February 1999, in Hashim, *Referendum*, p. 118.
91. Hashim, *Referendum*, p. 101.

92. Exclusive interview granted by Chairman Salamat Hashim to Greg Torode, *South China Morning Post*, and Peter Arford, *The Australian*, Camp Abubakre as-Siddique, 16 March 1999, in ibid., pp. 126–27.

93. Salamat Hashim, letter dated 24 December 1977 to Dr Ahmadu Karm Gaye, secretary-general of the OIC, Jeddah, cited in Che Man, *Muslim Separatism*, p. 85.

94. Hashim, *Referendum*, pp. 81–87.

95. Abhoud Syed Mansur Lingga, "The Political Thought of Salamat Hashim" (MA thesis, Institute of Islamic Studies, University of the Philippines, 1995), pp. 26, 59–60. Jihad, Hashim argues, is obligatory since Muslims in the country are being persecuted and oppressed. However, he clarifies that participation is not limited to battles but includes all efforts that will contribute to the goal of jihad.

96. Jubair, the pen name of MILF Central Committee member Mohager Iqbal, earned his master's degree in political science from Manuel Luis Quezon University in Manila. Soliman Santos, Jr. wrote this about Iqbal: "He typifies that segment of the MILF, like Murad and Jaafar, who come from the secular elite or professional sector, as distinguished from the religious elite or *ulama* sector like Hashim, Mimbantas and Pasigan. The former have been moderating and modernizing ... influences on the MILF" (Soliman Santos, Jr., email message to this writer, 22 January 2008). Just the same, Jubair qualified that although he had a secular education his upbringing was very religious. His father studied in Saudi Arabia during World War I when Saudi Arabia was still under the Turks. His grandfather headed the hajj that brought his father to Mecca, where his father stayed, served and learned from "the masters". He attests to a "religious consciousness", which somehow makes up for not being a religious scholar. Interview with Jubair/Iqbal, 6 November 2008, Maguindanao.

97. Defined by Baud and Rutten as those who emerge in the development of the social movement and who have the explicit vocation of promoting and developing a collective action frame to serve the movement, especially in the more "mature" stages of the movement. They include the core activists and leaders of the movement, and they may have been formally educated or have risen from the movement, which provided them the space to reflect upon life in a meaningful way. Michiel Baud and Rosanne Rutten, eds., "Popular Intellectuals and Social Movements: Framing Protest in Asia, Africa, and Latin America", *International Review of Social History* 49 (2004): 197–99.

98. Hashim, *The Bangsamoro Mujahid*, p. 26.

99. In 2010, Ustadz Umbra Kato left and organized his followers from the MILF's 105th Base Command into the BIFF. Kato had become impatient with the lack of progress in the peace negotiations and resented the discipline imposed on him for the civilian attacks he led in protest at the Supreme

Court decision junking the MOA-AD in 2008. The BIFF splintered into several groups, with one faction aligning itself with Jemaah Islamiyah — an al-Qaeda network in Southeast Asia — and later the Islamic State in Iraq and Syria (ISIS).

100. Formed in 2012 by brothers Abdullah and Omarkhayam Maute of Lanao del Sur.
101. In 2001 the ASG connected with operatives of Jemaah Islamiyah. Despite factionalism and descent to plain criminality in Sulu, the Basilan group led by Isnaji Hapilon appears to have kept intact the Islamist agenda of Abdurajak Janjalani, the founding father of the ASG. In July 2014, Hapilon pledged allegiance to ISIS.
102. Ibid., p. 89.
103. Nur Misuari, "The Bangsa Moro People's Struggle for Self-Determination (Towards an Understanding of the Roots of the Moro People's struggle)", *Philippine Development Forum* 6, no 2 (1992): 27, 25
104. Ibid., p. 25.
105. Salah Jubair, *Bangsamoro, A Nation under Endless Tyranny*, 3rd ed. (Kuala Lumpur: IQ Marin, 1999), p. 19.
106. Ibid., p. 24.
107. Ibid., pp. 88, 129–30.
108. Ibid., p. 78.
109. Ibid., p. 148.
110. Ibid., p. 262.
111. Ibid., pp. 146–47.
112. Ibid., p. 125.
113. Ibid., p. 259.
114. Ibid., pp. 14–15.
115. Ibid., pp. 262–63.
116. Ibid., p. 263.
117. 1986 *Midweek* interview with Salamat Hashim, in Hashim, *Referendum*, pp. 30–31.
118. MILF Technical Working Groups, "Position Papers of the Technical Working Groups on the Six Clustered Agenda", n.d., reprinted in *Kasarinlan: A Philippine Quarterly of Third World Studies* 15, no. 2 (2000): 254.
119. Salah Jubair, *The Long Road to Peace: Inside the GRP-MILF Peace Process* (Cotabato City: Institute of Islamic Studies, 2007), p. 166.
120. Ibid.
121. Ibid., p. 169.
122. Tripoli Agreement, in Office of the Presidential Adviser on the Peace Process, *GRP-MNLF Peace Process: A Compilation of Major Documents* (n.d.), pp. 105–10.

123. FAB, part 2, Governance Structure, no. 3. The 1996 GRP-MNLF Final Peace Agreement provided for cross-sectoral representation in the form of a deputy-governor each for Christians, Muslims and Highlanders — a classification that mixed up religion and ethnicity (*highlander* was a common appellate for indigenous cultural communities before *IP* became the standard reference).

124. 1996 Interim Peace Agreement, I, 2(a), in OPAPP, *GRP-MNLF Peace Process*, p. 151.

125. 1996 Final Peace Agreement, paras. 129 and 143 in OPAPP, *GRP-MNLF Peace Process*, pp. 99, 101.

126. This section will focus only on the women's question and not all aspects of gender relations.

127. Among them are Bainon Karon and Fatmawati Salapuddin, who were appointed to various posts, Norma Mohamad Amiril and Giobay Diocolano, who set up the Kadtabanga Foundation, and Bai Sandra Sema, who became an outspoken member of Congress.

128. Rosalie Alcala Hall and Joanna Parres Hoare, "Philippines", in *Women in Conflict and Peace*, edited by International Institute for Democracy and Electoral Assistance (Sweden: IDEA, 2015), p. 98.

129. Ibid.

130. Hashim, *The Bangsamoro Mujahid*, pp. 30–31.

131. Hall and Hoare, "Philippines", p. 106.

132. Ibid., p. 109.

133. Leslie Dwyer and Rufa Cagoco-Guiam, *Gender and Conflict in Mindanao* (Washington, DC: The Asia Foundation, n.d.). Field research was conducted in 2010.

134. Ibid., 19.

135. Mucha-Shim Quiling Arquiza, "Knowledge and Power in Bangsamoro Identity Politics: An Essay on Intersectionality of Ethnicity, Religion, Gender and Kinship as Determinants of Identity", draft discussion paper submitted to KonsultMindanaw, 15 June 2009 (copy provided by the author to this writer). Arquiza is the secretary-general of the Asian Muslim Action Network in the Philippines (AMANPHIL) and director of the Lumah Ma Dilaut Center for Living Traditions.

136. In a conference of *ulama* held on 29 January 2009, Amina Rasul, head of the Philippine Council for Islam and Democracy and chair of the conference, stepped off the stage after giving her remarks because she could not be seated beside the male religious leaders there.

137. Various conversations with women civil society leaders in Mindanao.

138. Hall and Hoare, "Philippines", p. 106.

139. Ibid.

140. Coeli Barry, ed., *The Many Ways of Being Muslim: Fiction by Muslim Filipinos* (Pasig City: Anvil, 2008), p. xvii.
141. McKenna, *Muslim Rulers and Rebels*, p. 329.
142. Arquiza, "Knowledge and Power".
143. Ibid.
144. As retold by Guiamel Alim, head of the Consortium of Bangsamoro Civil Society, based on his conversation with an MILF official who reportedly was apologetic about the decision. Conversation with Guiamel, March 2008, Hiroshima, Japan.
145. The specific provisions were: "The Autonomous Government in the area of autonomy advocates the equal opportunities for all inhabitants of the areas of autonomy regardless of ethnic origin, culture, sex, creed and religion." (Government of the Republic of the Philippines-Moro National Liberation Front Interim Peace Agreement, para. 2, vi); and "In addition to basic rights already enjoyed, the following rights of all citizens residing in the Bangsamoro bind the executive, legislature and judiciary as directly enforceable law and are guaranteed:... Right to equal opportunity and non-discrimination in social and economic activity and the public service, regardless of class, creed, disability, gender and ethnicity" (FAB, VI, 1, i). The use of *gender* instead of *sex* in the CAB was agreed on after MILF negotiator Datu Michael Mastura said that *sex* might be offensive to some of their *ulama*.
146. In the GPH-MILF's FAB, there is this quite famous clause on "the right of women to meaningful political participation" (see my account on the discussions on this provision during the peace talks in "Inclusion of 'Meaningful Participation' in the Moro Peace Process in the Philippines", in *Women's Meaningful Participation in Negotiating Peace and Implementing Peace Agreements: Report of the Experts Group Meeting Convened by UN Women*, 16–17 May 2018, p. 13). In addition, the CAB's 2013 Annex on Power Sharing mandates the future Bangsamoro autonomous government to establish appropriate mechanisms for consulting women and marginalized sectors — note that here, women are not lumped with 'other sectors' but is a distinct gender category. The CAB's 2014 Annex on Normalization mandated "access of women to eligible financing schemes, capacity building, institutional strengthening, impact programs to address imbalances in development and infrastructures, and economic facilitation for return to normal life".
147. Joint Communiqué between the United Nations Children's Fund (UNICEF) and the Moro Islamic Liberation Front (MILF) dated 14 April 2007. The document was signed by Dr Nicholas K. Alipui, then UNICEF country representative to the Philippines, and MILF chair Al-haj Murad Ebrahim,

based on discussions held on 12 February 2007 in Camp Darapanan, Sultan Kudarat, Maguindanao. See Salah Jubair, *The Long Road to Peace*, pp. 223–24.

148. One study noted that during conflict, men's mobility is restricted, whereas the opposite happens for women. To quote the study: "Men's mobility was frequently severely constrained by conflict, leading to feelings of frustration and marginalization, challenges to cultural definitions of masculinity, and long-term disadvantages, including curtailed education and less opportunity for formal employment or involvement in agricultural activities. For women, mobility is often increased, leading to enhanced opportunities for leadership, formal employment, and decision-making, but also greatly expanding the demands placed on women's time and safety." Dwyer and Cagoco-Guiam, *Gender and Conflict*, p. 9.

149. Ibid. pp. 21–23.

150. Hall and Hoare observed: "The MILF's adherence to conservative Islamic tenets that anchor the role of women in the home, and that see women's involvement in livelihood and community activities as secondary and supportive to men, does not reject the gains already made but affords more policy preference toward projects that do not contradict these tenets" ("Philippines", p. 104).

151. For example, the executive director of the United Youth of the Philippines-Women segment, Noraida Abo, is the daughter of MILF vice-chair for political affairs Ghazali Jaafar. MILF Panel Secretariat head Malik 'Jun' Mantawil's daughter, Baileng Utto Mantawil, founded the Bangsamoro Free Elections Movement, which independently monitored the plebiscite for the Bangsamoro law in January and February 2019. Former MILF peace negotiator Datu Michael Mastura's daughter, Mariam, is a judge.

152. Dwyer and Cagoco-Guiam, *Gender and Conflict*, p. 9.

153. See McKenna, *Muslim Rulers and Rebels*, pp. 227–28.

154. Arquiza, "Knowledge and Power". She also cited Arquiza, Alojamiento and Enriquez, "Evolving a Development Framework for the Sama Dilaut" (unpublished manuscript dated 2002) as one source in this excerpt.

155. Ahmad Aijaz, "Class and Colony in Mindanao", in *Rebels, Warlords and Ulama: A Reader on Muslim Separatism and the War in Southern Philippines*, edited by Kristina Gaerlan and Mara Stankovitch (Quezon City: Institute of Popular Democracy, 2000), p. 9. Aijaz is a Pakistani professor based in the United States who conducted fieldwork in Mindanao in the 1980s.

156. Ibid., pp. 8–9.

157. Arquiza, "Knowledge and Power". She made the same point against the MNLF leadership despite their earlier secular-inspired stance against datuism and social inequity. This perspective does not accord with McKenna's

view of the 1980s sermons he heard in Campo Muslim, of which he said the *ulama* threatened the sanctified inequality in Muslim society by proclaiming political equality and economic justice as "essential aspects of Islam". Whatever the actual impact of the preaching of *ulama*, it is true that their increased societal presence has, as McKenna noted of the situation back in the 1980s, explicitly challenged the Islamic authority of the traditional nobility (McKenna, *Muslim Rulers and Rebels*, pp. 232–33). But based on Arquiza's critique, it seems that both maintain elite status, the end result of which is the status quo of social inequality.

158. Arquiza, "Knowledge and Power".

159. On the progenitor role of the MNLF, we are informed by this observation that "some movements function early in the cycle as progenitor of master frames that provide the ideational and interpretative anchoring for subsequent movements later on in the cycle." David A. Snow, E. Burke Rochford, Jr., Steven K. Worden, and Robert D. Benford, "Frame Alignment Processes, Micromobilization, and Movement Participation", *American Sociological Review* 51 (August 1986): 477.

160. Defined by Fairclough as "how constituent parts (episodes, sentences) are meaningfully related so that the text as a whole makes sense" (*Discourse and Social Change*, p. 83). Text, in this sentence, is taken to mean the total discourse rather than any specific text.

161. Fairclough defined ideology as "significations/constructions of reality (the physical world, social relations, social identities) which are built into various dimensions of the forms/meanings of discursive practices, and which contribute to the production, reproduction or transformations of relations of domination" (*Discourse and Social Change*, p. 84). He emphasized that ideological processes appertain to discourses as whole social events between people, not just the texts (pp. 87–89).

162. In their accounts of the peace negotiations, the MILF divides the history of the talks into two phases: the domestic phase (1997–2001) and the international phase (2001–14), which began with the entry of Malaysia as facilitator of the talks.

163. Hashim, *The Bangsamoro Mujahid*, p. 6.

164. Ideological struggle, said Fairclough, is "a dimension of discursive practice to reshape such practices and ideologies built into them in the context of the restructuring or transformation of relations of domination (*Discourse and Social Change*, pp. 87–88).

5

Identity Ambivalence in the Pan-Cordillera Discourse

Three different nomenclatures have been used to refer to our unit of interest in this chapter. These are *Cordillera, Mountain Province* and *Igorot*. We have already used *Cordillera* to describe either the resistance movement and the resistance discourses or narratives. The term, moreover, is used to refer to the mountain range, the people inhabiting the territory, and the imagined nation. The term *Cordillera region* is likewise being used in different ways. It can refer to the state-defined administrative region, the unrealized autonomous region, or merely used as a spatial reference that vaguely encompasses a presumed territorial entity.

The geographic location of the Cordillera discourse is the Gran Cordillera Central mountain range in Northern Luzon. As we shall see, boundaries of this homeland, ancestral domains and/or the roots or origins of what we call today the Cordillera people(s) and Cordillera region have not been fixed but were rather porous. They have been constructed and reconstructed over time, both by state fiat and societal processes.

Then and now, the term *Igorot* is a highly contested term. Briefly, the term originated during the Spanish times. It was used by the Spaniards and the lowlanders as a collective, undifferentiated identity marker for most of the inhabitants of the Cordillera range.[1] Like the word *Moro*, *Ygorrotes/Igorots* (mountain people) came from outsiders, although the

151

American historian and long-time resident of Mountain Province William Henry Scott wrote that it was derived from local languages. *Igolot* in Tagalog means "dwellers in/people of a mountain chain". *Golod* or *golor* in Tagalog and *golot* in the language of the Bagos (descendants of Igorots who migrated to Ilocos) meant the mountain or a hill; and the prefix *i-* denotes place of origin.[2] Prill-Brett offers another possibility — that the name came from the Ilocano word *gerret*, which means "to cut off", and may have been inspired by the headhunting tradition among these mountain people.[3] The label, along with its negative and positive attributes, was carried on to the postcolonial period.

Mountain Province originally referred to the politico-administrative unit established by the American colonial regime in 1908. It was made up of seven sub-provinces; namely, Benguet, Ifugao, Bontoc, Apayao, Kalinga, Amburayan and Lepanto. In 1966 this unit gave birth to four provinces, including one that is also called Mountain Province. The other three were Benguet, Ifugao and Kalinga-Apayao.

Significantly, what is now the province of Abra was not included in the territorial scope of the original Mountain Province, nor did it figure in the 1966 administrative region. Since Spanish colonial rule, Abra had been governed as part of the Ilocos region. Bangued town, the capital of Abra, was founded as a mission town by the Spaniards in 1599. Colonial settlements were first established along the lower Abra river in the 1600s. Bangued and other areas close to the Ilocos provinces were Christianized and put under effective Spanish colonial control. On the other hand, the Spaniards were able to establish settlements in Benguet, Bontok, Tabuk, Tinglayan and Ifugao only in the 1800s. A 1731 reference indicated a customary distinction made by Spaniards and lowlanders between the *Tinguianes*, or the indigenous inhabitants of Abra, and the *Igorots*, the Spanish and lowlander term used to identify the other groups of people from the Cordillera mountain range.[4] The administrative and normative segregation created a measure of historical separation and differentiation in what were otherwise contiguous areas and intermingling cultures linked by rivers, valleys and mountains. Thus, in our historical rendering, when we refer to Igorot communities and the Cordillera region or mountain range during the Spanish colonial period, or to the Mountain Province created by the American regime, we have to bear in mind that Abra is not included, unless specified.

Abra's political and administrative affinity with the Cordillera provinces grew only during martial law. Ironically, this happened during a period, in 1973, when the Marcos martial law administration re-clustered the northern provinces of Luzon into two administrative regions: Region 1 (Benguet and Mountain Province with Abra, Pangasinan and the Ilocos provinces) and Region 2 (Kalinga-Apayao and Ifugao with Cagayan Valley, Isabela and Nueva Vizcaya). In 1988 the Aquino administration responded to the demands for regional autonomy and firmed up the official inclusion of Abra in the new Cordillera Administrative Region. The official Cordillera (administrative) region is now made up of the provinces of Benguet, Ifugao, Mountain Province, Apayao, Kalinga and Abra, and the chartered city of Baguio.

From *Igorot* to *Cordillera*

Scott found early references to Igorots in documents dated 1593 and 1594. The 1593 document reported on a Spanish expedition that began in Pampanga, passed through the Caraballo mountains (now known as Nueva Vizcaya) and traversed the Cagayan Valley all the way to Appari. The document noted sighting gold-mining *Ygolotes* in the mountains to the west.[5] Thus, *Igorot* may have preceded the Spaniards, who merely adopted the term used by indigenous lowlanders.

Interestingly, not one of the languages of the Cordillera provinces uses the word *golot* for mountain. The words for mountains are *filig/ bilig* in the Mountain Province and *biling* in Kalinga, *pugu* in Ifugao, *shontog/dontog* in Benguet.[6] *Ginolot* in Kankanaey means "native rice". In Kankanaey (or Lepanto), the word *golot* means native rice as opposed to the second crop called *topeng*. Also, the term was not used in myths and legends in these provinces, although the people there do use the prefix *i-* to indicate the place they came from.[7]

As colonization progressed, the term assumed negative connotations and was used interchangeably with *pagans*, *infidels*, *rebels*, and *bandits*. It differentiated those who had accepted incorporation into the Spanish regime. Thus, even Ilocanos from the neighbouring Ilocos region who rejected Spanish subjugation and escaped to the mountains were supposedly lumped under the term. Similar to the word *Moro*, the term *Igorot* perpetuated a negative and highly prejudiced image that was carried over to the postcolonial period. Many Filipino state leaders inherited the bias of the former colonizers. For instance, in his 1943 book *Mother America: A Living Story of Democracy*, former foreign secretary and World War II hero Carlos P. Romulo wrote that "the Igorot is not Filipino and we are not related.... These primitive black people are no more Filipino than the American Indian is representative of the United States citizen."[8]

Like the originally pejorative term *Moro*, the term *Igorot* was appropriated, turned upside down (from negative to positive) or inside out (from being an out-group reference to an in-group self-identification), and adopted with pride by the emerging ethnonationalists during the American colonial period. By the 1930s, a province-wide pan-ethnic consciousness had already manifested. A 1933 slogan demanded "Mountain Province for the Igorots!"[9]

The 1930s insider-identity entrepreneurs used two tracks in transforming *Igorot* into a positive group-identification. On the one hand, they fought for respect for and the preservation of their indigenous cultures. On the other, they demanded to be recognized as 'also Filipinos' by becoming 'more Filipino', such as converting to Christianity; going to schools in urban centres, where they interacted with lowlanders; 'modernizing' in their way of life and beliefs; and entering the bureaucracy and other state institutions, thereby earning their place as co-equals among the majority Filipinos. Thus, their articulations disdained the 'backwardness' of the state of their communities, and this backwardness was used as an argument to demand greater budgetary support from the state.

This approach is best manifested in the 1931 maiden speech of Dr Hilary Clapp, Mountain Province Representative to the National Assembly. In one part of the speech he pursued the 'Igorot are Filipinos' line: "The people I represent want to feel that they constitute a part of the Filipino nation instead of a distinct, isolated tribe. Despite their differences in customs, habits and religion they are conscious of the fact that they belong to one country."[10] In another part the pitch was made for more government support to elevate them from their inferior status. Thus, Clapp appealed "for help to give these poor backward Igorots more chance and encouragement so they can build better houses in place of their tiny huts and mud-holes; to enable them to procure more food to eat instead of *camotes* [sweet potatoes] only most of the year round, and so they can discard their traditional G-string and put on some clean clothes."[11]

Ambivalence with regard to their own cultures vis-à-vis the dominant Filipino culture has characterized the process of building group consciousness. This is further reflected in the saga of one prominent identity symbol, the G-string worn by males. Trousers, prescribed for the males who entered the Trinidad Farm School built by the Americans in 1916, soon became the new status symbol to the extent that when the school authorities requested a group of males to wear the G-string before a group of visitors, they rejected the imposition. This 1927 incident sparked a mini-revolt on the campus.[12]

Subsequently, the identity entrepreneurs imbued their native identity with pride. Some Igorot leaders would return to the G-string as a proud statement of identity. In 1964, Representative Lam-en attended the Northern Luzon fair held in Vigan, Ilocos Norte proudly wearing a G-string.[13] Of more recent vintage are mayors and House Representatives who showed up at the Baguio City Hall and in Congress in the wrap-around loincloth.[14] Despite the negative association of Igorots with fierceness and headhunting practices, the image of the head axe and shield to symbolize bravery and capacity to fight was used in a placard during a rally in Baguio in 1988.[15] Another placard read, "Mayor, we don't glorify war, but don't belittle our resolve to fight.[16]

Another telling event was the opposition raised by natives to House Bill 1441 filed by former House Representative Luis Hora of the third district of the old Mountain Province in 1958. The well-meaning bill sought to ban the use of *Moro* and *Igorot* because of the biases that have been built into the terms. The ill-fated bill proposed the use of *Muslim* and *Highlander* instead. In response an editorial of a Baguio newspaper argued: "If the measure is enacted into law, it will mean that the people of the province are ashamed to be called Igorots ... and that they are willing to turn their backs on their cultural heritage that is distinctly Igorot, superior in many of its aspects to that of other ethnic groups in the country."[17]

Other narratives emphasizing the Igorot's heroism (for example, during World War II) or academic competitiveness (because of the widespread use of good spoken English in urbanized centres in the region, good performance in state examinations, and entry into top educational institutions like state universities and the Philippine Military

Academy) produced positive images of the Igorot and supported affirmative Igorot identification.

The nationalist student movement that grew beginning in the 1950s supported the 'distinct but also Filipino' track. From joining Independence Day parades in order to advance recognition of 'Igorot heroes' who contributed to the fight against Western/Japanese colonialism, a segment of the Igorot youth took on more political causes and assumed an oppositional stance to the government. For example, their youth organizations in Manila and Baguio City condemned the suspension of the writ of habeas corpus in August 1971 by then Philippine president Ferdinand Marcos. Many were also drawn into libertarian, socialist and Marxist groupings, notably the Kabataan Makabayan led by the founding chair of the Communist Party of the Philippines, Jose Ma. Sison.

Interestingly, while the signifiers *Igorot* and *Kaigorotan* (a term that transposes the diverse Igorot ethnics into a singular people or collectivity) gained more positive connotations through the anti-discrimination efforts of Igorots themselves, politicized youthful Igorot groupings would experiment with alternative nomenclatures based on places/provinces. Others chose the more generic and neutral term, *Highlanders*.

A prominent place-name is *BIBAK*, which stands for their places of origin, the sub-provinces that made up Mountain Province until 1966. These are Benguet, Ifugao, Bontoc, Apayao and Kalinga. The BIBAK was formed in 1950 by some sixty highlander students attending the Baguio Colleges in order to unify "the different tribes in the Mountain Province".[18] The acronym BIBAK may have been inspired by the earlier BIBKA Association. Created in January 1941 and standing for the same sub-provinces, BIBKA came into the limelight for writing a letter to Commonwealth president Manuel Quezon that argued the natives' capability to serve as governors of their own provinces and in other provincial posts.[19] It may be said that both BIBKA and BIBAK were committed to building the unity of the people/tribes in the sub-provinces and promoting their political rights and general welfare. However, the BIBKA was born when the postcolonial political institutions were being transferred from the Americans to the Filipinos and the natives wanted to secure their places in these institutions. The BIBAK was the next generation's more confrontational response to continuing discrimination, and later to the growing political crisis in the country resulting from corrupt and tyrannical governance.

Both the BIBKA and the BIBAK were said to be basically assimilationist. However, the BIBKA represented the post-war, educated generation of the 1950s, who were "at one and the same time more highly ethnic and assimilationist in outlook".[20] Thus it was observed that the BIBKA avoided using the word *Igorot* in its documents and stuck to *natives* as a self-reference.[21] BIBAK, on the other hand, protested the negative representation of the Igorot in Romulo's 1943 book *Mother America*. Concerned by the possible loss of their own culture and the uncritical adoption of modern ways, the BIBAK played a leading role in what the *Baguio Midland Courier* referred to as "Igorot culture meetings". To promote their culture, members performed native dances in the annual state-sponsored festivities and cultural contests in the 1960s.[22]

The BIBAK Association was described as an "organization of Igorot students in Baguio City and its suburbs".[23] It drew its original base from the Baguio-Mountain Province Native Students' Association, and continued to grow in influence through members who secured the leadership in student governments in Baguio City's colleges.[24] It reflected youthful unity and reconciled equally significant prior and perhaps more intimate sub-Igorot identities. Conveniently, it adopted the existing politico-administrative divisions of the state, although these divisions may not accurately reflect actual ethnolinguistic boundaries.[25] In any case, it was a continuation of the traditional practice of being identified by place of origin, although traditionally that place was the *ili*, or village, rather than the bigger political/administrative units.

As student activism in Manila assumed a more radical posture against the Marcos presidency, *highlander* was privileged by the educated class, and later by the politicized youthful natives studying in Metro Manila. According to Finin, the term "was popularized during the American regime, along with natives, mountaineer, and non-Christian — terms that distinguished them from the generic Filipino, lowlander, and Christian, which was how the dominant cultural majorities were generally called and described. Educated Cordillera natives evidently preferred highlander and mountaineer, based on how they adopted it as self-reference in speeches, editorials and so on. They used it to distinguish themselves from the Ilocanos and other lowlanders who were recruited into the growing bureaucracy, and into the mining corporations by the Americans."[26]

In 1969 a loose Manila-based student organization of youth from the region chose the name Highlander Activists (HiAct). In October 1971 the

Alliance of Highlander Students, an organization of native students led by student leaders attending the Episcopal Trinity College in Quezon City, took to the streets to contradict the statement of the Mountain Province vice-governor that the province supported the suspension of the privilege of the writ of habeas corpus. In their statement they localized the impact of the suspension on the region. They demanded respect for civil liberties and asked that "Igorot students, unite!" Later, these activists reorganized into the Kilusang Kabataan ng Kabundukan (KKK, Mountain Youth Movement). The choice of KKK — which is the acronym of the revolutionary organization founded by the Tagalog Andres Bonifacio (Kataastaasan, Kagalanggalangang Katipunan, or Highest and Most Respectable Association) to fight Spanish rule — showed that by this time they were framing their opposition within the broader national political struggle against the looming dictatorship, even as they were giving it a distinct, ethnic or local flavour, as encapsulated in the Tagalog word *kabundukan*, which means mountain range.

The KKK soon after became the Kilusan ng Kabataan ng Kordileyra (Movement of the Cordillera Youth) — the first activist organization that used the *Cordillera* geographic reference, albeit spelled phonetically or transliterated in the Tagalog language. Indeed, one of its founders claimed the honour for the new KKK as "the militant Igorot student's movement which popularized the word Cordillera".[27] The organization used the house of historian William Henry Scott at St. Andrew's Seminary in Quezon City as its headquarters. In December 1971 it held the First Cordillera Congress for National Liberation in Bontoc. There, Scott presented the paper "The Creation of a National Minority", which traced the discrimination and historical differentiation of the highlanders. According to Victoria Tauli-Corpuz, who became a prominent, global indigenous people's rights activist, the basic framework of regional autonomy was already defined in this congress, including the notion of self-determination and the need for the delineation of ancestral territories.[28]

Organizing around the Cordillera Master Frame

So we find that by the 1970s the notion of a supra-tribal Igorot or Cordillera-wide collectivity was tapped as an organizing and mobilizing frame for radical political activism. The writings of Scott were apparently a major influence in popularizing the more inclusive term, *Cordillera*. Looking back, some thirty years later, the Cordillera Peoples Alliance (CPA) wrote: "The term 'Cordillera' which government identified with the progressive writings of Dr William Henry Scott and which were considered subversive, eventually became acceptable and were popularized."[29]

However, rather than being considered as a different category, for the most part *Cordillera* continued to be conflated or to be interchanged with *Igorot*. This can be gleaned in Tauli-Corpuz's account of the 1971 event: "In this Congress, we re-read our history, discussed our present situation as Igorots.... we already identified that Igorots who were then considered cultural minorities, are suffering from multiple burdens and levels of oppression."[30] Evidently, it was only in the 1980s, when resistance to the dam and Cellophil projects ballooned and reached as far as Kalinga and Abra, that the geographic mountain range reference *Cordillera* assumed pre-eminence in the framing of the collective resistance. As such, the Cordillera People's Democratic Front (CPDF) became the chosen name for the front that aimed to unite and broaden the resistance. Also, since 1981, Cordillera Day has been marked on 24 April to commemorate the murder of tribal leader Macli-ing Dulag in 1980. When the CPP forces split into two in 1986, the breakaway force likewise privileged Cordillera by adopting the name Cordillera People's Liberation Army (CPLA).[31]

We can surmise that one consideration for privileging *Cordillera* over *Igorot* was the inherent problem associated with the 'Igorot' and 'Kaigorotan' frame. For one, natives remained ambivalent toward the label. Second, and more importantly, it was a self-identification not shared by other tribes in the mountain range. Even now, the Ifugaos do not generally refer to themselves as Igorot. "[T]hey do not want to be called Igorots; they simply want to be called Ifugaos", wrote the Cordillera Schools Group.[32] Even among the southern Cordillera tribes there remained ambivalence towards the *Igorot* label, given the historical baggage associated with it. As such, it could not be the unifying term to encompass the social movement that grew beyond the core 'Igorot' provinces and Baguio City.

Notably, the Americans restricted the use of the label *Igorot* to the inhabitants in the southern Cordillera, which they also considered the more civilized culture group compared to those in the east, such as the Kalinga and the Apayao/Isneg.[33] These southern Cordillera tribes include the Bontoc, Kankanaey, Ibaloy and Aplay. Through anthropological studies that they financed, the colonial regime more systematically studied and adopted their policies to the fact of a multiplicity of tribes. They more consciously confined the use of *Igorot* to certain tribes only, although not without difficulty or confusion. As early as 1899, the Philippine Commission member and zoologist Dean C. Worcester noted how loosely the word *Igorot* was being applied. He wrote:

> The word 'Igorrote' which was originally the name of a single tribe, was extended to include all the headhunting peoples of Luzon, and later became synonymous with wild, so that when one speaks of Igorrotes at the present day, he refers to a number of fierce hill-tribes, which differ more or less inter se.[34]

After more fieldwork, in 1906, Worcester wrote more definitively, but not without the orientalism of the times:

> Any classification which unites strikingly different peoples as the peaceable, industrious and highly civilized Tinguians of Abra, the long-haired, warlike headhunting peoples of Banaue, Silipao and Mayaoyao, and the fierce and wild Kalingas in one 'ethnological group' seems to be fundamentally wrong.[35]

Similarly, T.W. Thomson, acting division superintendent of schools for Nueva Ecija, wrote, with special reference to the Tingguians:

> They are generally known by the name Igorrote, among the Americans and Filipinos, but among the better informed natives and among the Spanish they are called 'Tinguianes'. The word 'Bago' ['new'] is also applied to them by the Tagalogs and Ilokanos, to indicate that they are *new* Christians. Among themselves and among the Igorrotes proper, they are known as Itnegs.[36]

However, American period categories were also faulty in treating *Igorot* as referring to a tribe rather than as a supra-tribal appellate used to refer to and accepted by those who trace their origins to the Mountain Province and Benguet. But American writings did distinguish among these Igorots based on place — thus their sub-classifications like *Lepanto-Benguet* and *Bontoc Igorots*.[37] Today, *Igorot* is not used as a census category.

Up until now, this limited self-identification with the term by the tribes in the southwestern Cordillera and the non-identification among the Ifugao, Tingguian, Kalinga and Apayao appears to be the case. According to Aydinan, those who are generally called Igorots are the Benguet-Kankanaey, Ibalaoi, Bontoc and Balangaw from the eastern provinces.[38] However, many lowlanders continue to use *Igorot* as a generic term for the mountain tribes from this region/mountain range. Many even up to now may not even know the names of the different tribes due to ignorance and historical biases carried over from Spanish times.

A March 2000 informal survey conducted during an athletic meet attended by delegates from the Cordillera Administrative Region found that the Kalinga and Ifugao do not accept the label *Igorot* and that they prefer to be identified based on place/origin.[39] Those from the Mountain Province referred to themselves both as *Igorot* and based on their place/origin (*i-Besao*, *i-Natonin*, which are sub-provincial units). Curiously, many in Benguet felt strongly against the label — this, as the author noted, despite the fact they were probably the first to have been called *taga-golot o i-golot* because of their miners/traders from Tuba who traded gold with lowlanders using their own weighing system, even during pre-colonial times.[40]

Given the historical baggage and limiting frame of the term *Igorot*, *Cordillera* thus provided a more inclusive frame to pull together the different tribes in the mountain range who became part of the resistance to the Marcos dictatorship and who subsequently articulated their goals along the lines of an autonomy movement. *Cordillera* is "used to define our ancestral domain and also because there were those among us who did not like to be called Igorots" was how the eminent movement entrepreneur Tauli-Corpuz expressed this shift before members of the Igorot Global Association.[41]

In appropriating or keeping the name *Cordillera*, campaign groups claimed or aimed to represent and promote the perspectives of the Cordillera by Cordillerans. In the process, they generated affinity to a regional identity, a pan-ness or unity as a geographic-political bloc, of which the desired political expression is in the form of an autonomous region. The national democratic groups like the CPA were among the most vocal, politicized articulators of 'we, the Cordillera'. Its self-written twenty-five-year history of campaigns begins with this claim: "Since it was established in June 1984, [the] CPA has always been in the forefront of the Cordillera people's protests and struggles on major and continuing issues that affected the people of the region."

"Banbantay Cordillera" (Mountains of the Cordillera) is a song composed by the Dapayan ti Kordillera. Civil society groups had names like the Pan-Cordillera Women's Network for Peace and Development. The Cordillera People's Forum was formed to join the ranks of the CPA.

The frontloading of *Cordillera* as the resistance identity in this geographic space was not a complete shift, however. *Igorot* persisted as a self-reference, politically and culturally, and also because the identity entrepreneurs themselves perhaps unconsciously conflated the two categories and uncritically used *Igorot* and *Cordillera* interchangeably. In protest actions staged in Baguio City, where those associated with the *Igorot* appellate remain dominant, the term had resonance both as a cultural and political identity label. For example, in September 1988 an anti-Igorot remark about a 'lowlander' mayor engendered the writing of an "Igorot Manifesto" proclaiming the Igorots as a people who believe in peaceful coexistence with other people, and prompting shouts of "Kaigorotan lumaban" (Igorot people, fight) and "Mabuhay ang Kaigorotan" (Long live Igorothood) during the rally.[42] Also, those who self-identify as Igorot, including the diaspora community such as those organized under the Igorot Global Organization (IGO),[43] continue to engage in cultural self-reproduction. Children wear t-shirts emblazoned with "Igorotak" (I am Igorot), followed by a dictionary-like entry that says: "n.Bibakese* — a statement asserting ethnic identity".[44]

In picking up the 'Cordillera people' frame, the national democratic movement led by the CPP's New People's Army (NPA) and their allied organizations became the primary agents of this emergent pan-Cordillera identity-building project, even though early movement entrepreneurs from among the natives may have begun their political consciousness with *Igorot* as the enlightened self-identity. This much we can glean from Abrino Aydinan, an Ifugao native — an ethnic group that generally did not particularly identify with *Igorot*. "Dahil sa mulat" (because of social consciousness), Aydinan considered himself an Igorot. "Ako galing ako sa NPA (New People's Army), [kung saan] basta taga-Cordillera ay Igorot. Ganun yung hubog ko, kaya okay lang sa akin ang [Igorot]."[45]

On this issue, Aydinan recounted that it was debated within the CPP-NPA operating in Northern Luzon whether to adopt *Igorot* or *Cordillera*. Ironically, most of those from the Lumbaya Company, although most were from Kalinga, preferred *Igorot*. But Conrado Balweg, a Tingguian from Abra, was vocal about his preference for *Cordillera*. He reportedly went public with the CPLA as the name of the splinter organization and de facto settled the debate. Aydinan claims that the CPDF likewise stuck to *Cordillera* to more effectively counter the CPLA threat,[46] although, interestingly, at this time the CPP-NPA was still ambivalent about either *Cordillera* or *Igorot*.

After 1986 the state likewise picked up the new *Cordillera* discourse and constitutionalized the creation of an autonomous region that was referenced to it. The state reorganized administrative boundaries accordingly. As such, it too entered the terrain of regional identity construction. We may say in fact that there has been a bureaucratization, albeit one that lacks cohesion, of the Cordillera identity project.

Nonetheless, it is evident that the cultural and political content of the Cordillera region/people frame remained contested. The failure to institute an autonomous regional government reflects this contestation. According to Hilhorst, *Cordillera* remains a movement (political) identity that has not yet matured as a regional or indigenous (cultural) identity. She wrote:

> However, what happened in the regional movement in the Cordillera … cannot be explained as the maturation of a regional or indigenous identity. The regional identity became the most visible for some time, but was always contested by others. Moreover, it was also clear that many people who formed part of the movement had no indigenous identity at all. The movement attracted many followers, varying from national politicians, a range of anti-dictatorship activists, an organization for national liberation, to international advocates. What these people shared was not an indigenous identity, but rather a sense of identification with the movement.… I think it is more appropriate to speak of a process of identification rather than a collective identity, in reference to an issue or movement.[47]

Who are the Cordillera Peoples?

Who are the Cordillera peoples for whom the armed resistance was fought? What makes them a people, or peoples (a term that has gained greater currency as, paradoxically, it is deemed to highlight the distinctiveness of each grouping and in so doing offers a more inclusive orientation)? To reflect on this question, we will use as reference the CPDF's 1986 General Program and the 1986 CPLA position paper.

For the CPDF, the Cordillera people are "first and foremost Filipinos". As Filipinos they share similar characteristics: they belong to and are made up of the same democratic classes; namely, the workers, peasants, the petty bourgeoisie, women, youth and others who are exploited and oppressed. Thus they retain the essential class-divided characteristics of the Filipino nation, as typologized by the CPP-NDF-NPA. Among the indigenous are the rich peasants "who shall be allowed to retain their standard of living and shall be encouraged to utilize their surplus capital" for their economic improvement should the revolution be won. However, these rich peasants will have to decrease their reliance on hired labour. Confiscated land, vegetable farms and other agribusiness enterprises shall be subjected to distribution.[48]

Nonetheless, the document differentiated the inhabitants into two groupings: the minorities or indigenous, and the non-minorities. It noted that the peoples of the Cordilleras are "primarily indigenous peoples". From the alternating speaking voice in the CPDF document, we can surmise that, for the CPDF, legitimate Cordillera inhabitants include outsiders who fought for the Cordillera and non-native settlers present in significant numbers in Baguio City. While distinguishable from the natives, these "[n]on-minorities residing in the Cordillera who form a significant part of the city, municipal and provincial population, shall be represented adequately and accordingly in all government levels in the region. Their rights and privileges as citizens of the Republic shall be assured."[49]

The CPDF document also took note of a "Cordillera Minority diaspora" or those who have emigrated to other parts of the Cordillera or outside of the region.[50] But in elaborating its programme it had more to say about the "families of revolutionary martyrs and those who have rendered service to the revolution", the "capitalist farm-owners who have supported the revolution", and the supportive rich peasants, enlightened landlords and merchants.[51] The martyr-families shall be given priority to ownership of redistributed lands, while the others will be given opportunity to work closely with the state in raising and modernizing agricultural production and trade.

On the whole, the CPDF programme referred minimally to and only indirectly discussed other social divisions such as tribes, clans and different ethnic groups, evidently concerned that these social categories were divisive to the national democratic cause. Its solution to this danger is to foster equality among the tribes and clans in the future autonomous region. It pledged to eliminate all sources of conflict between these social units.[52] It may be said that the CPDF's perspective was akin to the modernization theory, which assumed that social and economic progression would eventually weaken traditional ties.

In sharp contrast, the CPLA framed the 'Cordillera Nation' in terms of ethnicity-based constituents. The "language groups and tribes composing the Cordillera Nation in their existing homelands in the Gran Cordillera Central and contiguous areas" include the:

- Tingguian, Kalinga and Bago groups
- Isnegs
- Malawegs
- Agtas-pugots
- Kankanaeys
- Ibalois
- Ipugaws-Itaulis
- Gaddangs
- Isinays
- Kalaguyyas-Ikadazans
- Karaws
- Balangaos
- Bontocs
- Katagoans
- Mandek-eys[53]

In addition, there are "similar tribal peoples in Northern Luzon that properly belong to the Cordillera Nation", such as the:

- Ilongot-Bugkalot peoples of the Caraballo mountain range
- Itaois and Dumagats of the Sierra Madre mountains

Among these groups, the Agtas-Pugots and Dumagats were recognized as the most marginalized.[54]

This listing is fairly consistent with anthropological data on the peoples of the Cordilleras.[55] The Cordillera Studies Group's more recent ethnographic listing collated by a group of social scientists overlaps considerably with the CPLA-CBA-MNS (Cordillera Bodong Administration; Montañosa National Solidarity) list. Shared by the two lists are the Kankanaey, Bontok, Balangao, Gaddang, Kalinga, Ibaloy, Bago, Ifugao, Isneg, Itneg/Tingguian, Kalanguya (spelled differently and hyphenated with the Ikadazan in the CPLA-CBA-MNS list). Not specified by the CPLA-CBA-MNS were the Masadiit and Maeng[56] and various other subgroups. Listed by the CPLA but not found in the Ethnographic Table are the Katagoan,[57] Karaws,[58] Agtas-Pugot, Malaweg,[59] and, understandably, the Ilongot-Bugkalot in the Caraballo mountain range, which lies at the foot of Nueva Vizcaya province, and the Itawis and Dumagat in the Sierra Madre mountains.

The irredentist accounting of the CPLA — notably its inclusion of Negrito subgroups (Agta, Dumagat) — is substantiated in earlier anthropological tracts as well as in more recent linguistic studies. For example, the 1906 article by Worcester published in the *Philippine Journal of Science* listed the Negritos among the seven tribes in Northern Luzon as:

1. Negritos
2. Ilongots (Ibalois)
3. Kalingas
4. Ifugaos
5. Bontoc Igorots
6. Lepanto-Benguet Iforots
7. Tingguians

Noticeably, Worcestor interchanged the Ilongots with the Ibalois.

Based on earlier fieldwork conducted in the early 1900s, anthropologist Faye Cooper Cole listed the Negritos among the tribes he found in the northwerstern region of Luzon:

1. Negritos — the Aetas, Agtas and Adangs;
2. Igorots (Igorottes);

3. Tingguans (Tinguianes, Tinggians, Tingians, Itneg, Burics) and Apayaos (Ishneg, Kalanasan);
4. Kalingas-Dadayag, Banaos [mixed with Igorots and Tinggian], Nagbayuganes, Guinaanes, Calauas.[60]

Negritos are hardly found now in the region. Cole's 1909 study noted that while previously present in the entire northwest of Luzon, he saw only a small band of Negritos along the southern border of Ilocos Sur and Abra; another band in the mountains south of Bangui in Ilocos Norte; considerable numbers along the Abulug river and its tributary, Rio Dommital, and also bordering the Pamplona river, and southwest of Mt. Tauit-Purak.[61] For this reason, except for the CPLA intellectuals, none of the twentieth century identity entrepreneurs articulated, much less conceived of, the Negritos as in any way part of the Cordillera identity.

Linguistic evidence nonetheless suggests that the Negritos were the original inhabitants of the region until migration from Taiwan 4,500 years ago introduced a new genetic pool, which later differentiated to form two major language groups, with one set spoken by those who settled in south-central Cordillera, the other in northern Cordillera.[62] Based on this data, those who now claim to be the indigenous peoples in the Cordillera were indigenous only up to 4,500 years ago. Moreover, their ancestors supposedly came from Taiwan. The presence of the Negritos has been dated to 50,000 years earlier, and they may have been pushed out of the region by the influx of migrants from the island of Taiwan. Thus, according to Reid, "Your [the Cordilleran peoples] ancestors were the first colonizers"![63]

The CPLA-CBA-MNS tried to reinstate the links to the Negritos, the most marginalized and dispersed grouping in the Philippine archipelago. However, the CPLA's organic intellectuals like Aydinan do not necessarily find the Taiwanese connection acceptable, nor do they concede having been preceded by the Negritos. He argued that the bows and arrows of the Agta are technologically superior to the spears of the Cordilleran tribes, who never practised archery. Thus, according to Aydinan, the Cordilleran IPs may have preceded the Agta. Moreover, the Agta are seafarers, which made it possible for them to move to other locations across the seas. On the other hand, he claimed, there is no tradition of seafaring among the Cordillera ethnic groups. He acknowledged similarities between the Ifugao and Ivatan[64] languages and that of the indigenous peoples of Taiwan, as well as similarity in the practice of building rice terraces to those of the tribal cultures in China. But Aydinan claimed that Ifugao oral literature — which traces tribal genealogy before the great flood — has no reference to crossing large bodies of water.[65] Thus, for him, the Ifugao people, who supposedly built the cultural centre of ancient Cordillera, have been there all along. But, as more recent anthropological findings suggest, even the grand Ifugao rice terraces may not be 2,000–3,000 years old, as earlier anthropological studies had dated them. Rather, more recent studies have found that intensified terraced wet-rice cultivation took place between AD 1600 and 1800, at the onset of and during the Spanish colonial regime in response to settlement shifts and the demands of more densely populated villages.[66]

The CPLA-CBA-MNS's Cordillera peoples also included tribes like the Ilongot-Bugkalot[67] and the Itawis[68] in the neighbouring Caraballo and Sierra Madre mountain ranges. These places had received Cordillera migrants or 'spillovers' in the course of time.

In all, the CPLA list can be considered very inclusive and ambitious in the incorporation of Negritos and tribes in neighbouring provinces that lie at the foot of other mountain ranges. Looking back, the choice of *Cordillera* has enabled this casting of a wider net than would have been possible under the earlier identity marker *Igorot* or the coined movement identity construct *Kaigorotan*. Notably, the word *Igorot* was not used in the CPLA-CBA-MNS document.

The Cordillera Bodong

As a counterpart to *Bangsa Moro* (Moro Nation) as the unifying identity, the choice of name by the CPLA for its nation is *bodong* — thus the Cordillera Bodong is the Cordillera Nation.

To the CPLA, the shared pan-Cordillera characteristics that constitute the identity of this Cordillera Bodong are communal stewardship and utilization of land, in contrast to the private proprietorship that defines lowland land relations; the practice of direct democracy through the village assemblies and council of elders; and the *bodong* (peace pacts among tribes) system as a 'supra-tribal expression' of the spirit of social cooperation.[69] Moreover, it characterized these features as 'socialistic'. This socialist way of life and moral order is supposedly indigenous to the peoples. Consequently, it demanded "respect [for] the integrity of the Cordillera national community" and that "the socialist way of life and moral order indigenous to its homelands" be allowed to develop.

This distillation of the essence of the Cordillera has been met with trepidation, including among those sympathetic to the cause of regional autonomy. It is argued that Cordillera natives' identity is rooted in their villages, with customs, beliefs and practices that differ from one village/tribe to another, rather than anything that is pan-regional. Anthropologists have pointed to the differences across the ethnolinguistic groups inhabiting the mountain ranges, from variations in house building techniques, house styles and spatial arrangement of villages to the design of tools and baskets, languages and epics (the *Ullalim* of Kalinga, the *Hudhud* and *Alim* of Ifugao). Mummification is found particularly among the Ibaloy of Kabayan but not among other groups, and the *ato/ator/dap-ay* institution is absent among the Kalinga, Ifugao, southern Kankanaey and Ibaloy.[70] Land-ownership patterns exhibit a mixture of private, clan, communal and other forms.

Reacting to the regionalized framing of the *bodong*, William Henry Scott cautioned against myth-making, or the romanticizing of a pan-Cordillera monolithic culture or a unifying form of government under a peace pact system, since these are not based on historical or ethnographic fact.[71] And yet it is this extension of a tribal practice of peace pacts into a pan-tribal identity and its transposition into the concept of a 'nation' that makes the CPLA document much more creative and rooted than the class-based orthodoxy of the CPDF document. In terms of the contest over framing between the two armed movements, the frontloading of the derivative of a 'nation' by the CPLA was likewise a direct challenge to the CPDF's national, Filipino-led revolution.

Why was the Kalinga *bodong* privileged among other traditional institutions? As already noted, the socio-political institution that is the peace pact is called *budong/badong* among the Kalinga, *pechen* among the Bontok, and *kalon* among the Tingguian. Also, peace pacts were traditionally bilateral in nature, between two tribes represented by their elders, and not multilateral or across several tribes. Contrary to claims that the making of peace pacts is found only among the above cultural groups, Aydinan argued that traditionally it was practised by all tribes but that it disappeared among other tribes during the American colonial regime.[72] Kalinga *bodong* holder Andres Ngao-i explained that *pechen* is one and the same word as *bodong*, except for the difference in the way sounds are pronounced by the Bontok and Tingguian.[73]

The proposed multilateral *bodong* is admittedly "a modernized version" of the *bodong*, but it is drawn from the same elements as the traditional practice. "The bodong is like the government structure. It has executive, judiciary and legislative functions. The bodong holders are like the executive branch. They implement the agreement.... In the bodong, we recognize respective claims to territory. There are prohibitions to kill, steal, and penal provisions.... The bodong is a small structure of government. So we also want the Cordillera to be something like that, an autonomous government."[74]

Of course, the privileging of the *bodong* was not an idea that sprouted from sheer imagination. Rather, it was a product of the process that saw inter-tribal unity forged in the course of the resistance, first against the Chico River Dam project and the Cellophil Resources timber plantation and later against the dictatorship at large. Such struggles enhanced the "awareness of a common Cordillera national identity", which was consolidated into the "Cordillera nationalism" and expressed in the multilateral *bodong*.[75] For the CPLA, the bilateral *bodong* was a living tradition, and the newer, multilateral *bodong* as fact already existed. The first manifestations of this multilateralism was the Kalinga-Bontok Peace Pact Holders Association (KBPPHA), which was formed in March 1982 in Bugnay, Tinglayan Kalinga, hometown of the revered tribal leader and peace pact holder Macli-ing Dulag. With the help of the CPP-NPA cadres operating in the region, the KBPPHA was expanded to include other provinces in the Cordillera. As we traced in the earlier chapter on Cordillera, its name was changed to the Cordillera Bodong Association (CBA) in a meeting on 23 January 1984, in Bontoc, Mountain Province. Later, when the CPLA split from the CPP-NPA, it took a chunk of the CBA membership, which it formed into the Cordillera Bodong Administration (then referred to as *CBAd*, but by the 2000s just *CBA*, since the CPP-NPA no longer organized along CBA lines).

Despite the asserted fact of the existence of a multilateral *bodong*, it took another imaginative turn on the part of the CPLA-CBA-MNS to transform what foremost was a traditional institution into the working concept for the future nation and (federal) state that was to be negotiated with the majoritarian Philippine republic. In doing so, it posed a challenge and a concrete alternative to the CPP-NPA's notion of alternative organs of state such as the people's revolutionary courts and people's councils, the lowest organs of the CPP's envisioned People's Democratic Republic.

Aydinan posited that the choice of the term *bodong* over the Bontok's *pechen* in the expanded association of peace pact holders was because the peace pact tradition is strongest in Kalinga. At the time of the interview in 2008, Ngao-i claimed that ninety per cent of tribes in Kalinga had a *bodong*.[76] Whether or not the basis for the transformed *bodong* and its valorization is myth-making or an evolved fact does not really matter. What made the Cordillera Bodong a novel idea is the frame it provided for a diverse but incorporated identity distinct from that of the Filipino majority.

However, the idea of the Cordillera Bodong, despite its novelty, seems to have fizzled along with the dissipation of the CPLA, indicating that, aside from the fact that the project was marred by the divisions among the progressive forces advancing Cordillera autonomy, it did not capture the imagination of the opinion- and decision-makers in the Cordillera, nor that of society at large.

Reclaiming Territory: Region and Homeland

What constitutes the envisioned Cordillera political entity? For the CPDF's autonomous region it was a matter of incorporating the six existing provinces (as delineated by their current territorial boundaries) that had converged under the Cordillera frame of resistance against the Marcos regime. These six provinces are the same ones that constitute the BIBAK cluster plus Abra; a grouping that gave rise to the newer acronym *BIBAKA* — for Benguet, Ifugao, Bontoc, Apayao, Kalinga and Abra.[77] The CPLA-CBA-MNS also adopted BIBAKA as the core of its proposed federal state. But consistent with its wider conception of who the Cordillera peoples are, it has extended its territorial claims to include outlying areas.

We will discuss the details of the CPLA-CBA-MNS 'homeland' claims later. But first let us examine the BIBAKA construct as the valorized claim of a spatial Cordillera.

As noted earlier, Abra's territorial inclusion was a product of the spatial and temporal proximity of the opposition to the Cellophil Resources and the Chico River Dam projects, and the conjoined resistance to these projects and the Marcos regime that grew under the leadership of the CPP-NPA and was transformed into a regional autonomy movement. President Corazon Aquino's administration, in response to the demands for regional autonomy, firmed up this inclusion by officially incorporating Abra in the new Cordillera Administrative Region (CAR).[78]

At the same time, Abra may be said to have merely rejoined the Cordillera, given the geographic and cultural ties that historically bound it to the rest of the Cordillera. The Americans kept the Spanish-designated Abra province separate from the original Mountain Province that it created in 1908 because of what they perceived as the Tingguian's more highly civilized culture. The Tingguians in the northern Cordillera were not included in this perception and were thus distinguished by the appellate *wild Tingguians* and put under the sub-province of Apayao. Since Abra was administered through Ilocos Sur, a governmental practice that continued up to the 1950s, the ties with the Ilocanos of the *educated Tingguians* in the lower areas grew (and vice versa) under colonialism. Meanwhile, the Tingguian villagers in the deep interior maintained their links with the nearby villages of Kalinga and Apayao.[79]

Anthropological and linguistic studies affirm an affinity or contiguity of the Tingguian in Abra and Ilocos with the (original) Cordillera (sans Abra) geographic and cultural region. Fieldwork in the early 1900s identified several mixed 'Tingguian-Igorot' municipalities and 'Igorot' and Kalinga settlements in Abra.[80] Among the Tingguians, segments moved to outlying areas. Tingguian settlements were found in Ilocos (although this may be a return, as it is possible they were there previously until they were pushed out), Mountain Province and Cagayan.[81]

Ilocano-Tingguian affinity is actually strong both ways. According to Cole, genealogical tables revealed that many of the leading Ilocano families of Bangued (the capital town of Abra) were only four or five generations removed from the Tingguian, and many of their customs and beliefs are almost identical with those of the Tingguian.[82] In this sense, the Ilocanos also enjoy cultural and linguistic affinity with the Cordillera through their strong Tingguian connection. Ilocano too has become the shared lingua franca in the Cordillera, having served historically as the language of trade between lowlanders and highlanders. However, despite the cultural affinity, the CPLA does not consider the Ilocanos as indigenous, probably because they have their own territory in the Ilocos region, have adapted more to the dominant Filipino culture, and were not geographically part of the Cordillera resistance movement that developed in the 1970s–80s. The Ilocanos are generally perceived to belong to the majority culture (the late president Ferdinand Marcos was an Ilocano), whereas the Tingguians are not.

This historical and cultural affinity of Abra to the Cordillera was restored by the contemporary movement history. As the Cordillera Peoples Alliance asserted: "Abra geographically and culturally belonged to the Cordillera".[83] Kalinga leader Andres Ngao-i similarly reasoned: "Abra is part of the Cordillera mountain range. The people in some of its municipalities are relatives of the Kalinga people. They are also from Kalinga. You see how they talk? The same. Mailed Molina [CPLA leader who was subsequently elected mayor in one town of Abra] and I understand each other [when we speak]. They are also Kalingan. Only politics divided us."[84]

Even then, Abra's historical affinity with the Cordillera and therefore its justifiable inclusion in a singular Cordillera region/nation/homeland and identity did not present itself as self-evident until the mid-1980s, when the question of autonomy was advanced in designing the post-Marcos polity and in peace negotiations between the government and the CPLA-CBA-MNS.

Interestingly, the Cordillera autonomy campaign was actually preceded by a 'regionalization' campaign mainly directed against the Marcos government's reshuffling of provinces. As noted earlier, during martial law the BIBAK provinces were put under two different regions. Benguet and Mountain Province were clustered with the Ilocos provinces to comprise Region 1 (Ilocos) along with Abra, while Kalinga-Apayao and Ifugao were grouped under Region 2 (Cagayan Valley) with the more developed provinces of Isabela and Cagayan. On being part of Region 2, the Kalingan Andres Ngao-i complained: "We were like second-class citizens."[85] The campaign of the politicians and activists then was for the restoration of the old BIBAK under one region.[86]

Thus, up to the 1980s the framing of the Cordillera region was still a contest between the old BIBAK spatial identity of the cultural-colonial period and the BIBAKA geographic identity of the 1970s political movement. But with movement entrepreneurs taking centre stage in negotiations with the new Philippine government in 1986, the BIBAKA territorial frame was sealed as pre-eminent, valorized in political activist discourse and institutionalized with the passage of laws and executive orders that created the Cordillera Administrative Region. The process could have paved the way finally for the Cordillera Autonomous Region made up of the BIBAKA provinces, thus consolidating the valorized spatial identity. However, as we know, this has not happened; to date, there is no such autonomous region, despite the imperative that has been mandated in the 1987 Constitution.

The CPLA's Original Expanded Claims

Historical and anthropological tracts show that the peoples in the Cordillera range were not isolated from the lowlands, and that within the territory, migration from one tribe to another tribal territory took place historically, as we have partly discussed in the previous section. A 1909 study concluded that intermarriages between tribes and tribal-migrant settlements in the other provinces also indicate that "these tribes flow into one another, so that sharp lines separating their habitats cannot be drawn".[87]

Trading activities flourished with the lower lying areas such as Ilocos, Cagayan, Nueva Viscaya and Isabela before and during Spanish colonial rule. Igorot communities were found settled in parts of these areas as well. In fact, in the eighteenth and nineteenth centuries the Igorots and the Christianized populations both claimed the foothills of Ilocos, Cagayan and Isabela as their traditional hunting grounds.[88] Many of these areas, including the Caraballo Sur mountains between Nueva Vizcaya and Nueva Ecija, were put under effective Spanish control much earlier. What distinguished the peoples in the Cordillera mountain range from the surrounding areas was the failure of the Spanish regime to penetrate and establish effective administrative control over their expansive territory. At best, by the late nineteenth century, the Spaniards were able to put in place dozens of military districts that were the objects of intermittent attacks by the indigenous population.[89]

Based on these historical tracts, one can claim that this cultural contiguity of what are now called the Cordillera tribes and languages extends to the Ilocos region, Nueva Viscaya and Cagayan — effectively a large chunk of Northern Luzon. Indeed, the CPLA tried to recover this scope with a more encompassing coverage of who constitutes the Cordillera peoples, and, by implication, a wider territorial scope for the envisioned autonomous/federal state. This marks a key difference with — and a further distancing from — the shared movement-based spatial and political identity of the CPP-NPA-CPDF in favour of a primordial, irredentist project to reclaim a cultural identity that is consistent with its ethnonationalist moorings.

The CPLA-CBA-MNS document did not however spell out the territories being claimed/reclaimed. Buendia tried to extrapolate the coverage based on the CPLA's listing of tribes and their location, as follows:

- the Kalanguya who traditionally lived in Ifugao and in four municipalities of Nueva Vizcaya, three barangays in one municipality of Nueva Ecija, and four sitios in a barangay in the municipality of San Nicolas, and another sitio in the municipality of Natividad, Pangasinan;
- the Kanakanaey and Maeng — who reside not only in Benguet and Abra but also in twelve municipalities of Ilocos Sur;
- the Yapayao, Pugit and Agta — whose abode stretches not only from Kalinga-Apayao to three municipalities of Bahayan and one municipality of Ilocos Norte;
- the Gran Cordillera Central language groups and tribes: Tinggian, Kalinga and Bago, Isneg, Malawegs, Agta-Pugots, Kanakanaeys, Ibalois, Ipugaw-Itualis, Gaddangs, Isinays, Kalanguya-Ikadazans, Kawar, Balangaos, Bonotks, Katagoans, Mandek-eys;
- the Ilongot-Bugkalot in the Caraballo mountain range;
- the Itawis and Dumagats in the Sierra Madre range; and
- other similar tribal people of Northern Luzon descent.[90]

Consequently, the proposed Cordillera Autonomous State under a federal system could possibly include the BIBAKA provinces and parts of Cagayan, Ilocos Norte, Ilocos Sur, Nueva Ecija, Nueva Vizcaya and Pangasinan.[91] According to Buendia, all of these should be included in the plebiscite for the Cordillera Autonomous Region in order to preserve "the integrity of [the] Cordillera national community".[92]

Aydinan and Ngao-i separately recounted that they had indeed held meetings with some of these tribal groups, such as the Kalanguya in Nueva Vizcaya, during the drafting of the CPLA-CBA-MNS document. The Kalanguya whom they talked to were reportedly interested in being part of an envisioned federal Cordillera territorial state. "They felt they were second-class citizens in their province.... They wanted to join even though we ourselves doubted the political viability. Maybe if they had arms, it would have been more possible", recalled Ngao-i.[93]

Aydinan explained the basis for the expanded claim thus: "The Bago can be found in 11 towns of Ilocos Norte. The Apayao spilled over to parts of Cagayan. The Ifguao ethnic groups — Tuwalie, Ayangan [and one more] — spilled over to Nueva Vizcaya. So the [Cordillera] land should be bigger. In our negotiations, the Cordillera as delineated now is supposed to be temporary but in our original demand, the other areas are included." Interestingly, Aydinan added not a cultural factor but a political movement factor to further buttress the claim of prior affinity. According to him, Ilocos and Pangasinan were the original areas of operation of the Lumbaya Company that split from the CPP-NPA; as such, they have extended their claim to the Caraballo Mountains. Nonetheless, he realizes the political difficulty of recovering parts of the other provinces where their cultural kin are located. In 1987 the CPLA-CBA-MNS effectively settled for a much smaller prospective coverage, the so-called BIBAKA, and even a lesser entity — an administrative region — in lieu of an autonomous government or a federal state.

The national democrats, for their part, acknowledge the same affinity. According to the Cordillera People's Alliance, "considerable portions of the populations of La Union and Nueva Vizcaya then consisted of mountain peoples".[94] But they did not complicate their right-to-autonomy claims by going beyond the already established political movement–conjured and administratively established BIBAKA provinces.

Nation, Homeland, Region or Ancestral Domain?

The term *homeland* was actually used only sparingly by the CPLA-CBA-MNS and never by the CPP-NPA-CPDF. Contemporary Cordillera resistance narratives do not prominently appropriate the concept of homeland. In the Cordillera discourse, therefore, nationhood, homeland or statehood claims are less developed compared to the Bangsamoro resistance discourse. This might be ironic because, despite the underdeveloped claims to an encompassing homeland, the natives have for the most part secured the majority of the Cordillera territory from settlers despite a century of colonial incursions and redrawing of administrative boundaries. In contrast, the former Moro provinces have been subdivided, with most areas demographically and politically taken over by non-Moro settlers, weakening the basis for any irredentist claim to a Bangsamoro homeland covering the whole of Mindanao, the Sulu island group and the southernmost parts of Palawan. On the other hand, one may say that the fact of severance or loss of the claimed Bangsamoro homeland had fed the fiercer attempt by the Moro nationaliststs to recover lost ground or to secure whatever is left.

In conducting this research, one question I wanted to answer was why a pan-Cordillera identity developed belatedly compared to that of the Bangsamoro, resulting in the relatively underdeveloped 'nation' and 'homeland' claims. My tentative answer rests on the pre-eminence of *ili* (village) autonomy as the basic socio-political principle on which the different tribes and villages established peaceful coexistence.

Traditionally, the *ili* was the highest political unit within the Cordillera tribal communities. In contrast, the Moros have their Islamic sultanates predating the existence of the Philippine republic. In the Cordillera, there was no bigger political unit that could claim 'statehood' or 'nationhood' over larger territories and ethnolinguistic groups prior to the creation of the Philippine state. Thus, there was no history of 'statehood' — one that is represented by a political authority that exercised control over significantly large populations and territory — on which to build independence and the demand for a singular homeland. There was no tradition of an army or groups of armed men who were mobilized beyond the defence of their respective villages.

The size and formation of the *ili* varied across the region.[95] Territorial boundaries and political jurisdiction were found to be more defined in the larger settlements of the Ibaloy, Kankanaey, Kalinga and Bontok, where wet rice agriculture was practised.[96] An *ili* is governed by a group of elders. Each has their own 'citizenship' customs that define who are considered 'citizens' — or, more accurately, the members of the tribal land — with their corresponding rights and obligations. These terms include the right to the resources within the *ili* and the obligation to observe bilateral pacts with other tribal villages. The *ili* forged intricate diplomatic relations with other *ili* to seek retribution for infractions against a member by a resident of another *ili*, to settle boundary and other disputes,[97] and to agree on trading arrangements. In this system, the peace pact was an important mechanism for forging settlements. By setting areas of responsibility, the peace pact institution further defined and reinforced the concepts of territory and jurisdiction.[98] Based on the content of peace pact treaties, Prill-Brett concluded that the Kalinga and Bontok have the most developed indigenous political concept of territory.[99]

Interestingly, the *ili* generally practised what is called 'third party neutrality' in matters involving other *ili*. In other words it did not build political alliances with one or more *ili* against another *ili*. It left the other *ili* to settle matters with the others, and did not demand support from an *ili* with whom it enjoys a pact to support its interests in relation to another *ili*. Instances of alliances were short-lived and were on a per incident basis.[100] The sayings "your enemy is my enemy" or "the friend of my friend is my friend" apparently were not operative, given the bilateral nature of the alliances.

This practice of 'third-party neutrality', we can surmise, helped foster the autonomous development of each *ili*. Members enjoyed freedom from subjugation by another *ili*. Murders were dealt with harshly by the *ili* of the victim. Traditionally, deaths would have to be settled evenly, after which peace negotiations would follow and the two *ili* would be reconciled (a case of justice before reconciliation). These customary laws that relate to justice, dispute settlement and capital punishment allowed each *ili* to protect their respective ways of life with dignity. They exploited and cared for their resources according to their respective systems of production, resource management and property relations. For the longest time, the autonomy fostered peace and the well-being of each *ili*, but not the evolution of a pan-Cordillera identity or institutions, nor a popular notion of a singular statehood or homeland.

The traditional autonomy that governed each *ili* and the bilateral relations with other *ili* were the core values and sources of security that were threatened by subsequent state incursions. Eventually, the threat coming from a supra-*ili* institution (the state) created the impetus to put up a multilateral, pan-*ili* defence. But rather than claims for statehood and a homeland, what dominated the discourse was the 'regional autonomy' frame.

I am tempted to think that the CPLA's rare and ambitious use of *homeland* was part of the attempt to elevate the indigenist Cordillera movement to the status of the Bangsamoro struggle, with its more established and developed Bangsamoro homeland claims, although the Cordillera movement for its part was never separatist.

The same may be said of the use by the CPLA-CBA-MNS of *Cordillera Nation*. However, their concept of nation was inspired by their re-examination of what the *bodong* has meant to them. While the Moro nationalists used *nation* in the established sense of *bangsa* (people, sovereignty and territory), the CPLA-CBA-MNS indigenists were apparently translating/transforming the *bodong* into an English term/concept, and *nation* came closest. Ngao-i recounted how the leap from *bodong* to *nation* happened in their discussions: "Why nation? Because the *bodong* has structures similar to a nation, so instead of just Cordillera Bodong, might as well go for Cordillera Nation. The structure is similar." Ngao-i said he in fact questioned Balweg about this. "Are we asking to be separated from the Filipino nation?" Balweg allegedly replied they were not and explained, "No we will just modernize the bodong and call it nation."[101]

However, neither the concept of a Cordillera homeland nor of a nation took off, and the two terms remained confined to the CPLA-CBA-MNS discourse. Then and now, the term *region* provided the common ground. *Region* framed much of the discourse of both the state and non-state forces, although it may have been used differently or its use evolved from largely an administrative concept to an identity-based one. The established state use of the term is with reference to administrative regions, which are really coordinative structures with no distinct executive, legislative or juridical entities. Even the 'regionalization' campaign against the Marcos government's gerrymandering of the Northern Luzon provinces was directed against the splitting up of BIBAK into two separate administrative regions.

By the second half of the 1980s, the notion of a Cordillera region assumed an identity and the quality of a political movement, especially when the political project adopted regional autonomy as a goal. Although the CPLA-CBA-MNS went one step further by calling for a federal state, they also settled for the regional autonomy frame when this was adopted by the 1986 drafters in the Constitutional Commission and subsequently legislated and institutionalized in the new Philippine Constitution ratified in February 1987. Under this charter, the rights to regional autonomy and to a regional autonomous government granted to the Cordillera and Muslim Mindanao were justified on the basis of their unique cultural and historical characteristics. Thus, instead of *homeland* or *nation, region* as the pre-eminent supra-*ili* unit achieved hegemonic standing.[102]

It can be said that the aspiration for autonomy of the resistance articulators drew its strength from the long-established tradition of *ili* autonomy. But *ili* autonomy is still different from regional autonomy. The lack of nationhood and prior institutions of statehood over a larger territory beyond the *ili* have made efforts to construct regional autonomy and a regional autonomous government in the Cordillera difficult — even as identity as 'a people' or as a distinct collective of 'peoples' has gained traction and the territorial boundaries (the six provinces, including Abra) have been institutionalized by current state practice. Today, although the discourse has not completely died down, there is no longer a strong current underpinned by a movement from the inside to transform the evolved pan-*ili* consciousness into a full-blown autonomous regional governance framework.

Interestingly, after about three decades of trying (unsuccessfully) to institutionalize regional autonomy, the 'regional' discourse has been tempered by an emerging re-emphasis on *ili* and *ili* autonomy. The movement discourse has shifted towards local autonomy and the 'land is life' narrative, as encapsulated in the new normative — as well as legal — frame of 'ancestral domain'. The advantage of the ancestral domain frame is that its territorial and political constructs are defined more by the traditional *ili* than any supra-*ili* frame like the region (or nation or homeland). Thus, it has more cultural resources to build on and to undertake the political struggle for land and cultural security. Moreover, the right to indigenous peoples' ancestral domain and ancestral lands is an established legal framework in the country. The right is constitutionally guaranteed and the enabling legislation, the Indigenous People's Rights Act, has set off new institutions and legal processes for recognition at the levels of clan, tribe and village.

This shows that the *ili*, its proud tradition of autonomy and its foundation on established land tenure and customary practices, although varied across *ili*, continue to be at the core of the local peoples' narratives. This 'tradition of locality' embedded at the village, tribe or even at the larger supra-tribal (such as 'Igorot') levels seems to have a stronger hold than the pan-Cordillera identity fashioned from the social and political movement of the 1970s–80s. Locality — as "a sense of space" or of "communality and group identity that arises from affective, social and economic interdependence" — was strong in the traditional community structure because of the "defined territorial nature of the village [*ili*] and its function as a closed social and ecological system".[103] Land rights was the glue that bound this *ili*, "an organized agricultural community ... defined by territorial boundaries and [having] control over its own social, political and religious institutions".[104]

The Right to Self-Determination and IP Rights

While the CPLA's demands expressed all the elements of the UN-recognized rights of minorities, they did not explicitly refer to these rights as such. On the other hand the 1986 CPDF programme explicitly stated its goal to "Eliminate national oppression and assert the right to self-determination." Yet it was evident that the CPP subordinated the Cordillera peoples' right to self-determination to its broader struggle against the Philippine state. Its 'national struggle' is one directed against US imperialism/neocolonialism. In this schema, class struggle is essential to achieving the national liberation of the whole Filipino people — that is, from the oppression and exploitation of a 'semi-colonial, semi-feudal regime'.

Nonetheless, the appropriation of the right to self-determination of national minorities by the CPP-CPDF in its documents indicated that they were borrowing heavily from progressive global discourses and putting forward their own ideological interpretation. Even with its radical thinking along the lines of the right to self-determination and national minorities, it still largely operated from the viewpoint of its national democratic revolution, which in turn drew its ideological moorings from "Marxism-Leninism-Mao Tse Tung Thought". One can find in one of the CPP-led Moro Revolutionary Organization (MORO)[105] documents, for example, the argument that "Among the broad masses of the Moro people, especially among the working class and the peasantry, there is no point in struggle for national self-determination if this is not substantiated by a democratic revolution." Similar to its stance on Cordillera autonomy, it argues that the Moro people "can opt for regional autonomy only in a people's democratic state which can guarantee the quality of nations in the Philippine archipelago".[106]

The CPP, however, gave more leeway to the Moro struggle to lead to an independent Moro state ahead of the victory of the people's democratic revolution. But, should this happen, "they should always be willing to unite, cooperate and coordinate with the Filipino people in fighting for common interests and aspirations against the same enemies". This option of independence was not given to the Cordillera.

But more than the 'national minorities' discourse, the greater success in the CPP's reframing of its discourse is in its appropriation of the more contemporary and currently more powerful discourse on indigenous peoples and ancestral domain in its repertoire of claims, even as it remained within the ambit of the orthodox national democratic discourse. In doing so, the CPDF has managed to survive and persist despite its ideological orthodoxy and the challenges coming from the CPLA, the state and the changing world.

In the early 1980s, as we noted, the IP frame was in its infancy. The CPDF and the CPLA documents of this period hardly used the terms *indigenous populations/peoples*. The CPLA-CBA-MNS Position Paper did mention *indigenous peoples*, but not as a proper noun. Rather, the word *indigenous* served merely as an adjective — as a description for people, ways of life, institutions, systems, et cetera. It was the same case with the CPDF programme. The CPLA-CBA-MNS more often used terms like *minority people, uncolonized people, unsettled peoples, Cordillerans* or *peoples of the Cordillera nation*, which it referenced against the *majority*. The CPDF for the most part used *Cordillera people*, and linked this in a subsidiary way to *Filipino people*.

However, the CPP-NPA significantly reconstructed its approach to the Cordillera struggle in light of the international context of the late 1980s that saw the 'indigenous peoples' (IP) discourse gain ascendancy, and, corollary to it, the notion of ancestral domain. Even within the constricting ideology of the CPP-NPA-CPDF, the new IP language was accommodated and utilized to frame campaigns. The 'cause-oriented groups' (as political and social movement groups were called in the early 1980s in the Philippines) and intellectuals of the movement in fact managed to implant the IP frame in the deliberations of the 1986 Constitutional Commission, an effort that formalized the recognition of the rights of 'indigenous cultural communities', such as rights to their ancestral lands/domains.

In a way, the rootedness of IP rights on the land question accorded well with the basic agrarian issues that the CPP was comfortable with. Besides, recognition of ancestral domain was several steps removed from independence, and the IP rights movement did not necessarily translate to separatism. Indeed, for the most part, IP movements were not separatist. In Latin America during the same period the activism of the indigenous peoples had strong Marxist currents and they were mainly mobilized from within workers' and peasants' movements.

Perhaps the strongest influence that led to the incorporation of the discourse in the CPP-led national democratic movement was that of the national democratic movement entrepreneurs who participated in and were among the leaders of the campaign for the recognition of IP rights in the United Nations. They appropriated, but also elaborated on and promoted, the IP discourse, both domestically and internationally.

Networked organizing among IP groups in North America, Australia, Latin America, the Caribbean, New Zealand and the Philippines began in the 1970s. The first event that brought these disparate efforts together took place in Guyana, in 1974, under the auspices of the World Council of Indigenous Peoples. The event was also attended by IP leaders and activists from North America, New Zealand, Australia, Latin America, Norway, Denmark, Sweden and Finland.[107]

By 1982, when the UN set up the UN Working Group on Indigenous Peoples, whose mandate was to develop minimum standards to protect IP rights, Filipinos, particularly national democratic activists from the Cordillera, were actively participating in the global initiative. Joji Carino, an Ibaloi, attended the 1982 meeting. The CPA, formed in 1983, continued to participate in this body and other subsequent ones until the 1993 adoption of the draft Declaration on the Rights of IPs and the proclamation of the International Decade of the World's Indigenous Peoples.[108] It sustained its involvement until the Declaration was adopted by the United Nations in 2007. Victoria Tauli-Corpuz eventually played a leading role in the international campaign. Like Carino, Tauli-Corpuz was politicized in the 1960s and early 1970s and was involved in the opposition to the Chico River Dam in Kalinga and Bontoc.[109]

This period of engagement with the UN saw the birth of a global indigenous peoples' movement, with the CPP-led Cordillera movement actively part of it. That it is global "is a logical development because the construct of 'indigenous peoples' is linked with colonial history which is itself an international project".[110]

The codification of IP rights into the UN Declaration on the Rights of Indigenous Peoples involved a power struggle with states and among IP groups over the substance and process of institutionalizing IP rights, as can be gleaned from the account of the UN process by Tauli-Corpuz. As chair of the UN Permanent Forum on Indigenous Issues, she was in the thick of the formation of the UN forum and the lobbying of governments to endorse the IP-driven discourse encapsulated in the Declaration.[111]

Domestically, the global advance in acknowledging and institutionalizing IP rights alongside the new domestic challenges that saw the defeat of the regional autonomy movement resulted in a reshaping of the thrusts in the open (legal) Cordillera movement by the time of the 1990s. The IP rights discourse became more prominent than the regional autonomy frame, with its contentious links to the 1980s split in the CPP that gave birth to the CPLA.

Indeed, despite the orthodoxy of the CPP-NPA-CPDF with regard to the basic tenets of the national democratic revolution — the primacy of the armed struggle against US imperialism, bureaucratic capitalism and feudalism — its adherents have always had enough leeway to pragmatically integrate the new discourses alongside legal or parliamentary-based campaigns, especially in the open mass movement arena. The effect is hybridity in their social movement discourses despite the overall orthodoxy in the armed movement's ideological framework.

CPDF: Reframing within the Orthodox Master Frame

National democratic activists continue to rearticulate the Cordillera struggle. To use this time the language of social scientists doing work on the 'framing' of social movements, they engaged in various forms of frame alignment to cope with the challenges of the times, including the threat from the CPLA, the new government, and the emerging global discourses. Such frame alignment was achieved by 'frame bridging'[112] or the linking of two or more ideologically congruent but structurally unconnected frames regarding a particular issue or problem, such as the national democratic movement's developed democratic language on human rights and anti-militarization, and the globalized IP frame. As the CPA claimed, it recovered from the damage caused by the CPLA and state militarization in the 1980s "through its perseverance and consistent advocacy on human rights and indigenous peoples rights at the local, national and international levels".[113]

They also utilized 'frame amplification', whereby the newer value of ancestral domain has been emphasized over regional autonomy; and 'frame extension', or the extension of the movement's primary national democratic revolution framework to encompass interests that are "incidental to its primary objectives" — in this case the victory of the national democratic revolution and the overthrow of the reactionary state — "but of considerable salience to potential adherents" such as the Cordillera IPs who seek to preserve the autonomy of their *ili* and ways of life. The CPA was thus at the forefront of localizing the UN Decade of Indigenous Peoples (1994–2003), during which time it campaigned against open-pit mining in Benguet, other large-scale mines, the San Roque mega-dam project, and the adverse impact of official development assistance in the region. Prior to this it was co-organizer of various international initiatives such as the Asia Indigenous Peoples' Pact, the Asia Indigenous Women's Network, and the International Alliance of Indigenous/Tribal Peoples of the Tropical Forest.

As noted earlier, regional autonomy was given less emphasis in favour of the more generic right to self-determination. Thus the CPA's slogan tapped two defining points of the global IP movement: self-determination and the defence of ancestral domain.[114] Bridging this self-determination slogan with its anti-imperialist stance, it framed its movement as "the Cordillera indigenous peoples' movement against national oppression and imperialist globalization and for self-determination"[115] — as such, amplifying the core nationalist (that is, anti-imperialist) content of the national democratic movement.

However, despite this multiple positioning, there was no transformation or systematic alteration of the master frame of the national democratic revolution itself. In 1992 the CPP leadership issued its so-called Reaffirm document.[116] Those who had doubts, left the organization, while those who stayed professed to the national democratic orthodoxy even as they engaged in various other forms of frame alignment to be able to hold on to and expand the movement's base of adherents.[117]

For its part, the CPLA-CBA-MNS adopted what one might consider, by the late-1980s, the old-fashioned language of 'majority-minority' relations. In doing so it sought to downplay the influences of the national democratic frame and 'indigenize' the discourse. The CPLA cadres were not as exposed to the emerging international discourse at that time. Most of them were guerrillas lodged in the mountain fastness of the Cordillera. The MNS intellectuals were Manila-based and most of their reading fare was on left-wing politics. Aydinan, the principal author of the CPLA-CBA-MNS document, was in jail from November 1971 to 1977, from where he discussed with fellow political detainees his disagreements with the CPP's dogmatic analysis of the Cordillera situation and brainstormed alternative approaches for the movement in the Cordillera.[118] He carried with him the weight of the early 1970s party debates that turned down proposals to create an Igorot Liberation Army and the motion to build an anti-dam alliance that would have a broader basis of unity than that of the NDF (wherein unity is based on adherence to the CPP-led armed struggle and national democracy). He and his colleagues were for the most part trying to shape an indigenous socialism that would apply in general to Filipinos and distinctly to ethnic groups like those in the Cordillera.

Aydinan, a University of the Philippines civil engineering student who dropped out of school to join the underground movement full-time, recalled a book on African socialism that he read when he headed the security force guarding CPP founding chair Jose Ma. Sison. The main thesis of the book was that socialism was not invented by Marx, because its elements were already present in South Africa. That set him thinking about the elements of socialism being practised in the Cordillera. The book belonged to Sison's library. When Juliet de Lima, wife of Sison, saw him reading this and other books, she allegedly told him to stop reading them because he would only get confused. In any case, this was the seed of the 'indigenous socialism' track that was integrated into the CPLA-CBA-MNS document. Out of jail in the early 1980s, Aydinan continued his explorations of ethnicity and socialism in the Filipino Socialist Movement. His ideas on direct democracy came from readings on the cantons in Switzerland. He then read up on ethnic nationalism later. All these became useful when the CPLA-CBA-MNS documents were written, putting together ideas such as the federal concept of Balweg and getting affirmation through consultations with ground forces, elders and the communities where the Lumbaya company operated.

No new articulation from the CPLA-CBA-MNS has surfaced in recent decades to reflect how their discourse has evolved. The organization has been preoccupied mainly with livelihood concerns for former guerrillas. It laid claim to a settlement area for former CPLA combatants in Kalinga, which it named the Conrado Balweg Camp.[119] From 2011 to 2015 the Armed Forces of the Philippines integrated a total of 332 former CPLA combatants or their kin, 15 of whom were officers, and 888 members entered the civilian auxiliary force. Livelihood programmes were awarded to 408 CPLA members.[120] In November 2015 the AFP and the CPLA, represented by Marcelina Bahatan and Arsenio Huminding, signed an agreement testifying to the full implementation of the integration programme for the CPLA.[121] In addition the government allocated 220.41 million pesos for the implementation of eighty-one community development projects, and the Batwagan Bridge and Access Road were constructed.[122]

So, while the national democrats have appropriated local, regional, national and international discourses into their own all-encompassing and pragmatic discursive practice, the CPLA-CBA-MNS dug deeper on the ground and focused on localized, village-level to provincial-level concerns such as livelihood projects and addressing tribal wars through peace pacts, with some former members winning seats as mayors, provincial board members or barangay officials, in Abra and Kalinga. Given its scarce resources, factionalization, absence of a strong leadership, a weak presence in national public affairs, and the aging base of guerrillas — whose main concern now is improving their economic situation — it is unlikely that the CPLA-CBA-MNS will be able to play as prominent a regional or national role as it did in the mid-1980s. At best, its allied organizations and individuals will remain significant at the village, municipality or provincial levels, since their leaders remain influential there.

Despite its capacity to weave various discourses into its own discursive practice, neither is the CPP-NPA emerging as the most influential actor in the region. As things stand, the power struggle over both the Cordillera discourse and governance has not been won by any one of the two alternative forces. At the same time, although the state has institutionalized in laws and institutions elements of the resistance discourse such as regional autonomy, IP rights and ancestral domain rights, the state has been unable to effectively deliver on these, nor has it been able to suppress the armed challenge.

Lost Momentum

In all, the region-wide political movement in the Cordillera has lost its momentum. The Cordillera collective identity can be considered today as primarily a name or label for a *geographic-cultural* identity-cluster. This is evident in the wave of academic studies, courses and books using the Cordillera geographic-cum-cultural frame. Baguio Colleges Foundation was recently renamed the University of Cordillera. The University of the Philippines in Baguio City established the Cordillera Studies Center, which regularly organizes the Cordillera Studies Conference. In 2009 it launched the academic journal *The Cordillera Review: Journal of Philippine Culture and Society* and held the Second Cordillera Creative Writing Workshop for budding writers of the region writing in the different Cordillera languages. There is a Cordillera Career Development College. The tourist city of Baguio is packaged as the "gateway to the Cordillera".

Interestingly, identity entrepreneurs and political activists still conflate or interchange *Cordillera* with *Igorot*, showing a situationalist response to the challenge of mobilizing a constituency around their political ideals. Some scholars appear to have carried over this vagueness. Finin, for example, plotted in one continuous line the Igorot/Mountain Province administrative grid into the Cordillera 'grid'.[123] Finin ignored this transformation by conflating *Igorot* and *Cordillera* to mean one and the same thing in his book, when the two are distinguishable and represent a marked but stunted evolution.

To round up, it is evident the Cordillera regional autonomy frame has not been as vibrant in terms of a political project compared to the older Moro advocacy that began in the late 1960s and saw a resurgence in the 1990s. Proof of this is the success in finally legislating a Bangsamoro Organic Law in 2018, four years after the

Comprehensive Agreement on the Bangsamoro was signed, whereas bills filed in Congress to create a Cordillera autonomous region have had no traction either inside or outside the legislature. The saliency of the 'Cordillera' frame as a political project would require much more concerted effort and consensus-building among the political elites in and from the region, the social movement forces on the ground, and the communities themselves.

Notes

1. It is argued that differentiation among the Igorots took place in cases where there was frequent contact between the Spaniards and a group, such as in armed confrontations. Thus, that the Spaniards differentiated the *Quianganes*, as reflected in Spanish accounts, may be due to the group's frequent raids on lowland missions and resistance to the establishment of Spanish missions. One other Spanish account referred to *Igorrotes de Benguet*, but only to qualify place of origin. On the whole the Spanish apparently had no adequate knowledge "for them to construct ethnic boundaries" among the so-called Igorots. See the undated monograph by Maria Nela B. Florendo, *Cordillera Historiography and the Crisis of Identity*. Florenda is a professor at the University of the Philippines in Baguio/Northern Luzon.
2. William Henry Scott, *Of Igorots and Independence: Two Essays* (Baguio City: Era, 1993), pp. 44–45. See also "The Word Igorot", *Philippine Studies* 10, no. 2 (April 1962): 235.
3. Cited in Gerard Finin, *The Making of the Igorot: Contours of Cordillera Consciousness* (Quezon City: Ateneo de Manila University Press, 2005), p. 11.
4. Scott, *Of Igorots and Independence*, p. 10.
5. William Henry Scott, *Cracks in the Parchment Curtain* (Quezon City, 1982), pp. 8–9.
6. Kate Chollipas Botengan, "Who Are the Igorots: Shadows of the Past Falling onto the Present and Reaching into the Future" (paper presented at the Third Igorot International Consultation, Baguio City, 26–29 April 2000).
7. Ibid. However, according to the author, some accounts use *Igorot* in the process of narration, but not in speaking parts of the characters.
8. Cited in Scott, *Of Igorots and Independence*, p. 69.
9. Ibid., p. 59.

10. Cited in Finin, *The Making of the Igorot*, p. 118.

11. Ibid.

12. Ibid., p. 82.

13. Ibid., pp. 199–200. However, as governor in 1964, Lam-en would ban tattooing of men's foreheads, cheeks or chins, although this practice traditionally marked bravery. He also criticized non-church weddings and the practice of *bodong* because it impoverished the whole family, who had to prepare the food for the rituals or may have had to pay indemnification (pp. 201–2).

14. Several times during his three, three-year terms — from 2010 to 2019 — Ifugao House Representative Teodoro Baguilat, Jr attended the yearly re-opening of Congress wearing his *bahag* (loincloth), when the president would deliver his State of the Nation Address.

15. Cited in Finin, *The Making of the Igorot*, p. 3.

16. Cited in ibid., pp. 3, 4.

17. Cited in Scott, *Of Igorots and Independence*, p. 66. We presume the other ethnic groups referred to here are the other minoritized cultural minorities, not the dominant, lowlander ethnic groups.

18. Finin, *The Making of the Igorot*, p. 161.

19. Ibid., p. 135. BIBKA's qualifications for membership were: native, educated or, if illiterate, a landowner and taxpayer.

20. Ibid., pp. 177–78.

21. Ibid., p. 135.

22. Ibid., pp. 183–85, 204–5. Finin observed that they "danced, sang and played musical instruments in a fashion that suggested they were all the same" and, even as they strove to meet the contest criteria of "genuineness, realism and authenticity", the dances were more elaborate than those performed in their home villages, and they were devoid of their socio-religious significance (pp. 204–5).

23. Cited in Scott, *Of Igorots and Independence*, p. 69.

24. Finin, *The Making of the Igorot*, pp. 163–64.

25. Ibid., p. 161.

26. Ibid., pp. 62–63. Moreover, long-time Ilocano residents in the Mountain Province were qualified as "mountaineer-lowlander", to distinguish them from the "true highlander" (p. 67).

27. Vicky Tauli-Corpuz, "Igorot Initiatives and Achievements Here and Abroad: Past, Present and Future" (paper presented at the International Igorot Conference, Baguio City, 26–28 April 2000). In this paper, Tauli-Corpuz stated that the KKKordilyera was formed before the suspension of the writ of habeas corpus.

28. Ibid.

29. Cordillera Peoples Alliance, "The Igorot Diaspora and the Present Cordillera Situation" (paper prepared for the Third Igorot International Conference, Baguio City, 26–28 April 2000). As noted in the earlier chapter on the Cordillera, the CPA originally spelled its name as *People's*. In other tracts it is spelled as *Peoples'*. All versions appear in Internet searches.
30. Tauli-Corpuz, "Igorot Initiatives".
31. In some references, the *P* in the CPLA is spelled as *Peoples*.
32. Cordillera Schools Group, Inc., *Ethnography of the Major Ethnolinguistic Groups in the Cordillera* (Quezon City: New Day, 2003), p. 73. If the theory of Ifugao historian Manuel Dulawan (1999; cited in the Cordillera Studies Group volume) that the Ifugao originally were from the Bauko-Tadian area in western Mountain Province and have language and cultural affinities with the Kankanaey (particularly the Kankanaey language as spoken by the Aplay) is true, this disdain of being identified with the Igorot is interesting.
33. Florendo, *Cordillera Historiography*.
34. Cited in Finin, *The Making of the Igorot*, pp. 26–27.
35. Cited in ibid., p. 34.
36. Cited in ibid., p. 30.
37. Worcester used it to refer to the tribes concentrated in Lepanto-Benguet and Bontoc, or what now constitutes the provinces of Benguet and Mountain Province. However, Worcester distinguished the Ibaloi, who are often classified among the Igorot.
38. Interview with Abrino Aydinan, 20 October 2008, Quezon City.
39. Cited in Botengan, "Who Are the Igorots".
40. Ibid.
41. Tauli-Corpuz, "Igorot Initiatives".
42. Finin, *The Making of the Igorot*, pp. 4–6.
43. The draft constitution of the IGO dated 25 April 2000 opened its membership to any individual who subscribes to the purposes of the IGO and has a relationship to the Cordillera provinces. "Such relationship may be by birth, affinity, residence, heritage or choice." It did not define what the Cordillera provinces are; the current administrative, regional composition must have been assumed as the base.
44. Cited by Jimmy Fong, "Change and Identity in Ibaloi Pop Songs", in *Towards Understanding Peoples of the Cordillera: A Review of Research on History, Governance, Resources, Institutions and Living Traditions*, vol. 1 (Baguio City: Cordillera Studies Center, University of the Philippines Baguio, 2008). *Bibakese* was coined from *BIBAK*.
45. Interview with Abrino Aydinan, 20 October 2008, Quezon City. Loose translation: "Being politically aware, I considered myself an Igorot even

though I am a native of Ifugao.... I came from the NPA, where all people from the Cordillera region were called Igorot. I was moulded into that [practice], so Igorot is okay with me."

46. Interview with Abrino Aydinan, 20 October 2008, Quezon City.
47. Dorothea Hilhorst, *The Real World of NGOs: Discourses, Diversity and Development* (Quezon City: Ateneo de Manila University Press, 2003), p. 32.
48. CPDF Program, no. 4, paras. 6 and 10.
49. Ibid., point no. 6, para. 14.
50. Ibid., point no. 6, paras. 5 and 6.
51. Ibid., point no. 4, paras. 9, 10 and 14.
52. Ibid., point no. 6, para. 7.
53. Recommendation no. 1 in "Towards the Solution of the Cordillera Problem: Statement of Position", presented to Her Excellency Corazon C. Aquino, President of the Republic of the Philippines, during the Cordillera Peace Talk held on 13 September 1986 at Mt. Data Lodge, Bauko, Cordillera, by the Cordillera Bodong Administration, Cordillera People's Liberation Army, and Montañosa National Solidarity. Henceforth referred to as the 1986 CPLA-CBS-MNS position paper.
54. Ibid., para. 31.
55. Botengan ("Who Are the Igorots") claims there are 96 tribes in the Cordillera Administrative Region (CAR), out of 353 in the country, with the biggest being the Ifugao tribe (Ifugao province); Kalinga tribe (Kalinga); Itneg/Isneg tribe (Apayao); the Bontoc, Kankanaey and Aplya tribes (Mountain Province); and Ilbaloy and Kankanaey tribes (Benguet). In 1998 there were 1,252,962 such "ethnic Filipinos" in the Cordillera Administrative Region.
56. The Masadiit and Maeng are in Abra near the Kalinga border, thus they enjoy affinity with both the Tingguian and Kalinga.
57. The Katagoan is a group living in Kalinga, as can be ascertained from a news report of the Philippine Information Agency (PIA) about livelihood assistance given by the Department of Labor and Employment in Kalinga to the Katagoan Association. See Gigi Domallig, "DOLE Kalinga allotted P0.7 million for livelihood", PIA Daily News Reader, 13 February 2006, http://www.pia.gov.ph (accessed 4 February 2009).
58. The Karaw (sometimes spelled Karaos) language is a language of the Philippines spoken by the people of the region of Karao and Ekip, Bokod, in eastern Benguet Province, according to the "Karaw language" entry in http://e.wikipilipinas.org/ (accessed 4 February 2009).
59. The Malaweg are found in parts of Cagayan and Kalinga-Apayao provinces and are said to be culturally closer to the Itawit and Ibanag in Cagayan.

60. Fay Cooper Cole, "Distribution of the Non-Christian Tribes of Northwestern Luzon", *American Anthropologist* 11, no. 3 (July–September 1909): 331.
61. Ibid., p. 331. Cooper reported seeing many Negritos of mixed descent who had adopted the practices of their neighbours.
62. Lawrence Reid, "Who are the Indigenous? Origins and Transformations" (paper presented at the First International Conference on Cordillera Studies, UP, Baguio City, 7–9 February 2008). I attended the conference. The paper was later published as Lawrence A. Reid, "Who are the Indigenous? Origins and Transformation", *Cordillera Review: Journal of Philippine Culture and Society* 1, no. 1 (March 2009): 3–25.
63. Ibid.
64. The Ivatan ethnolinguistic group live on the Batanes islands at the northernmost tip of the Philippine archipelago, from where islands of Taiwan may be sighted.
65. Interview with Abrino Aydinan, 20 October 2008, Quezon City. The unacceptability of having originated from migrants from the northern seas is also evident among pro-CPDF personalities in the Cordillera, as can be surmised from the contentious remark raised during the open forum of Reid's presentation during the 2008 Cordillera Studies Conference, questioning his findings.
66. Stephen Acabado, Marlon Martin, and Adama Lauer, "The Ifugao Archaeological Project", *Backdirt* 24 (2015): 54–61, https://www.ifugao-archaeological-project.org/about.html (accessed 15 February 2019). The authors' individual and joint academic publications may also be found at this website.
67. The Ilongot or Bugkalot today are found in Nueva Ecija, Nueva Vizcaya, Quirino and Aurora provinces in the Sierra Madre mountain range, all outside but sharing borders with the present administrative Cordillera region. When the Ambuklao dam was built, displaced Ibaloi and Ifugao families were moved to Bugkalot domain in Nueva Vizcaya. A transfusion of cultures and intermarriages took place, as well as displacement of some Bugkalots, who retreated deeper into the forest. See Pedro V. Salgado, *The Ilongots 1591–1994* (Sampaloc, Manila: Lucky Press, 1994); see also the excerpted documentary on the Bugkalot at http://www.youtube.com/watch?v=balrxpHPOXU made by the Philippine Center for Investigative Journalism, and the book, *Katutubo: Memory of Dances* by the Philippine Center for Investigative Journalism, 2002.
68. The Itawis, Itaois, Itawit live in southern Cagayan province in Luzon, along the watershed areas of the Chico and Matalag rivers. Their language is said to be related to that of the Ibanag, a large indigenous ethnolinguistic

group in the Cagayan Valley that is not included in the CPLA list. This poses a problem as to where the boundary should lie, as it can be extended farther and farther.

69. 1986 CPLA-CBS-MNS position paper.

70. June Prill-Brett, various writings, including the "Cultural Heritage Development in the Cordillera" (paper presented at the Third International Consultation/Conference, Baguio City, 26–28 April 2000) and "Preliminary Perspectives on Local Territorial Boundaries and Resource Control", Cordillera Studies Working Paper Series no. 6 (Cordillera Studies Center, University of the Philippines College of Baguio, 1988).

71. William Henry Scott, "Foreword" in June Prill-Brett, "Preliminary Perspectives on Local Territorial Boundaries and Resource Control", Cordillera Studies Working Paper Series no. 6 (Cordillera Studies Center, University of the Philippines College of Baguio, 1988).

72. Interview with Abrino Aydinan, 20 October 2008, Quezon City.

73. Interview with Andres Ngao-i, 7 November 2008, Tabuk, Kalinga.

74. Ibid. It seems this notion of a confederation of *bodong* as the expression of a nation and state came from Conrado Balweg, but the framing of the idea into a document came from the efforts of Aydinan and his colleagues.

75. Quotations were taken from the 1986 CPLA-CBS-MNS position paper, paras. 26 and 27. Para. 26 reads: "The fairly recent struggles waged by various language groups and tribes against threats to their lands and social lives have enhanced their awareness of a common Cordillera national identity." Para. 27 reads: "Such national consciousness became consolidated into the Cordillera nationalism which has seen the emergence of the Cordillera Bodong Administration (CBA) and the Cordillera People's Liberation Army (CPLA)."

76. The terms of the *pagta* (agreement/peace pact) across *bodongs* may vary. Ngao-i said they were currently codifying a standard *pagta* to be observed across such bilateral agreements. In particular, they want all *pagta* to do away with retaliatory killings, as was the traditional practice, in favour of paying damages. But getting all tribes to agree to modify this established standard of "an eye for an eye" was difficult. Interview with Ngao-i, 7 November 2008, Tabuk, Kalinga.

77. The chartered city of Baguio, the political and cultural centre of the region, is presumed to be included.

78. The Cordillera Administrative Region today is officially made up of the provinces of Mountain Province (comprising ten municipalities, including Bontoc, its capital), Ifugao, Benguet, Kalinga, Apayao and Abra. The Kalinga-Apayao province became the two provinces of Kalinga and Apayao in 1995.

79. See Finin, *The Making of the Igorot*, pp. 42, 161–62, 217–18.

80. See Fay Cooper Cole, "The Tinggian", *Philippine Journal of Science* 3, no. 4 (September 1908): 198. Cole identified Manabo as the last pure Tinggian municipality in the south; Barit, Amtuagan, Gayaman and Luluno are Tinggian with Igorot from Agawa and Sagada municipalities. Villaviciosa was an Igorot settlement from Sagada, but Bulilising near Villaviciosa was reportedly strongly Tinggian.

81. Ibid., p. 199.

82. Ibid., p. 211.

83. "Cordillera Political Map", http://www.cpahphils.org/cordillera/cordimap_pol.htm/ (accessed 26 November 2005).

84. Interview with Andres Ngao-i, 7 November 2008, Tabuk, Kalinga. In his reasoning, the Tingguian are Kalingan, and not vice versa.

85. Interview with Ngao-i, 7 November 2008, Tabuk, Kalinga.

86. The 1985 parliamentary bills filed by Assemblyman Honorato Aquino of Baguio City and Jesus Paredes of Ifugao proposed the creation of a Cordillera Region composed of the five provinces (BIBAK). The proposal gained support from provincial governments; several organizations from the Cordillera and beyond formed the Task Force Regionalization to support the move. See Rizal G. Buendia, "The Cordillera Autonomy and the Quest for Nation-building: Prospects in the Philippines", *Philippine Journal of Public Administration* 34, no. 4 (October 1991): 335–36. For a more detailed account, see Athena Lydia Casambre, *Discourses on Cordillera Autonomy* (Baguio City: Cordillera Studies Center, University of the Philippines Baguio, 2010): 21, 58–70). A corollary campaign was to break up Kalinga-Apayao again into two separate provinces. It was hard for Kalingas to have to campaign for electoral posts in Apayao and vice versa, and this made elections very expensive, according to engineer and peace pact holder Andres Ngao-i, who was a provincial board member of Kalinga-Apayao in 1985, shortly before the 1986 overthrow of Marcos. Interview with Andres Ngao-i, 7 November 2008, Tabuk, Kalinga.

87. Cole, "Distribution of the Non-Christian Tribes", p. 347.

88. Scott, *Of Igorots and Independence*, p. 11.

89. Various short-lived forts were built in the 1600s in places like Boa, Antamok, Mankayana and Lepanto, and a road passing between Pangasinan and Cagayan was opened up in the 1700s. In the 1890s, permanent troops were stationed in Kalinga and Ifugao. An 1898 Spanish census claimed that 120,444 pagans in these places recognized vassalage to the King of Spain, with inhabitants of Benguet, Lepanto and Bontoc among the first to be officially listed as Spanish subjects (ibid., pp. 13, 35–36). Colonial settlements were set up first along the lower Abra River in the 1600s,

and in Benguet, Bontok, Tabuk, Tinglayan Ifugao and other areas in the 1800s.

90. Buendia, "The Cordillera Autonomy", p. 355.
91. Ibid., p. 363.
92. Ibid., p. 356.
93. Interview with Andres Ngao-i, 7 November 2008, Tabuk, Kalinga.
94. "Cordillera Political Map", http://www.cpahphils.org/cordillera/cordimap_pol.htm/ (accessed 26 November 2005).
95. An *ili* in Bontok ranged from 600 to 3,000 people organized into 3–18 wards; while in Kalinga an *ili* was more kinship-based, and was made up of 1–8 settlements, each with about 20 houses. See June Prill-Brett, "A Survey of Cordillera Indigenous Political Institutes", Cordillera Studies Working Paper Series no. 5 (Cordillera Studies Center, University of the Philippines College of Baguio, 1995), pp. 9–10, 13–14. The paper is a revised version of one delivered during the Conference on Issues on Cordillera Autonomy, 22–24 May 1987, Baguio City.
96. Ibid., p. 17.
97. It was noted that territorial boundaries and political jurisdiction were more defined in the larger settlements of the Ibaloy, Kankanaey, Kalinga and Bontok, where wet rice-agriculture was practised, and, moreover, that the peace pact institution further defined and reinforced their concept of territory and jurisdiction (ibid.).
98. Ibid., p. 20.
99. Ibid.
100. Prill-Brett wrote: "The cooperation of two armed groups against a common enemy has been observed practice among the Bontoks, northern Kankanaeys, Ifugaos and Kalinga. However, these alliances are traditionally never of long-term duration. It is for the purpose of one activity, and the agreement is generally not binding after that purpose has been attained" (ibid., p. 20).
101. Interview with Andres Ngao-i, 7 November 2008, Tabuk, Kalinga.
102. The MILF for the longest time disdained *region* as the unit for their envisioned self-government. This gave rise to terms like the *Bangsamoro Juridical Entity*, the *New Political Entity* or just *the Bangsamoro* in the draft MOA-AD and the FAB/CAB. Eventually the MILF settled for the name, Bangsamoro Autonomous Region in Muslim Mindanao (BARMM).
103. Deirdre McKay, "Locality, Place, and Globalization on the Cordillera: Building on the Work of June Prill-Brett", *Cordillera in June: Essays Celebrating June Prill-Brett, Anthropologist*, edited by B.P. Tapang (Quezon City: University of the Philippines Press, 2007), pp. 149–50.
104. June Prill-Brett (1987) cited in ibid., p. 150. Prill-Brett distinguishes the community referred to in the state's administrative language from the *ili*:

"What is called 'the community' may provide no substantial social basis for collective action. Rather, it may be a more geographic entity labeled as a village or community by external agencies for administrative purposes" (ibid., p. 155).

105. The MORO is a member of the CPP-led NDF.
106. These and other quotations were sourced from "The MORO Manifesto" as reprinted in W.K. Che Man, *Muslim Separatism: The Moros of Southern Philippines and the Malays of Southern Thailand* (Quezon City: Ateneo de Manila University Press, 1990), pp. 200–208.
107. Victoria Tauli-Corpuz, "Internationalizing the Indigenous Peoples' Movement and Indigenous People's Rights" (plenary paper presented at the First International Conference on Cordillera Studies, "Indigenous Peoples and Local Communities in Transition", 7–9 February 2008, University of the Philippines, Baguio City). Tauli-Corpuz founded and heads the TEBTEBBA (Indigenous Peoples' International Centre for Policy Research and Education) and was among the early national democratic activists from the Cordillera. She is currently chair of the UN Permanent Forum on Indigenous Issues and convener of the Asia Indigenous Women's Network. In the same paper, she defined the international IP movement as "the global convergence of various IPs' formations and movements from the local, national and regional levels to work towards common goals of social justice and emancipation".
108. Tauli-Corpuz, "Igorot Initiatives".
109. Tauli-Corpuz ("Internationalizing the Indigenous") recounted her involvement in the Cordillera resistance in the late 1970s: "I had the privilege of going to Bugnay [in Kalinga] several times to meet with Macli-ing Dulag, the Kalinga leader who was assassinated [in 1980] for his opposition to the project. I also participated in the various pan-Cordillera Bodong (Peace Pact) rituals where the Kalinga and Bontoc forged unity between themselves and between them and other indigenous peoples and support groups against the project." While Tauli-Corpuz focused on the UN process, Carino became more active in the World Commission on Dams created by the World Bank to guide its financial policies for projects where tribal peoples are located.
110. Tauli-Corpuz, "Internationalizing the Indigenous".
111. Among the struggles won by the IP activists were allowing IP representatives to sit in the intergovernmental bodies like the Working Group on the Draft Declaration, and the adoption of most of the provisions of the draft declaration as already endorsed by the Sub Commission on Human Rights. They also had to struggle with other IP groups who wanted to move in a different direction, especially on basic points such as the right

to self-determination, ownership of resources, and free and informed prior consent. Tauli-Corpuz, "Internationalizing the Indigenous".

112. The four types of frame alignment — frame bridging, frame amplification, frame extension and frame transformation — and their respective descriptions were taken from David A. Snow, E. Burke Rochford, Jr, Steven K. Worden, and Robert D. Benford, "Frame Alignment Processes, Micromobilization, and Movement Participation", *American Sociological Review* (August 1986): 467–76.
113. Cordillera Peoples' Alliance (CPA), "CPA through the Years", http://www.cpaphils.org/campaigns/ (accessed 18 March 2009).
114. See http://www.cpaphils.org/.
115. CPA, "CPA through the Years".
116. The 1992 CPP Central Committee document, "Reaffirm Our Basic Principles and Rectify Efforts", blamed party losses on petty bourgeois impetuosity and subjectiveness resulting in deviations from strategy, among others.
117. An excellent account of multiple positioning of national democratic NGOs in the Cordillera is provided in Hilhorst, *The Real World of NGOs*.
118. Among the leading national democrat leaders with whom he discussed these matters in jail were Saturnino Ocampo and former priest Edicio de la Torre. According to Aydinan, they were sympathetic to his ideas, but when they got out of jail they stuck to the party line. Interview with Abrino Aydinan, 20 October 2008, Quezon City. Dela Torre, however, consequently pursued the line of 'popular democracy'.
119. Interview with Juanita Chulsi, 7 November 2008, Tabuk, Kalinga.
120. Joint Declaration on the Successful Completion of the Military Integration Component of Executive Order No 49, dated 9 November 2015. The AFP was represented by Major General Lysander Suerte of the 5th Infantry Division. EO 49 was signed in July 2011 mandating the full implementation of the closure agreement called "Towards the Final Disposition of the CPLAs Arms and Forces and Its Transformation into a Potent Socio-Economic and Unarmed Force".
121. Ibid. Not all of the remaining CPLA acknowledged Bahatan as their representative. Andres Ngao-i contested the process.
122. A peer-reviewed write-up of the CBA-CPLA story was completed in 2014. Office of the Presidential Adviser on the Peace Process, "Frequently Asked Questions on the GPH-CBA-CPLA Peace Process", http://peace.gov.ph/cba-cpla/faqs/.
123. Finin, *The Making of the Igorot*.

6

Conclusion

In this book we have examined the respective discourses of two armed ethnopolitical mobilizations in the south and north of the Philippines; namely, the Moro and Cordillera movements. We traced how some core elements of these articulations have become valorized and accepted as gospel truths by their respective politicized masses of adherents. At the same time, we saw how the movement organizations modified their framings and appropriated elements from global and other domestic discourses, showing how creatively and pragmatically movement intellectuals adapted to new ideas and the changed conditions over the forty-year period since their movements emerged.

We followed the MNLF intellectuals in founding their claim to a separate/autonomous Bangsa Moro and statehood. The MILF enriched this core Moro ethnonationalist discursive practice by further highlighting Islam as an organizational and ideological platform, effectively distinguishing itself from its more secular mother organization, the MNLF. In the 1990s the MILF complemented their two-axis discourse on nation and Islam with a third axis that maximized the language of ancestral domain and IP rights.

Meanwhile, we saw how the Cordillera struggle for regional autonomy emerged in the mid-1970s from the popular opposition to several development programmes instituted by the Marcos regime. The popular opposition was harvested and later led by the CPP operating in the region. The CPP-led CPDF, which became the underground organizational expression of the movement, espoused a Marxist ideology and dovetailed the popular opposition to support the national democratic revolution whose class-based struggle tended to subordinate ethnonationalist aspirations. The CPLA that split from the CPP was dominated by cadres who were natives of the Cordillera provinces. These leading cadres espoused a more decisively ethnonationalist platform that stressed the oppression of the Cordillera cultural communities by the Filipino majority. In this aspect, their discourse veered more closely to that of the Moro ethnonationalists. In the same vein, they elevated the notion of a Cordillera (administrative and political) region to a 'nation' and had irredentist claims to wider territories and ethnic groupings. They also favoured a federal state that drew features from their cultural practices and institutions such as the *bodong* (peace pact), as against a regional autonomy movement that was subordinated to the larger national democratic agenda of the CPP-CPDF.

In all, we saw how the intellectuals of the MNLF and the MILF and of the CPDF and the CPLA shared common assumptions on state oppression and the distinctiveness of the Moro/Cordillera peoples. We followed how, from there, they drew their claims to the right to self-determination, distinct identities and the territorial or spatial location where such a right and identity would be fully lived. However, as they negotiated power relations between themselves (the MNLF vis-à-vis the MILF, the CPDF vis-à-vis the CPLA) and against or before the state, they continued to build on the legal, historical and normative arguments that justified their cause and enabled them to assume multiple positions as contexts changed.

A Thriving Bangsamoro Master Frame

To be sure, the proper nouns *Moro* and *Cordillera* have established themselves as identity markers with ardent supporters and believers beyond the immediate membership of the movement organizations. However, the movement intellectuals' valorized interpretations of their respective histories and societies not only had a need to compete for hegemonic acceptance vis-à-vis the advantage of the state's and the dominant society's systems of thought. They were also encumbered by counter-discourses within their constituencies. Nonetheless, we find that well into the first decades of the twenty-first century, the Bangsamoro movement has flourished.

If Filipino nationalism imagined all language and social groups from Jolo to Appari as constituting one people and then wrote the history of the Filipino nation based on this assumption, Moro nationalism in turn championed the cause of a singular, unified Bangsa Moro. On the Bangsamoro historical master frame, scholars like McKenna have pointed out "that the myth of Morohood has been professed as historical fact by various scholars. Their retellings of the myth of Morohood obscure for their readers the historical complexity and cultural diversity."[1] Moreover, the dominant theme of resistance can also be juxtaposed with collaboration. Mendick, another scholar, wrote: "Far from violently objecting to inclusion within the Philippine nation, or remaining passive to it, there has been enthusiastic acceptance of the forms of national government, and, even more surprising, an extreme [manifestation] of political activity. Voting is heavy, campaign expenditure[s] are large, and candidates are many. Politics played in terms of the national system have become almost an obsession."[2] One Filipino scholar, although a Bangsamoro advocate himself, pragmatically observed: "Many Moro leaders … sought to retain their positions of influence and privilege by supporting and participating within the established political framework."[3]

There is also concern that officialized Bangsamoro history has downplayed the diversity in local histories and practices in an effort to compress Moro-ness into a single, historical timeline with attributes (events, features, personalities) largely drawn from the numerically and politically dominant Moro ethnic groups; namely, the Tausug, Maguindanao and Maranao. Even within and among the three dominant language/ethnic groups, there are tensions. The cleavage between the Tausug islanders and the mainland-led MILF movement was blatantly manifested during the January 2019 plebiscite for the Bangsamoro Autonomous Region in Muslim Mindanaao (BARMM law). An overwhelming majority in the Maranao province of Lanao del Sur and Marawi City and the Maguindanao province voted in favour of inclusion in the BARMM, while *No* votes garnered the majority in Sulu province. There has also been a resurgence among Tausug intellectuals of identity building around the 'Tau Sug' construct. In Lanao del Norte, the elite Dimaporo clan opposed inclusion of the six municipalities in the BARMM, even as the residents in these municipalities wanted it.

Critical voices have also called attention to the invisibility of class and gender-sensitive elements in Bangsa Moro/Bangsamoro discourse. Indeed, this composite Moro ideological struggle remains contested — in the past, during the war years, as well as at present, during the period of peace negotiations and the drawn-out phases of implementing the Final Peace Agreement with the MNLF and the Comprehensive Agreement on the Bangsamoro with the MILF.

Notwithstanding the critics, and to the credit of the adherents mobilized around the valorized history and constituted identity of the Bangsa Moro/Bangsamoro, the movement remained significant as they waged war — and now peace — in order to justly retrieve and secure for themselves a measure of their claimed lost sovereignty and territory based on the right to self-determination, now under the terms of the negotiated agreements. An active, politicized Bangsamoro constituency across three generations continues to organize and maintain visibility around the identity project. Self-ascribed Bangsamoro civil society organizations, blogs, websites and so on have grown extensively in the process of entrenching their claims through political negotiations and by law, altogether leading to the establishment of the Bangsamoro Transition Authority in February 2019.

A Return to Locality in the Cordillera

In contrast, the ideological frames utilized by both the CPP-led CPDF and the breakaway CPLA to campaign for regional autonomy have foundered. The two plebiscites in a span of eight years failed to ratify the organic act that would have created a Cordillera autonomous region. Although efforts to produce a new Cordillera autonomy law were buoyed recently by the success of the Bangsamoro autonomy project, these initiatives have been touch-and-go. Several factors that have been attributed to the failure to advance the autonomy project include intra-ethnic group distrust and open hostility between the CPLA and the CPDF.[4] But a crucial factor, as we traced in Chapter 3, was the felt lack in the discursive content and overall practice that defined the campaign for regional autonomy. As Casambre argued, the project was unable to gain popular acceptance due to the alien construct of regional autonomy whose origin lies in bigger political/ideological projects — the national democratic revolution of the CPP, the socialist-cum-federalist politics of the CPLA, and the bureaucratic-legalistic framework of the state when it appropriated the agenda.[5] Counter-proposals for arrangements that combine local autonomy with regional autonomy to ensure respect for the variety of property relations, indigenous practices and ways of life in the region, and to give more recognition to the *ili* as the seat of a traditional and stronger sense of identity, have consequently been suggested, but without much traction so far.

Despite the large-scale mobilization in the Cordillera against the Marcos regime, the transposition of the anti-dictatorship resistance into the regional autonomy frame had not been as vibrant as the older, Moro advocacy that began in the late 1960s and which saw a resurgence in the 1990s.[6] From a social movement identity that generated the pan-Cordillera autonomy struggle, *Cordillera* today appears to be relegated to a geographic-administrative (name-place) and social (cluster of tribes/ peoples) category. Instead, the older *Igorot* identity formation has gained renewed momentum, as witnessed by the more profuse and passionate production of cultural resources under this frame. The campaign for regional autonomy has taken a back seat to the more generic IP rights and ancestral domain campaigns, the locus of which are located at the level of *ili* (village) or tribal groupings.

Locality refers to "the sense of community and group identity that arises from affective, social and economic interdependence, forms of relation that have historically been strongest when contained in a defined territorial space".[7] The more immediate and functional affinity provided by the *ili*, or the *ili* as part of a province, remains evident in areas of the Cordillera where populations remain generally homogenous and the observance of customary laws remains strong. Indigenous communities in Abra (Tinguians and other smaller groups) for the most part organize around groups that are either tribal or locally based, despite their having been integrated administratively and in terms of the political movement into the Cordillera frame since the late 1980s. The same is true for those in Kalinga, where the *bodong* (peace pact-making) continues to be the strongest socio-political institution at the grass roots that maintains the peace between tribes with their respective *bugis* or ancestral territories. Through the Kalinga Bodong Congress, the peace pact holders and other tribal elders have been brought together, creating a provincial-administrative and inter-tribal-cultural sense of belongingness and cohesion around the Kalinga frame. This second-level identity, while still articulated by some of their leaders as part and parcel of the Cordillera autonomy ideal, has a far more solid and deeply rooted societal base that would withstand the test of time regardless of the fate of the idealized Cordillera project.

As has been said, locality is not only rooted in territorial space, although it has historically been strongest when contained in a defined, physical space. As a phenomenological quality, it can be constituted by a "sense of social immediacy", "technologies of interaction" and the relativity of context.[8] Thus, it can persist even as many of the region's educated youth have left their villages to study and work in metropolitan centres; even as many middle-aged professionals have migrated to foreign shores with their young children; and despite the disrupted practices and tenurial arrangements due to state laws and incursions of the cash economy. It persists if its materiality is maintained through regular work,[9] or through social practices. Overseas self-ascribed Igorots, for example, have organized the Igorot Global Association, which holds annual conferences in different parts of the world. During such conferences, they dress in native garb and perform their songs and dances. Many parents use these occasions to expose their children to their customs, since these young people no longer experienced childhood in their *ili*.

The Internet, in particular, has become a very potent technology of interaction to maintain the materiality of locality, even if only virtually. A survey made of Internet sites found robust identity reproduction along *ili*, province, tribe/ethnolinguistic group and supra-tribal categories like Igorot and BIBAK.[10] Terms in their local languages are often used in the written exchanges. Wegan noted that this use of the vernacular and of the websites as medium not only function as venues for identity assertion but also for 'performing' their identity. Like the CPLA indigenist intellectuals, terms are sometimes given new meaning to suit the global location of their users. For example, the *dap-ay* or the circular formation wherein elders discuss community matters "is appropriated in this space to encompass the world" or the global forum that is created through the Internet.[11]

Fong also discovered a robust local industry of music CD production of songs in the vernacular growing in towns like Buguias.[12] Many of these songs addressed the challenge of coping with the demands of tradition and the modern world. One genre of songs is called *kinnoboyan* — whose root word is *cowboy* — a cultural resource that assimilated well into the Igorot physical and cultural setting. Native film-makers are also generating their own indie films that are written, directed, acted and spoken in the vernacular by the 'Igorots' themselves. Ruth Tindaan studied these vernacular films, with titles like *Kedaw* (The request), *Din Sungbat* (The Answer), *Gasat* (The Fate), and *Laton Pay Dedan* (It Will Be Alright).[13] In all, there is a vibrant Igorot pop culture being nurtured at the interstices of the highlands and in the Igorot diaspora.

The acronym *BIBAK* also continues to linger as a collective identity label that is closely related to the Igorot. A small makeshift canteen near Burnham Pak in Baguio City is so named. There are several chapters of the BIBAK Association in the United States and Canada. There are also chapters in Europe and the Middle East. Most members are based in different parts of the Philippines, and most originated from Benguet and Bontoc. Most of these chapters have their respective Facebook accounts. Among the Ifugao — who, as discussed in earlier chapters, do not generally self-identify as Igorot — there has been a similar surge in tribal consciousness revolving around the famed rice terraces.[14]

The *Igorot* identity marker evidently enjoys the highest visibility among all these open-ended nomenclatures. Indeed, *Cordillera* seems to have been relegated to a concurrent, secondary *geographic-cultural* identity. Sometimes the two are conflated, since the Igorot identity after all traverses several Cordillera provinces. A good example of the interchangeability of the two terms among self-ascribed Igorots is the Facebook page @igorotcordilleran, which describes itself as a "place of reunion among Cordillerans, where we can celebrate our unique identity in this modern times". Eager to represent themselves as a "thriving tribe", the account holder called for support in their campaign "to defy the centuries old misperception about Igorots", and ended with the heterogeneous mixture of a battle cry, "Viva Cordillera Kaigorotan".

Meanwhile, many of the products of the 1970s–80s anti-Marcos activism continue to be politically active in the region through the CPA. The underground CPDF continues to build a support base to further the national democratic agenda, which includes pursuing political negotiations with the government. In their more recent discourse we also see a conflation of both *Cordillera* and *Kaigorotan* in the same texts, with the latter more decisively referring to peoplehood, and the former apparently referring to the region and the residents therein, whether natives or not. For example, a video recording of the reading of a CPDF statement by its spokesperson Simon Naogsan referenced their constituency as the "national minorities and people of the Cordillera".[15] A November 2018 protest statement of the CPA was entitled "Kaigorotan stands with the Lumad: Free our human rights defenders unjustly detained in Talaingod."[16] In this statement, *Kaigorotan* is put at par with the Lumad or Mindanao natives as indigenous groupings, and thus the expression of people-to-people solidarity.

Commemorating the annual Cordillera Day in April — on the date of the 1980 killing of tribal chieftain Macli-ing Dulag — has not achieved any status beyond that of an activity led by the Cordillera Peoples Alliance, failing to become a Cordillera-wide event owned by a broader constituency. The CPA's 2018 Cordillera Day statement condemned the Duterte administration's militarism in the region and ended with a call to intensify "our struggle against the fascist and dictatorial US-Duterte regime".[17] Recalling the context of the killing thirty-four years ago when the call for the right to self-determination was at its peak, it paid lip service to this right, which it qualified as "a right to self-determination from national oppression and imperialism".[18] This national oppression, according to CPDF spokesperson Simon Naogsan in a July 2018 newspaper interview, "is perpetrated by the reactionary state ruled by big landlords, comprador bourgeoisie and US imperialism".[19]

In all, the CPDF and the CPA have stayed committed to the orthodoxy of the national democratic movement. They have not dropped the regional autonomy agenda. However, they are not keen to revive the autonomy project. In 2017 the CPA rejected efforts to resuscitate the drafting of a new autonomy law, saying that "there is no popular clamor for Regional Autonomy". It argued that the bill "does not address the problem of national oppression of indigenous peoples, development aggression, land grabbing and plunder of ancestral lands and resources; is divisive instead of uniting the Cordillera people; and would only serve the present unjust system of the ruling class and their foreign masters".[20] As far as the regional autonomy agenda goes, the CPA will only settle for the almost unattainable *GRA* — its acronym for "Genuine Regional Autonomy". Presumably, that GRA will only be achieved upon the victory of the national democratic movement.

Over the course of half a century we have witnessed the vibrancy of discourses that have given life to revolutionary movements. These articulations did not go uncontested within the movements themselves. We saw how the developed 'master frames' ebbed and flowed with time, securing niches in the legal and state discourses as well. Such dynamics bear watching because they reflect how articulators are continuously engaged with the evolving contexts and the discourses therein.

According to Fairclough, such changes in the orders of discourse have happened and will continue to happen "as producers and interpreters combine discursive conventions, codes, and elements in new ways in innovatory discursive events, in effect cumulatively producing structural changes in orders of discourse, disarticulating existing orders, and rearticulating new orders, new discursive hegemonies".[21] Along this line it can only be expected that, some time in the future, upcoming identity entrepreneurs may articulate alternative identity constructs or revive fallen ones. Correspondingly, they may breathe life into political projects that have been left behind or into entirely new ones, similar to what the MNLF, MILF, CPDF and CPLA intellectuals and ideologues had done and struggled for during their prime.

Notes

1. Thomas McKenna, *Muslim Rulers and Rebels: Everyday Politics and Armed Separatism in the Southern Philippines* (Manila: Anvil, 1998), p. 84.
2. Melvin Mendick, "Sultans and Mayors: The Relation of a National to an Indigenous Political System", in *The Muslim Filipinos: Their History, Society and Contemporary Problems*, edited by Peter Gowing and Robert McAmis (Manila: Solidaridad, 1974), p. 226, cited in William Larousse, *Walking Together Seeking Peace: The Local Church of Mindanao-Sulu: Journeying in Dialogue with the Muslim Community (1965–2000)* (Quezon City: Claretian, 2001), p. 92.
3. J. De Los Santos, "Towards a Solution to the Moro Problem", *Dansalan Quarterly* 1, no. 4 (1980): 221, cited in Larousse, *Walking Together*, p. 95.
4. According to Casambre, "the specter of intra-ethnic group competition" and their lack of trust of each other as to who would exercise executive

power over the region helped doom the regional autonomy project. See Athena Lydia Casambre, "Autonomous Regions: The Cordillera Autonomous Region", in *Philippine Politics and Governance: An Introduction*, edited by Noel Morada and Teresa Encarnacion-Tadem (Quezon City: Department of Political Science, University of the Philippines, 2006), pp. 442–43.

5. Athena Lydia Casambre, "The Failure of Autonomy for the Cordillera Region, Northern Luzon, Philippines", in *Towards Understanding Peoples of the Cordilleras: A Review of Research on History, Governance, Resources, Institutions and Living Traditions*, vol. 1 (Baguio City: Cordillera Studies Center, 2001), pp. 21–26.

6. For someone who followed the events in the late 1970s and 1980s as a young adult, I cannot but feel a sense of nostalgia and loss, given the lives that were devoted to it and the inspiration it generated in battling not only the Marcos dictatorship but also powerful multilateral agencies like the World Bank.

7. Deirdre McKay, "Locality, Place and Globalization on the Cordillera: Building on the Work of June Prill-Brett", in *Cordillera in June: Essays Celebrating June Prill-Brett, Anthropologist*, editd by B.P. Tapang (Quezon City: University of the Philippines Press, 2007), p. 149. The author also cited the definition provided by Appadurai (1995): "a phenomenological quality, constituted by links between a sense of social immediacy, technologies of interaction, and the relativity of contexts" (p. 149).

8. Appadurai (1995), cited in ibid., p. 149.

9. Ibid., p. 149.

10. Blogs and websites based on Igorot identity or Igorot-named are Igorotblogger. com, "Bontoc Ikholot", "Full Blooded Igorot", "Proudly Igorot", "Haggiyo", "Kala Ngoy Ya", and "Nan Tawid Mi". Sacha Garah Weygan, "Virtual Communities: Identity Projects by Igorots in the Diaspora", *Ti Similla, Official Newsletter of the Academic Staff, UP Baguio*, May 2009, p. 10.

11. Weygan, "Virtual Communities".

12. Jimmy Fong, "Constructing Igorotness in Popular Culture" (paper presented at the First International Conference on Cordillera Studies, UP, Baguio City, 7–9 February 2008. It would be interesting to find out whether USB flash drives or other modes have now replaced CDs.

13. Ruth Tindaan, "Imaging the Igorot in Vernacular Films Produced in the Cordillera" (paper presented at the First International Conference on Cordillera Studies, UP, Baguio City, 7–9 February 2008). Like the songs, they featured tensions brought about by competing values and demands. They challenged stereotypical representations found in mainstream films such as *Mumbaki* and the much older *Igorota*. As Tindaan said, the latter films tended to exoticize the people and their 'primitive' ways of life, thereby reinforcing stereotypes

and prejudice. In contrast to the sentimentalization of mainstream films, Igorot film-making incorporated a historical consciousness and firmly located Igorots in their social settings. Many films foregrounded the lives of poor Igorot farmers, who are never shown in mainstream movies. The use of the narratives of multiple elders as a film technique effectively tapped into their collective oral traditions. The film-makers eschewed a typical hero-dominated narrative. By casting Igorots, actors represented themselves. But, according to Tindaan, the films have not become radically emancipatory because they reinforce the subordination of the natives, particularly to local Christian protagonists. Many of the films demonized native priests and juxtaposed rituals with boisterous chants, brawls and blood oozing from animals sacrificed. Lowlanders are likewise stereotyped as the harbingers of vice, although reverse discrimination is more ambivalent, as the lowland is both desired and resisted. Tindaan concludes that Igorot film-making remains a host of contradictions, with possibilities and constraints.

14. According to Acabado, "The past decade ... has seen the re-emergence of an Ifugao identity in the midst of integration into wider Philippine society (and globalisation), with a revival of both tangible and intangible heritage. This is evident in the resurgent importance given to the terraces and rituals associated with Ifugao farming." Stephen Acabado, "The Ifugao Agricultural Landscapes: Agrocultural Complexes and the Intensification Debate", *Journal of Southeast Asian Studies* 43 (2012): 503, http://journals.cambridge.org/abstract_S0022463412000367.

15. ICR Media, "Cordillera People's Democratic Front Spokesperson Ka Filiw Naogsan Talks about Escalataing [*sic*] Oplan Bayanihan Manuevers of the AFP Despite Pres. Duterte's Ceasefire Order for the Ongoing Peace Talks", 27 November 2016, https://www.youtube.com/watch?v=nMnvfzWRHao.

16. Talaingod is a municipality in Davao del Norte. A fact-finding mission was organized by Bayan Muna and allied organizations in November 2018 to investigate alleged harassment by the military of the Lumad Manobo tribe in the area. During their mission they were temporarily detained by the military. See https://www.cpaphils.org/kaigorotan-stands-with-the-lumad.html.

17. Cordillera Peoples Alliance, "Cordillera Day 2018 Central Statement: Unite to Resist Tyranny! Assert Our Right to Self-determination! *Agkaykaysa a Rupaken ti Tiraniya! Ilaban ti Karbengan iti Bukod a Pangngeddeng!*, 21 April 2018, https://www.cpaphils.org/cd2018.html.

18. Ibid.

19. Artemio Dumlao, Cordillera Rebels Reject 'Localized' Peace Talks", 9 July 2018, https://www.philstar.com/nation/2018/07/09/1831998/cordillera-rebels-reject-localized-peace-talks.

20. Cordillera Peoples Alliance, "CPA Statement on OPAPP's Attempt to Create a Cordillera Autonomy Bill", 6 November 2017, https://www.cpaphils.org/cpa-statement-on-opapps-attempt-to-create-a-cordillera-autonomy-bill.html.
21. Norman Fairclough, *Discourse and Social Change* (Cambridge: Polity Press, 1992), p. 97.

Bibliography

A. Books, Journals, Periodicals and Pamphlets

Abdulhaqq, Nu'ain, ed. 2005. *"We Must Win the Struggle!" by Ash-Shayk, Ash-Shaheed Salamat Hashim*. Camp Abubakre as-Siddique, Mindanao: Agency for Youth Affairs–Moro Islamic Liberation Front.

Abinales, Patricio N. 2000. *Making Mindanao, Cotabato and Davao in the Formation of the Philippine Nation-State*. Quezon City: Ateneo de Manila University Press.

Acabado, Stephen. 2012. "The Ifugao Agricultural Landscapes: Agrocultural Complexes and the Intensification Debate". *Journal of Southeast Asian Studies* 43, no. 3: 500–522.

Agbayani, Rene. 1987. "The Political Movement in the Cordillera". *Diliman Review* 35, nos. 5–6: 15–25.

Aijaz, Ahmad. 2000. "Class and Colony in Mindanao". In *Rebels, Warlords and Ulama*, edited by Kristina Gaerlan and Mara Stankovitch, pp. 1–20. Quezon City: Institute of Popular Democracy.

Ayoub, Mahmoud M. 2004. *Islam, Faith and History*. Oxford: Oneworld Publications.

Azurin, Arnold. 1998. *Beyond the Cult of Dissidence in Southern Philippines and Wartorn Zones in the Global Village*. Quezon City: University of Philippines Center for Integrative and Development Studies and UP Press.

Bagader, Abubaker A. 1994. "Contemporary Islamic Movements in the Arab World". In *Islam, Globalization and Postmodernity*, edited by Akbar S. Ahmed and Hasting S. Donnan. London: Routledge.

Baguilat, Teodoro. 2014. "Do the Cordillerans Really Want Autonomy?", inquirer. net, 16 July 2013, https://newsinfo.inquirer.net/446367/do-cordillerans-really-want-autonomy#ixzz5fbXv7xYb.

Bajunid, Omar Farouk. 1989. "Islamic Revitalization in ASEAN: A Survey of Source Materials". In *Islamic Revitalization in ASEAN Countries: Proceedings of the Third ASEAN Forum for Muslim Social Scientists*, pp. 27–44, held at the University of the Philippines Asian Institute of Tourism, Quezon City and Mindanao State University, Marawi City, 25–30 September.

Banlaoi, Rommel. 2007. "'Radical Muslim Terrorism' in the Philippines". In *Handbook on Terrorism and Insurgency in Southeast Asia*, edited by Andrew T.H. Tan, pp. 194–222. Cheltenham: Elgar.

Barry, Coeli, ed. 2008. *The Many Ways of Being Muslim*. Pasig City: Anvil.

Baud, Michiel, and Rosanne Rutten, eds. 2004. *Popular Intellectuals and Social Movements: Framing Protest in Asia, Africa, and Latin America*, International Review of Social History Supplements.

Boquiren, Arturo C. 1994. *Advancing Regional Autonomy in the Cordillera: A Source Book*. Baguio City: Cordillera Studies Center, University of the Philippines; Manila: Friedrich Ebert Stiftung.

Borrows, John. 2005. "Indigenous Legal Traditions in Canada". *Washington University Journal of Law and Policy* 19 (January): 167–223.

Brenneis, Donald. 1996. "Telling Troubles: Narrative, Conflict, and Experience". In *Disorderly Discourse: Narrative, Conflict and Inequality*, edited by Charles L. Briggs. New York: Oxford University Press.

Briggs, Charles L., ed. 1996. *Disorderly Discourse: Narrative, Conflict and Inequality*. New York; Oxford University Press.

Brownlie, Ian. 1992. *Treaties and Indigenous Populations: The Robb Lectures*. Oxford: Oxford University Press.

Buendia, Rizal G. 1991. "The Cordillera Autonomy and the Quest for Nation-Building: Prospects in the Philippines". *Philippine Journal of Public Administration* 34, no. 4 (October): 335–68.

Burger, Julian. 1994. "United Nations Working Group on Indigenous Peoples". In *Indigenous Peoples and International Organisations*, edited by Lydia Van de Fliert. Nottingham: Spokesman.

Burman, Erica, and Ian Parker, eds. 1993. *Discourse Analytic Research*. London: Routledge.

Caballero, Evelyn. 2001. "Strategies of Survival for a Community of Traditional Small-Scale Miners". In *Towards Understanding Peoples of the Cordillera: A Review of Research on History, Governance, Resources, Institution and Living Traditions*, vol. 1, pp. 171–81. Baguio City: Cordillera Studies Center, University of the Philippines Baguio.

Caluza, Desiree. 2008. "Kin of Ibaloi Leader Want John Hay Named after Him". *Philippine Daily Inquirer*, 2 September 2008, p. A15.

Canoy, Reuben. 1987. *Mindanao: The Quest for Independence*. Cagayan de Oro City: Mindanao Post Publishing Company.

Carino, Joanna K. 2009. "Cordillera Indigenous Peoples' Struggles in Defense of Life, Land, Livelihood and Resources". In *Ti Daga Ket Biag = Land is Life: Selected Papers from Three Cordillera Multisectoral Land Congresses (1983, 1994 and 2001)*, pp. 215–24. Baguio City: Cordillera Peoples Alliance.

Casambre, Athena Lydia. 2001. "The Failure of Autonomy for the Cordillera Region, Northern Luzon, Philippines". In *Towards Understanding Peoples of the Cordilleras: A Review of Research on History, Governance, Resources, Institutions and Living Traditions*, vol. 1, pp. 17–27. Baguio City: Cordillera Studies Center.

———. 2006. "Autonomous Regions: The Cordillera Autonomous Region". In *Philippine Politics and Governance: An Introduction*, edited by Noel Morada and Teresa Encarnacion-Tadem. Quezon City: Department of Political Science, University of the Philippines.

———. 2010. *Discourses on Cordillera Autonomy*. Baguio City: Cordillera Studies Center, University of the Philippines Baguio.

Castro, Nestor T. 1987. "The Zigzag Route to Self-determination". *Diliman Review* 35, nos. 5–6: 26–34.

———. 1994. "Ang Kilusang Komunista sa Kordilyera: Pagtatagpo ng taal at katutubong kultura". *Philippine Social Science Review*, special issue on Ang Kiulusang Masa sa Kasaysayang Pilipino 1900–1992 (January–December): 191–238.

———. 2000. "Three Years of the Indigenous Peoples Rights Act: Its Impact on Indigenous Communities". *Kasarinlan: A Philippine Journal of Third World Studies* 15, no. 2: 35–54.

Cawed, Carmencita. 1981. *The Culture of the Bontoc Igorot*. Manila: Communication Foundation for Asia.

Chaliand, Gerard, ed. 1989. *Minority Peoples in the Age of Nation-States*. London: Pluto Press.

Chaloping, Minerva M. 1992. "Recognizing and Protecting Rights to Ancestral Domain: A Core Element of Cordillera Regional Autonomy". In *Building Local Administrative Capability for Regional Autonomy in the Cordillera: Some Implementing Guidelines*, edited by Lorelei Crisologo Mendoza. Baguio City: Cordillera Studies Center, University of the Philippines, Baguio; Manila: Friedrich Ebert Stiftung.

Che Man, W.K. 1990. *Muslim Separatism: The Moros of Southern Philippines and the Malays of Southern Thailand*. Quezon City: Ateneo de Manila University Press.

Cooper Cole, Fay. 1908. "The Tinggian". *Philippine Journal of Science* 3, no. 4 (September): 197–211.

———. 1909. "Distribution of the Non-Christian Tribes of Northern Luzon". *American Anthropologist* 11, no. 3 (July–September): 329–47.

Cordillera Bodong Administration, Cordillera People's Liberation Army, and Montanosa National Solidarity. 1989. "Towards the Solution of the

Cordillera Problem: Statement of Position", presented to Her Excellency Corazon C. Aquino, President of the Republic of the Philippines, during the Cordillera Peace Talk held on 13 September 1986 at Mt. Data Lodge, Bauko, Cordillera. In *Waging Peace in the Philippines*, edited by Ed Garcia and Carol Hernandez, pp. 207–13. Quezon City: Ateneo Center for Social Policy, UP Center for Integrative and Development Studies, International Alert and Coalition for Peace.

Cordillera Peoples' Democratic Front. 1986. *General Program of the Cordillera Peoples' Democratic Front, Revised Draft*. CPDF Provisional Secretariat.

Cordillera Schools Group, Inc. 2003. *Ethnography of the Major Ethnolinguistic Groups in the Cordillera*. Quezon City: New Day.

Coronel Ferrer, Miriam, ed. 1997. *The Southern Philippines Council for Peace and Development: A Response to the Controversy*. Quezon City: University of the Philippines Center for Integrative and Development Studies.

———. 2005. "The Moro and Cordillera Conflicts in the Philippines and the Struggle for Autonomy". In *Ethnic Conflicts in Southeast Asia*, edited by Kusuma Snitwongse and W. Scott Thompson, pp. 109–50. Singapore: Institute of Southeast Asian Studies.

———. 2005. "The Philippine State and Moro Resistance: Dynamics of a Persistent Conflict". In *The Mindanao Conflict*, edited by Kamarulzaman Askandar and Ayesah Abubakar, pp. 2–28. Penang, Malaysia: Southeast Asian Conflict Studies Network, University Sains Malaysia.

———. 2006. "Autonomous Regions: The Search for a Viable Autonomy in Mindanao/Southern Philippines". In *Philippine Politics and Governance: An Introduction*, edited by Noel M. Morada and Teresa S. Encarnacion Tadem. Quezon City: Department of Political Science, University of the Philippines.

———. 2007. "The Communist Insurgency". In *A Handbook of Terrorism and Insurgency in Southeast Asia*, edited by Andrew T.H. Tan, pp. 405–34. Cheltenham: Elgar.

———. 2016. "Forging a Peace Settlement for the Bangsamoro: Compromises and Challenges". In *Mindanao: The Long Journey to Peace and Prosperity*, edited by Paul D. Hutchroft, pp. 99–131. Mandaluyong City: Anvil.

Davis, Selton H. 1994."The World Bank and Operational Directive 4.20". In *Indigenous Peoples and International Organisations*, edited by Lydia Van de Fliert. Nottingham: Spokesman.

Diliman Review Editorial Staff. 1987. "Forum: Interviews with Joanna Carino, Abrino Aydinan, Conrado Balweg and Andres Fernandez, CPDF Spokesperson". *Diliman Review* 35, nos. 5–6: 36–49.

Dumlao, Artemio. 2018. "Cordillera Rebels Reject 'Localized' Peace Talks". *Philstar*, 9 July, https://www.philstar.com/nation/2018/07/09/1831998/cordillera-rebels-reject-localized-peace-talks.

Dwyer, Leslie, and Rufa Cagoco-Guiam, n.d. *Gender and Conflict in Mindanao*. Washington, DC: The Asia Foundation.

Fairclough, Norman. 1989. *Language and Power*. London: Longman.

―――. 1992. *Discourse and Social Change*. Cambridge: Polity Press.

―――. 2003. *Analysing Discourse: Textual Analysis for Social Research*. London: Routledge.

―――. 2003. "'Political Correctness': The Politics of Culture and Change". *Discourse and Society* 14, no. 1: 17–28.

Finin, Gerard. 2005. *The Making of the Igorot: Contours of Cordillera Consciousness*. Quezon City: Ateneo de Manila University Press.

―――. 2008. "'Igorotism', Rebellion, and Regional Autonomy in the Cordillera". In *Brokering a Revolution: Cadres in a Philippines Insurgency*, edited by Rosanne Rutten, pp. 77–123. Quezon City: Ateneo de Manila University Press.

Florendo, Maria Nela B. 1994. "The Movement for Regional Autonomy in the Cordillera". In Arturo C. Boquiren, *Advancing Regional Autonomy in the Cordillera: A Source Book*, pp. 30–48. Baguio City: Cordillera Studies Center, University of the Philippines; Manila: Friedrich Ebert Stiftung, October.

Fong, Jimmy. 2001. "Change and Identity in Ibaloi Pop Songs". In *Towards Understanding Peoples of the Cordillera: A Review of Research on History, Governance, Resources, Institutions and Living Traditions*, vol. 1, pp. 211–25. Baguio City: Cordillera Studies Center, University of the Philippines Baguio.

Geneva Call. 2002. "Report of the Geneva Call Mission to the Moro Islamic Liberation Front", http://www.genevacall.org/resources/test-publications/gc-03may02-milf.pdf/.

Gowing, Peter Gordon. 1983. *Mandate in Moroland: The American Government of Muslim Filipinos 1899–1920*. Quezon City: New Day.

Hall, Rosalie Alcala, and Joanna Parres Hoar. 2015. "Philippines". In *Women in Conflict and Peace*, by the International Institute for Democracy and Electoral Assistance (IDEA), pp. 88–122. Sweden: IDEA.

Halliday, Fred. 1994. "The Politics of Islamic Fundamentalism: Iran, Tunisia and the Challenge to the Secular State". In *Islam, Globalization and Postmodernity*, edited by Akbar S. Ahmed and Hasting S. Donnan. London: Routledge.

Hashim, Salamat. 1985. *The Bangsamoro Mujahid: His Objectives and Responsibilities*. Mindanao, Bangsamoro: Bangsamoro Publications.

―――. 2002. *Referendum: Peaceful, Civilized, Diplomatic and Democratic Means of Solving the Mindanao Conflict*. Camp Abubakre as-Siddique, Mindanao: Agency for Youth Affairs–MILF.

Hilhorst, Dorothea. 2003. *The Real World of NGOs: Discourses, Diversity and Development*. Quezon City: Ateneo de Manila University Press.

Hutchcroft, Paul D., ed. 2016. *Mindanao: The Long Journey to Peace and Prosperity.* Mandaluyong City: Anvil.

International Crisis Group. 2004. "Jemaah Islamiyah in Southeast Asia: Damaged but Still Dangerous". Asia Report no. 63. Jakarta and Brussels: International Crisis Group, http://www.crisigroup.org.

———. 2004. "Southern Philippines Backgrounder: Terrorism and the Peace Process". Asia Report no. 80. Singapore and Brussels: International Crisis Group, http://www.crisigroup.org.

Johnston, Hank. 2002. "Verification and Proof in Frame and Discourse Analysis". In *Methods of Social Movement Research,* edited by Bert Klandermans and Suzanne Staggenborg, pp. 62–91. Minneapolis: University of Minnesota Press.

Jubair, Salah. 1997. *A Nation under Endless Tyranny,* 2nd ed. Lahore: Islamic Research Academy.

———. 1999. *Bangsamoro, A Nation under Endless Tyranny,* 3rd ed. Kuala Lumpur: IQ Marin.

———. 2007. *The Long Road to Peace: Inside the GRP-MILF Peace Process.* Cotabato City: Institute of Bangsamoro Studies.

Kiefer, Thomas M. 2001. "The Tausug Polity and the Sultanate of Sulu: A Segmentary State in the Southern Philippines". In *People of the Current: Selected Papers from Sulu Studies,* by the National Commission for Culture and the Arts. Manila: National Commission for Culture and the Arts.

Kottler, Amanda, and Carol Long. 1997. "Shifting Sands and Shifting Selves: Affirmations and Betrayals in the Process of Institutional Transformation". In *Culture, Power and Difference: Discourse Analysis in South Africa,* edited by Ann Levett, Amanda Kottler, Erica Burman, and Ian Parker, pp. 45–61. London, New Jersey and Cape Town: Zed Books and University of Cape Town Press.

Labrador, Roderick N. 1997. "Subordination and Resistances: Ethnicity in the Highland Communities of the Cordillera Autonomous Region, Northern Luzon, Philippines". *Explorations in Southeast Asian Studies: A Journal of the Southeast Asian Studies Student Association* 1, no. 1 (Spring), http://www.Hawai/edu/cseas/pubcs/explore/v1/v1n1-art4.html/.

Lacaba, Jose F. 2002. "The Bangsamoro Agenda: Interview with Salamat Hashim". *Midweek,* 10 December 1986. Reprinted in *Referendum: Peaceful, Civilized, Diplomatic and Democratic Means of Solving the Mindanao Conflict,* by Salamat Hashim, pp. 30–39. Camp Abubakre as-Siddique, Mindanao: Agency for Youth Affairs–MILF.

Larousse, William. 2001. *Walking Together Seeking Peace: The Local Church of Mindanao-Sulu Journeying in Dialogue with the Muslim Community (1965–2000).* Quezon City: Claretian Publications.

Lieblich, Amai, Rivka Tuval-Masciach, and Tamar Zilber. 1991. *Narrative Research: Reading, Analysis and Interpretation*. Thousand Oaks, CA: Sage.

Macnaghten, Philip. 1993. "Discourses of Nature: Argumentation and Power". In *Discourse Analytic Research*, edited by Erica Burman and Ian Parker. London: Routledge.

Maiello, Amedeo. 1996. "Ethnic Conflict in Post-colonial India". In *The Post-colonial Question: Common Skies, Divided Horizons*, edited by Iain Chambers and Lidia Curti, pp. 99–114. London: Routledge.

Majul, Cesar Adib. 1996. *The Political and Constitutional Ideas of the Philippine Revolution*, 2nd ed. Quezon City: University of the Philippines Press.

———. 1999. *Muslims in the Philippines*. Quezon City: University of the Philippines Press.

Maranan, Ed. "Development and Minoritization". *Diliman Review* 35, nos. 5–6: 7–14

McKay, Deirdee. 2007. "Locality, Place and Globalization on the Cordillera: Building on the Work of June Prill-Brett". In *Cordillera in June: Essays Celebrating June Prill-Brett, Anthropologist*, edited by B.P. Tapang. Quezon City: University of the Philippines Press.

McKenna, Thomas. 1998. *Muslim Rulers and Rebels: Everyday Politics and Armed Separatism in the Southern Philippines*. Manila: Anvil.

Mendoza, Lorelei Crisologo, ed. 1992. *Building Local Administrative Capability for Regional Autonomy in the Cordillera: Some Implementing Guidelines*. Baguio City: Cordillera Studies Center, University of the Philippines, Baguio; Manila: Friedrich Ebert Stiftung.

Mindanao (formerly Muslim) Independence Movement. 1999. "MIM Draft Constitution and By-laws" [1969]. In *Bangsamoro: A Nation under Endless Tyranny*, by Salah Jubair, pp. 309–13. Kuala Lumpur: IQ Marin.

Misuari, Nur. 1992. "The Bangsa Moro People's Struggle for Self-Determination (Towards an Understanding of the Roots of the Moro People's Struggle)". *Philippine Development Forum* 6, no. 2: 1–42.

———. 1992. "Appeal to Islamic World for Support of the Moro People in Southern Philippines" [1975]. *Philippine Development Forum* 6, no. 2: 61–94.

———. 1998. "Speech of Chairman Nur Misuari during the Opening Ceremony of the Formal Peace Talks" [1993]. In *Beyond the Cult of Dissidence in Southern Philippines and Wartorn Zones in the Global Village*, by Arnold Azurin, pp. 306–11. Quezon City: University of Philippines Center for Integrative and Development Studies and UP Press.

Moro Islamic Liberation Front Peace Panel. 2010. "GRP-MILF Peace Process, Compilation of signed Agreements & Other Related Documents (1997–2010)". MILF Peace Panel and The Asia Foundation.

———. 2015. *Third Party Facilitation Phase (2001–2008): Journey to the Bangsamoro*, vol. 2. Philippines: MILF Peace Panel.

———. 2015. *The Comprehensive Agreement on the Bangsamoro and the Expanded Peace Process Architecture Phase (2009–2014): Journey to the Bangsamoro*, vol. 3. Philippines: MILF Peace Panel.

Moro Islamic Liberation Front (MILF) Technical Working Groups. n.d. "Position Papers of the [MILF] Technical Working Groups on the Six Clustered Agenda". Reprinted in *Kasarinlan: A Philippine Quarterly of Third World Studies* 15, no. 2 (2000): 245–70.

Moro National Liberation Front Reformist Group. 1990. "The Nine-Point Proposal of the Reformist Group" [March 1983]. In *Muslim Separatism: The Moros of Southern Philippines and the Malays of Southern Thailand*, by W.K. Che Man, p. 197. Quezon City: Ateneo de Manila University Press.

Moro Revolutionary Organization (MORO). 1990. "The MORO Manifesto" [December 1982]. In *Muslim Separatism: The Moros of Southern Philippines and the Malays of Southern Thailand*, by W.K. Che Man, pp. 200–208. Quezon City: Ateneo de Manila University Press.

Murad, Ebrahim. 2005. "Foreword: Tribute to a Great Hero of the Bangsamoro and Muslim Ummah". In *"We Must Win the Struggle!" by Ash-Shayk, Ash-Shaheed Salamat Hashim*, edited by Nu'ain bin Abdulhaqq, pp. v–vii. Camp Abubakre as-Siddique, Mindanao: Agency for Youth Affairs–MILF.

Muslim Independence Movement. 1990. "The Manifesto of the Muslim Independence Movement" [1969]. In *Muslim Separatism: The Moros of Southern Philippines and the Malays of Southern Thailand*, by W.K. Che Man, pp. 187–88. Quezon City: Ateneo de Manila University Press.

Muslim, Macapado Abaton. 1994. *The Moro Armed Struggle in the Philippines: The Non-Violent Autonomy Alternative*. Marawi City: Mindanao State University.

Mutalib, Hussin. 1989. "Islamic Revitalization in ASEAN: The Political Dimension". In *Islamic Revitalization in ASEAN Countries: Proceedings of the Third ASEAN Forum for Muslim Social Scientists*, pp. 45–60, held at the University of the Philippines Asian Institute of Tourism, Quezon City and Mindanao State University, Marawi City, 25–30 September.

Noble, Leila G. 1994. "Muslim Politics and Policies". In *Patterns of Power and Politics in the Philippines: Implications for Development*, edited by James F. Eder and Robert Youngblood, pp. 15–42. Tempe: Arizona State University.

Parpan-Pagusara, Mariflor. 2009. "The Kalinga Ili: Cultural-Ecological Reflections on Indigenous Theoria and Praxis of Man-Nature Relationship". In *Ti Daga Ket Biag = Land is Life: Selected Papers from Three Cordillera Multi-Sectoral*

Land Congresses (1983, 1994 and 2001), pp. 31–50. Baguio City: Cordillera Peoples Alliance.

Pavlova, Elena. "Jemaah Islamiya according to PUPJI". In *Handbook on Terrorism and Insurgency in Southeast Asia*, edited by Andrew T.H. Tan, pp. 76–103. Cheltenham: Elgar.

Pawid, Zenaida Hamada. 2009. "Indigenous Patterns of Land Use and Public Policy in Benguet". In *Ti Daga Ket Biag = Land is Life: Selected Papers from Three Cordillera Multisectoral Land Congresses (1983, 1994 and 2001)*, pp. 19–24. Baguio City: Cordillera Peoples Alliance.

Philippine Campaign to Ban Landmines et al. 2001. *Full Conference Proceedings: Engaging Non-state Actors in a Landmine Ban; A Pioneering Conference*. Quezon City: Conference organizers.

———. 2004. *Towards the 2004 Review Conference on the Ottawa Treaty: From a Perspective of Engaging Non-State Armed Groups*. Quezon City: Philippine Campaign to Ban Landmines.

Philippine Human Development Report 2005: Peace, Human Security and Human Development in the Philippines. 2005. Metro Manila: Human Development Network, United Nations Development Programme and New Zealand Agency for International Development.

Philippine Office of the Presidential Economic Staff. 1969. *Province Profile of the Mountain Province*.

Phillips, Louise, and Marianne W. Jorgensen. 2002. *Discourse Analysis as Theory and Method*. London: Sage.

Prill-Brett, June. 1995. "A Survey of Cordillera Indigenous Political Institutes", Cordillera Studies Working Paper Series no. 5. Cordillera Studies Center, University of the Philippines College of Baguio.

———. 1997. "Preliminary Perspectives on Local Territorial Boundaries and Resource Control", Cordillera Studies Working Paper Series no. 6. Cordillera Studies Center, University of the Philippines College of Baguio.

Reid, Lawrence A. 2009. "Who Are the Indigenous? Origins and Transformation". *Cordillera Review: Journal of Philippine Culture and Society* 1, no. 1 (March): 3–25.

Rodell, Paul A. 2007. "Separatist Insurgency in the Philippines". In *Handbook on Terrorism and Insurgency in Southeast Asia*, edited by Andrew T.H. Tan, pp. 225–47. Cheltenham: Elgar.

Rodil, B.R. 1999. "The Tripeople Relationship and the Peace Process in Mindanao". In *Journeying Together Towards a Culture of Peace in Mindanao: The Bishops-Ulama Forum 1996–1998; A Report of the First Two Years*, edited by Antonio Ledesma, Hamid Barra, and Hilario Gomez. Iligan: Bishop-Ulama Forum Secretariat.

————. 2001. *Kalinaw Mindanaw: The Story of the GRP-MNLF Peace Process, 1975–1996*. Davao City: Alternative Forum for Research in Mindanao.

————. 2004. *The Minoritization of the Indigenous Communities of Mindanao and the Sulu Archipelago*, rev. ed. Davao City: Alternate Forum for Research in Mindanao.

Ronen, Dov. 1979. *The Quest for Self-Determination*. New Haven: Yale University Press.

Salgado, Pedro V. 1994. *The Ilongots 1591–1994*. Sampaloc, Manila: Lucky Press.

Santos, Soliman M., Jr. 2001. *The Moro Islamic Challenge: Constitutional Rethinking for the Mindanao Peace Process*. Quezon City: University of the Philippines Press.

————. 2010. *Constructively Engaging Non-state Armed Groups in Asia: Minding the Gaps, Harnessing Southern Perspectives*, South-South Network for Non-State Armed Group Engagement (SSN) Monograph no. 1.

Scott, William Henry. 1962. "The Word Igorot". *Philippine Studies* 10, no. 2 (April): 234–48.

————. 1982. *Cracks in the Parchment Curtain*. Quezon City.

————. 1993. *Of Igorots and Independence: Two Essays*. Baguio City: Era.

————. 1994. *Barangay: Sixteenth Century Philippine Culture and Society*. Quezon City: Ateneo de Manila University Press.

Snow, David A., E. Burke Rochford, Jr., Steven K. Worden, and Robert D. Benford. 1986. "Frame Alignment Processes, Micromobilization, and Movement Participation". *American Sociological Review* 51, no. 4 (August): 464–81.

Sweptson, Lee, and Manuela Tomei. 1994. "The International Labor Organisation and Convention 169". In *Indigenous Peoples and International Organizations*, edited by Lydia Van de Fliert. Nottingham: Spokesman.

Tapang, B.P., ed. 2007. *Cordillera in June: Essays Celebrating June Prill-Brett, Anthropologist*. Quezon City: University of the Philippines Press.

Taya, Shamsuddin L. 2017. "The Political Strategies of the Moro Islamic Liberation Front for Self-Determination in the Philippines". *Intellectual Discourse* 15, no. 1: 59–84.

Thornberry, Patrick. 1995. "The UN Declaration on the Rights of Persons Belonging to National or Ethnic, Religious and Linguistic Minorities: Background, Analysis, Observations and an Update". In *Universal Minority Rights*, edited by Alan Phillips and Allan Rosas. Turku/Abo and London: Abo Akademi University Institute for Human Rights and Minority Rights Group.

UN Women. 2018. *Women's Meaningful Participation in Negotiating Peace and Implementing Peace Agreements: Report of the Experts Group Meeting Convened by UN Women*. New York: UN Women.

Van de Fliert, Lydia, ed. 1994. *Indigenous Peoples and International Organisations*. Nottingham: Spokesman.

Van Dijk, Teun A., ed. 1985. *Handbook of Discourse Analysis*, vol. 2, *Dimensions of Discourse*. London: Academic Press.

Vitug, Marites, and Glenda Gloria. 2000. *Under the Crescent Moon*. Metro Manila: Anvil.

Warren, James Francis. 1985. *The Sulu Zone, 1768–1898*. Quezon City: New Day.

Weygan, Sacha Garah. 2009. "Virtual Communities: Identity Projects by Igorots in the Diaspora". *Ti Similla: Official Newsleter of the Academic Staff, UP Baguio* (May): 9–10.

B. Unpublished Manuscripts and Papers

Arquiza, Mucha-Shim Quiling. 2009. "Knowledge and Power in Bangsamoro Identity Politics: An Essay on Intersectionality of Ethnicity, Religion, Gender and Kinship as Determinants of Identity". Draft discussion paper submitted to Konsult Mindanaw (15 June).

Bahatan, Fernando D., Jr. 2004. "They Saw, They Fought, They Remembered". Unpublished manuscript (May).

Bahatan, Fernando D., Jr., and Gabino P. Ganggangan. 2004. "Struggle for a Cordillera Nation (CBA-CPLA Struggle for a New Socio-Economic Political Order in the Cordillera". Unpublished manuscript (May).

Brady-de Raedt, Carol H.M. "To Know the Meaning of the Chico Project". n.d. Photocopy held at UP Baguio library.

Caouette, Dominique. 2014. "Persevering Revolutionaries — Armed Struggle in the 21st Century: Exploring the Revolution of the Communist Party of the Philippines". PhD dissertation, Cornell University.

Cholipas Botengan, Kate. 2000. "Who Are the Igorots: Shadows of the Past Falling onto the Present and Reaching into the Future". Paper presented at the Third Igorot International Consultation, Baguio City, Philippines, 26–29 April.

Cordillera Peoples' Alliance. 2000. "The Igorot Diaspora and the Present Cordillera Situation". Paper prepared for the Third Igorot International Conference, Baguio City, 26–28 April.

Cordillera Peoples' Democratic Front. 1987. "Resolution against Reactionary Reformism and Counter-revolution". Paper presented at the First Political Congress of the CPDF, Sagada, Mountain Province, 17 January.

———. 1987. "Resolution on Genuine Regional Autonomy". Draft resolution presented at the First Political Congress of the CPDF (January).

———. n.d. An Interview with the CPDF spokespersons on the CPDF program, on the Cordillera people's agenda for peace held on 14 December 1986, in Benguet. Baguio City: Center for Nationalist Studies of Northern Luzon.

————. 1987. Resolution for a Genuine People's Army, presented on 17 January 1987 at the First Political Congress of the Cordillera People's Democratic Front.

Coronel Ferrer, Miriam. 2009. "Remapping Mindanao: Expanding the Frontiers of Autonomous Governance". Paper delivered at the 2009 Philippine Political Science Association Conference. Dumaguete, Negros Occidental.

Florendo, Maria Nela B. n.d. "Cordillera Historiography and the Crisis of Identity".

Fong, Jimmy. 2008. "Constructing Igorotness in Popular Culture". Paper presented at the First International Conference on Cordillera Studies, University of the Philippines Baguio City, 7–9 February.

Hataman, Mujiv S. 2008. Anak Mindanao Party List Representative Statement entitled "On being a Moro and a Muslim".

Igorot Global Organization. 2000. *Constitution of the Igorot Global Association.* Draft prepared by Edwin Abeya (dated 25 April).

International Labour Organization. 1957. The Convention Concerning the Protection and Integration of Indigenous and Other Tribal and Semi-Tribal Populations in Independent Countries (Convention No. 107).

Islamic Council of Foreign Ministers. 2008. 35th Islamic Council of Foreign Ministers Resolution no. 2/35-MM on the Question of Muslims in Southern Philippines, passed in Kampala, Republic of Uganda during the 18–20 June ICFM session.

Lingga, Abhoud Syed Mansur. 1995. "The Political Thought of Salamat Hashim". MA Thesis submitted to the University of the Philippines Institute of Islamic Studies, 1995.

————. 2002. "Understanding Bangsamoro Independence as a Mode of Self-determination". Paper delivered at the Forum on Mindanao Peace sponsored by the University of the Philippines in Mindanao Department of Social Sciences, the Philippine Development Assistance Programme and the Association of Mindanao State University Alumni on 28 February, Davao City, Philippines.

Memorandum of Agreement on Ancestral Domain Aspect of the GRP-MILF Tripoli Agreement in Peace of 2001. 2008. Certified true copy, embargoed until 5 August 2008. Sourced from the Office of the Presidential Adviser on the Peace Process.

Office of the Presidential Adviser on the Peace Process. 1988. "Nurturing a Culture of Peace in the Cordillera: Facilitator's Manual for Community-Based Peace Education". Metro Manila: OPAPP in coordination with peace partners in the CAR and the Association for Nontraditional Education in the Philippines (October draft).

Prill-Brett, June. 2000. "Cultural Heritage Development in the Cordillera". Paper presented at the Third International Consultation/Conference, Baguio City, 26–28 April.

Reid, Lawrence A. 2008. "Who are the Indigenous? Origins and Transformation". Paper delivered at the First International Conference on Cordillera Studies, UP, Baguio City, 7–9 February.

Santos, Soliman M., Jr. 2018. "Jihad and International Humanitarian Law: The Case of Three Moro Rebel Groups in the Philippines". Unpublished manuscript (6 May).

Snow, David A., and Robert D. Benford. n.d. "Clarifying the Relationship between Framing and Ideology in the Study of Social Movements: A Comment on Oliver and Johnston". Unpublished manuscript.

Suling, Francisco A. n.d. "Once More to the Breach: More Destructive Dams in Kalinga-Apayao". Photocopy held at UP Baguio library.

———. n.d. "Chronology of Events and Military Activities and Harassments in the Chico Dam Area from January to April 1980". Photocopy held at UP Baguio library.

Tauli-Corpuz, Victoria. 2000. "Igorot Initiatives and Achievements Here and Abroad: Past, Present and Future". Paper presented at the International Igorot Conference, Baguio City, 26–28 April.

———. 2008. "Internationalizing the Indigenous Peoples' Movement and Indigenous People's Rights". Plenary paper presented at the 1st International Conference on Cordillera Studies, "Indigenous Peoples and Local Communities in Transition", University of the Philippines, Baguio City, 7–9 February.

Tindaaan, Ruth. 2008. "Imaging the Igorot in Vernacular Films Produced in the Cordillera". Paper presented at the First International Conference on Cordillera Studies, UP, Baguio City, 7–9 February.

Wadi, Julkipli. 2000. "Strategic Intelligence Analysis of Philippine National Security, Muslim Secessionism and Fundamentalism". Paper presented at the Strategy and Conflict Studies of the Command and General Staff College Training and Doctrine Command, Philippine Army, Makati City, 14 June.

C. Philippine Laws and International Conventions

1987 Constitution of the Philippines.

Republic Act No. 782. The Public Land Act (1962).

Republic Act No. 6734. Organic Act for the Autonomous Region in Muslim Mindanao (1988).

Republic Act No. 6766. Organic Act for the Cordillera Autonomous Region (1989).

Republic Act No. 8371. Indigenous Peoples' Rights Act (1997).

Republic Act No. 8438. An Act to Establish the Cordillera Autonomous Region (1997).

Republic Act 9054. Amendments to RA No. 6734 (2001).

United Nations. Charter of the United Nations (1945).

———. International Covenant on Civil and Political Rights (adopted by the General Assembly in 1966 and entered into force in 1976).

———. International Covenant on Economic, Social and Cultural Rights (1966).

United Nation General Assembly. Declaration on the Granting of Independence to Colonial Countries and Peoples, or UN General Assembly Resolution 1514 (XV) (adopted 14 December 1960).

United Nations Working Group on Minorities. Commentary to the United Nations Declaration on the Rights of Persons Belonging to National, or Cultural, Religious and Ethnic Minorities, adopted at its 10th session in 2004.

D. Main Interviews

Interview with Abrino Aydinan, founder of Montanosa Solidarity Network and former political detainee and member of the CPP. Quezon City, 20 October 2008.

Interview with Andres Ngao-i, Kalinga bodong holder and secretary-general of the Kalinga Bodong Congress (KBC). Tabuk, Kalinga, 7 November 2008; and Tabuk, Kalinga, 28 May 2019, with Gerry Donaal, KBC Program Coordinator.

Interview with Juanita Chulsi, deputy chief of the CPLA. Tabuk, Kalinga, 8 November 2008.

Interview with Salah Jubair (pseud.)/Mohagher Iqbal (pseudo.)/Datucan M. Abas. Camp Darapanan, Crossing Simuay, Sultan Kudarat, Maguindanao, 7 November 2008.

Interview with Abhoud Syed Lingga, director of the Institute of Bangsamoro Studies in Cotabato City and secretary-general of the Bangsamoro Consultative Assembly. Cotabato City, 5 November 2008.

Interview by phone with Abul Kayhr Alonto. 14 December 2010.

E. Websites, Online Accounts

Abrenian.com, http://www.abrenian.com/

BIBAK, http://www.bibak.org/

Cordillera Idiosyncracies (blog), http://jmagreda.blogspot.com/

Cordillera Peoples Alliance, http://www.cpaphils.org/

Floss World Education (blog), http://www.lamundofloss.blogspot.com

The Igorot Facebook page, https://facebook.com/igorotcordilleran/

Inquirer.net, https://www.inquirer.net/

Intellectual Discourses (blog), http://www.mafatihulhikmah.blogspot.com
KusogMindanaw e-group
Mindanews, http://www.mindanews.com/
Moro Islamic Liberation Front, http://www.luwaran.com/
Morolaw (blog), http://morolaw.blogspot.com
National Democratic Front of the Philippines, http://www.philippinerevolution.org/
Philippine Council for Islam and Democracy, http://www.pcid.org.ph/
Philippine Information Agency, http://www.pia.gov.ph/
Philstar, https//www.philstar.com
Ubbog Cordillera Young Writers (blog), http://ubbogcordillera.blogspot.com/
WikiPilipinas, http://e.wikipilipinas.org/
Young Moro Professionals Network, http://www.ympn.org/ and http://www.
    bangsamoro.com/

Index

Note: Page numbers followed by "n" refer to endnotes.

g-string/bahag, 155, 190n14
Glang, Alunan C., 47n32
Golod, 152
golor, 152
golot, 153
G-string, 155
Guerrero, Amado, 85

H
Hapilon, Isnaji, 146n101, 117
Hassan, Lumet, 25
Hi-Act. *See* Highland Activists (Hi-Act)
Highland Activists (Hi-Act), 66, 157
highlanders, 155–58
Hilhorst, Dorothea, 163
Hora, Luis, 155
House Bill 1441, 155
human rights, 17, 75, 98–99, 100–101,
    105, 109, 136n19, 185
Huminding, Arsenio, 187
Hussein, Farouk, 26

I
Ibaloi, 68, 83, 88n35, 160, 165–66, 177,
    191n37, 196n97
Ibanag, 192n59, 193n68
Iligan, 44n9
ICAR. *See* Interim Cordillera
    Autonomous Region (ICAR)
ICCPR. *See* International Covenant on
    Civil and Political Rights (ICCPR)
Ifugaos, 58, 152, 159, 161, 166, 176,
    191n32, 192n45, 192n55, 196n100
  Ipugaws/Itaulis, 165
  oral literature, 168
  province, 151, 153, 156, 171
  rice terraces, 168
IGO. *See* Igorot Global Organization
    (IGO)
Igorot Global Organization (IGO),
    161–62, 204
Igorot Liberation Army, 186
Igorots, 8, 151–53, 188
  as ascribed identity marker, 58,
    151–53, 159, 160–61

as census category, 62, 88n21
conflation with "Cordillera", 159,
    162, 188, 205
cultural pride, 155–56, 162, 190n22,
    205
diaspora community, 162, 191n43
differentiation among, 189n1,
    190n26, 191n37
discrimination against, 153–55
as self-identification, 154–55, 159,
    161, 162
as supra-tribal political identity, 161
as supra tribal socio-cultural
    identity, 181, 204
"Igorot Manifesto", 162
Kaigorotan, 156, 162, 205
resurgence as identity marker, 205
IHL. *See* international humanitarian
    law (IHL)
Ikadazan, 166
Ilaga, 43n1
ILO. *See* International Labour
    Organization (ILO)
Ilocano/Ilokano, 62, 152, 153, 160,
    172–73
Ilocano-Tingguian affinity, 172
Ilocos, 61, 152, 155, 167, 174, 176
Ilongot, 193n67
Ilongot-Bugkalot, 165–66, 175, 193n67
indigenous peoples
  definition, 139n31
  lumad (non-Moro indigenous
    peoples), 117–19, 122–23
  rights, 181–84
Indigenous People's Rights Act, 180
Interim Cordillera Autonomous
    Region (ICAR), 79–80
intermarriages, 174
International Covenant on Civil and
    Political Rights (ICCPR), 136n18,
    136n19, 137n23
international humanitarian law (IHL),
    109–11, 133
International Igorot Conference,
    190n27, 191n29

International Labour Organization
(ILO), 103, 139n30
Iqbal, Mohager, 6, 11n15, 35, 46n23
Isabela, 153, 173–74
Isinays, 165
ISIS. *See* Islamic State in Iraq and Syria
(ISIS)
Islamic Directorate of the Philippines,
22
organizers, 47–48n34
Islamic State in Iraq and Syria (ISIS),
146n99
Isnaji, Alaverez, 25, 49n55
Itaois/Itawis/Itawit, 165, 175, 192n59,
193n68
Itneg/Isneg, 160, 165–66, 192n55
Ivatan, 193n64

J
Jaafar, Ghadzali, 39–40, 52n89, 145n96,
149n151
Jabidah Massacre, 17, 20, 45n17, 45n18
Jajurie, Raisa, 129
Jamasali, Abdurahman, 25
Janjalani, Khadaffy, 142n63
Jeddah Accord, 33
Jemaah Islamiya, 145n99, 146n101
Jolo, 26, 44n9
Jubair, Salah, 6, 19, 25, 11n13, 14, 22,
40, 46n23, 52n80, 53n105, 114, 116,
119–22, 145n96

K
Kabataan Makabayan, 23, 74, 89n39,
91n61, 156
kabundukan, 158
Kadtabanga Foundation, 147n127
KAGUMA. *See* Katipunan ng mga
Gurong Makabayan (KAGUMA)
Kalanguya/Kalaguyya-Ikadazan,
165–66, 175, 176
Kalinga, 67–68, 153, 157, 159, 160,
165–67, 171, 177, 192n55, 196n95,
196n97, 196n100

Kalinga-Apayao province, 86n11, 157
Kalinga *bodong*, 169–171
Kalinga-Bontok Peace Pact Holders
Association (KBPPHA), 70, 170
Kankanaey, 153, 160, 165, 175, 177,
191n32, 196n95, 196n100
Karaw, 165, 192n58
Karon, Bainon, 147n127
Katagoan, 165,192n57
Katipunan ng mga Gurong
Makabayan (KAGUMA), 73
Kato, Umbra, 41, 145n99
Kedat, 83
KBPPHA. *See* Kalinga-Bontok
Peace Pact Holders Association
(KBPPHA)
Kilusang Kabataan ng Kabundukan
(KKK), 66, 158
KKK. *See* Kilusang Kabataan ng
Kabundukan (KKK)
Kusogmindanaw, 21
Kutawato Revolutionary Committee
(jurisdiction), 31

L
LAB. *See* Liga ng Agham para sa
Sambayanan (LAB)
Lam-en, 155, 190n13
Land Settlement and Development
Corporation, 14–15
Lanao/Ranao, 19, 24, 30–31, 44n9
La Union, 176
Lepanto, 152, 161, 191n37
Lepanto-Bontoc province, 86n10
Libya, 18, 26–27, 31, 51n73
Liga ng Agham para sa Sambayanan
(LAB), 73
Lima, Juliet de, 186
Lingga, Abhoud Syed, 21, 32, 34–35
locality, 181, 202–4,
Loong, Saleh, 49n58
Lucman, Rashid, 24–25, 47n34, 50n66
Lucman, Tarhata, 25
"Lumad-ARMM", 141n50

Sali, Dambong, 25
Sama/Samal, 25, 132
Sama Dilaut, 131
Sangki, Abdullah, 20–21
Santos, Soliman Jr., 32, 11n16, 110–11
Saudi Arabia, 116
Sawatang (CPLA Commander), 81
Sungar (NPA Commander), 90n59
Scott, William Henry, 152, 153, 158, 159, 169
Sema, Muslimin, 25, 49n5
Sema, Sandra, 49n55, 147n127
Siasi, 44n9
Sierra Madre, 165, 193n67
Silipao, 160
Sison, Jose Ma., 156, 186
Spanish colonial rule, 151–53, 174, 189n1
Sultanates, 177
Sultan Kudarat, 31
Sulu, 9, 24, 30, 44n9, 45n17, 146n101, 177
Sumulong, Juan, 44n12

T
Tabuk, 152
Tagalogs, 62, 160
Taiwan, 167, 193n64
Talaingod, Davao del Norte, 209n16
Tamano, Mamintal, 47n34
Tamano, Zorayda, 47n34
Tan sisters, Desdemona and Eleonora Rohaida, 26, 50n63
Tapul Island, 25
Tauli-Corpuz, Victoria, 139n32, 158, 159, 161, 183, 184, 197n107, 197n109
Tausug, 25, 30, 33
Tawitawi, 26
Thomson, T.W., 160
Tindaan, Ruth, 205, 208n13
Tinglayan, 152
Tinguianes, 152, 160, 163, 165–67, 172, 192n55, 195n80, 203

Tiruray, 43n1
topeng, 153
Trinidad Farm School, 155
Tripeople Mindanao, 134
Tripoli Agreement (MNLF) of 1976, 28, 29, 33, 53n105
Tripoli Agreement on Peace (MILF) of 2001, 102, 109
Tun Mustpha, 26, 50n65

U
UN. *See* United Nations (UN)
UN Declaration on the Rights of Indigenous Peoples, 184
UNESCO. *See* United Nations Educational, Scientific and Cultural Organization (UNESCO)
UNICEF. *See* United Nations Children's Fund (UNICEF)
United Nations (UN), 133, 183–84
United Nations Children's Fund (UNICEF), 110, 130, 139n30, 142n61
United Nations Economic and Social Council (ECOSOC), 103
United Nations Educational, Scientific and Cultural Organization (UNESCO), 104
United States colonial regime, 152, 155, 169–61
  Bureau of Non-Christian Tribes, 58, 87n16, 87n18
  Cordillera polices, 58–60
  granting of independence, 19
  Lanao leaders letter, 19
  Mindanao policies, 14–18

V
Valerio, Nilo, SVD, 90n60, 93n93
Vigan, 155

W
Wadi, Julkipli, 114
Wali, Sali, 25

About the Author

Miriam Coronel Ferrer is a professor at the Department of Political Science, University of the Philippines, where she has taught courses on and published articles on the governments and politics of Southeast Asia, peace processes, human rights and international humanitarian law, civil society and democratization, among others. She chaired the government negotiating panel that signed the Comprehensive Agreement on the Bangsamoro with the Moro Islamic Liberation Front in 2014. She is currently Senior Mediation Adviser at the United Nations.

www.ingramcontent.com/pod-product-compliance
Lightning Source LLC
Chambersburg PA
CBHW071853270326
41929CB00013B/2210